TWELVE
EVENTS
THAT
CHANGED
OUR
WORLD

OTHER BOOKS BY
GEORGE WALTON

THE WASTED GENERATION

LET'S END THE DRAFT MESS

FORT LEAVENWORTH—
SENTINEL ON THE PLAINS

CO-AUTHOR OF

THE DEVIL'S BRIGADE
(with Robert Adleman)

FAINT THE TRUMPET SOUNDS
(with John Terrell)

ROME FELL TODAY
(with Robert Adleman)

THE CHAMPAGNE CAMPAIGN
(with Robert Adleman)

TWELVE
EVENTS
THAT
CHANGED
OUR
WORLD

GEORGE WALTON

COWLES BOOK COMPANY, INC.

NEW YORK

Copyright ©1970 by George Walton

SBN 402-12391-3

Library of Congress Catalog Card Number 72-102814

Cowles Book Company, Inc.
A subsidiary of Cowles Communications, Inc.

Published simultaneously in Canada by
General Publishing Company, Ltd., 30 Lesmill Road,
Don Mills, Toronto, Ontario

Printed in the United States of America

First Edition

For
Helen—with love

ACKNOWLEDGMENTS

The writing of a work of nonfiction would appear to be a form of conceit, for the author, in effect, holds out that he alone is capable of winnowing out all the facts and finally arriving at conclusions of some significance. Actually it is not that way, for there are a host of knowledgeable friends who are willing to generously give their time and counsel in the preparation of such a book.

To name all who helped in the writing of *TWELVE EVENTS THAT CHANGED OUR WORLD* would be impossible, for the list is endless. However, there are some whose contributions have been so great that were I not to acknowledge their help, I would indeed be an ingrate.

The late Edward D. Blodgett, a friend of many years' standing and a distinguished scientist, was not only responsible for leading me through the tortuous channels of the early history of television, but made many suggestions as to the results that flowed from the other events here recorded. In the late stages of a fatal illness, he not only gave me his time, but the advantage of his brilliant mind. I shall always remember him on the couch in his home in Haddonfield, New Jersey, saying, in his slow and gentle voice, "Now George, I cannot agree with that." He saved me from a number of pitfalls.

Had it not been for Helen, my wife, whose mind is far keener than mine, this book would not even have made its postponed deadline. Not only did she type and re-type draft after draft after draft, which ran into the hundreds of thousands of words, but many of her suggested changes became a part of the final manuscript. Her help was invaluable. The editorial assistance of my son, Frank, was also of great help. His criticism was constructive and his thoughts helpful.

The production of a final clean copy of the manuscript was made possible by my good friend, Harry Moser, and his capable secretary, Polly Modesitt.

I should also mention the tireless efforts of Jeanne Plitt and her staff at the Alexandria, Virginia, Public Library. I am particularly indebted to Margaret D. Calhoun, Chief of the Library's reference section.

The illustrations are the joint product of Major Kenneth J. Offen and Mrs. Donna Traxler of the Office of Public Information, Department of the Army; Lieutenant Colonel John Walton (no relation, although I would be proud if this were true) and Mrs. Fran Louis of the Office of Public Information, Department of the Air Force; Robert Carlisle of the Media Relations Division, Department of the Navy, and Miss Josephine Motylewski of the National Archives. I wish also to express my thanks to Mr. William G. Sartain, Head of the Readers Service Section of the Library of Congress. Dr. John E. Scott of the United States Public Health Service kindly read that part of the manuscript describing the discovery of polio vaccine and made helpful suggestions.

I also wish to express my appreciation for the gracious hospitality of my cousin, Elwood Austin Marshall, in whose home part of this book was written.

For all their help which went far and beyond the call of duty, I am truly grateful.

Washington, D.C.   GEORGE WALTON
April 25, 1970

CONTENTS

TWELVE EVENTS THAT CHANGED OUR WORLD

1.

DAY OF INFAMY— PEARL HARBOR

Entering its last month, 1941 had been the best and worst of years. It had witnessed the seemingly impossible in the survival of Britain. The indomitable courage of that "little nation of shopkeepers" had astounded the world. Standing alone, it had defied the greatest power of evil modern man had yet known. The fortitude, the sacrifices of her people in that dark year of adversity would be remembered as long as recorded history was read. It was, in truth, Britain's "finest hour."

Assisted by her Commonwealths, Great Britain had not restricted herself solely to the defense of her "tight little isle." On a score of fronts, she had defied the fantastic might of the Axis powers, not always successfully, but with courage. In spite of Rommel's victories, she still held Egypt and the Suez Canal. How long this would continue was problematical.

Nevertheless, the British had rallied to the defense of a new ally, when on 22 June, disregarding the advice of his generals, Hitler made his greatest mistake and attacked the USSR. Striking swiftly, the Wehrmacht achieved strategic surprise. Within a month Nazi Panzers had penetrated three hundred miles into the Soviet Union and taken Smolensk. By November, German troops were holding a 2,300–mile front deep within Mother Russia. The bear had been hurt, perhaps mortally, but as 1941 waned, Russia still held Leningrad and Kiev, and the German armies were stalled before Moscow.

The heroic sacrifices of the British and Russian peoples **and of** the Allied troops were not enough. The Third Reich stood a razor's edge from victory—from world domination—and a "thousand years' Reich" did not seem to be an idle boast. More Axis successes in the battle of the Atlantic or on any one of a multitude of fronts might well cause a complete Allied collapse.

In these United States, eloquently dubbed the "arsenal of democracy," the fall of 1941 found the nation irrevocably divided. It was a curious union of pro-fascists, pacifists, and the always isolationist liberals.

The America First Committee strenuously protested sending aid to the Allies and claimed it was unpatriotic to defend the nation beyond its borders. Charles A. Lindbergh, speaking as an air military authority on January 28, told the House Foreign Affairs Committee that aid to Britain would accomplish nothing and only prolong the war. His words were acclaimed by Senators Wheeler of Montana, Tydings of Maryland, and Johnson of Colorado.

A vast campaign against those who would aid the Allies was put into motion with funds supplied by the late Henry Ford; the late General Robert E. Wood, Board Chairman of Sears Roebuck; Julius Rosenwald; and the late Joseph Kennedy. Full page advertisements appeared in *The New York Times* and other papers throughout the country charging the President and those they called the interventionists with being warmongers who would send American boys across the sea to die in a foreign cause. Mass meetings were held throughout the country protesting aid to Britain and later Russia. Crowds were addressed by such luminaries as Lindbergh, General Hugh S. ("Old Ironpants") Johnson of Spread Eagle fame, and Senator McCarran of Nevada.

While the vast majority of Americans unquestionably wanted to stay out of war, many favored continued help to Great Britain. In March, Roosevelt, fresh from his November victory over the "barefoot boy from Wall Street," Wendell Willkie, secured the passage of Lend–Lease by Congress and an appropriation of $7 billion to carry out the Act.

Willkie himself became an apostate in the eyes of the America Firsters by endorsing the President's foreign policy. Willkie had gone to England during the height of the blitz. His trip, given daily front page coverage, convinced him of the necessity of aid to

Britain. Willkie wasn't at all reticent in expressing his support for Lend–Lease.

Not deterred by the passage of the Lend–Lease Act, or the defection of Willkie, the America Firsters continued their efforts. They came close to success when, in the House of Representatives, the extension of the Draft Act was passed by a slim one-vote margin. Booth Mooney best describes it in his essay on Sam Rayburn in his book, *Mr. Speaker:*

> Rayburn experienced a grueling test of his leadership on the preparedness issue less than a year after he had become Speaker. The date was August 12, 1941, and the question up for decision was whether the Selective Service Act should be extended.
>
> The law, which had been enacted in the preceding September, provided for the drafting of 600,000 men into the Army for one year. Now, as the time drew near to discharge the first draftees, parents of many of the affected soldiers called for their release. They were joined in this cry, of course, by the isolationists and their organizations. On the other hand, the War Department warned that to disband the Army might well prove to be disastrous for the nation.
>
> The pressure on Congress was heavy. Congressmen found it hard to resist the pleas of flag-carrying women, with tear-streaked faces, who buttonholed them in their offices and in the corridors of the Capitol to plead that their sons be sent home. The result of the bitter floor fight, carried on for three days, was in doubt to the last moment.
>
> Rayburn conducted his own intensive campaign for votes to extend the draft. He went directly to the members he knew were on the fence and appealed to them on whatever basis he thought likely to be most effective. This was a time, he later admitted, when it became necessary, he did not hesitate to make the ultimate plea: "Do this for me. I won't forget it."
>
> The hour of decision arrived. At the conclusion of the tense roll-call vote, the tally clerk handed Rayburn a slip of paper. The Speaker, his face expressionless, glanced at it, and raised his gavel.
>
> "On this vote," he announced tersely, "203 members [a majority] have voted aye."
>
> The poised gavel fell. Rayburn had acted quickly to take

3

advantage of the rule that no member may change his vote once the result of a roll call is announced.

A recapitulation of the vote could be asked, however, and Dewey Short, Missouri Republican, promptly demanded that. At the conclusion of the review, the Speaker—without pause, almost without punctuation—declared: "No correction in the vote, the vote stands, and the bill is passed, and without objection a motion to reconsider is laid on the table."

And the gavel fell again.

Sixty-five Democrats had combined with one hundred and thirty-three Republicans and four representatives of minor parties to almost bring about the defeat of the Draft Bill. Had such a catastrophe occurred, the defense effort would unquestionably have been delayed by at least a year. The Second World War would have been prolonged by an equal period. It is not inconceivable that the one-vote margin represented the difference between victory and defeat in the subsequent global conflict.

The Congressmen had been reading their mail as well as listening to flag-carrying mothers, all bitterly opposed to conscription. The Representatives concluded there were votes to be had in opposing the draft. As Charles Wolverton of the First Congressional District of New Jersey cynically remarked at a luncheon the next day, "Those who favored an extension of the draft will soon forget how I voted, but those who were opposed will remember."

In June of 1941, when Mussolini charged that the United States was already in the war, he was not far from being right. Only a few days earlier, it had been announced that in May, without warning, a German submarine had torpedoed the *Robin Moor*, a United States Merchant Ship enroute to Capetown, South Africa. President Roosevelt called the action "intimidation to which we do not intend to yield."

The U.S. government had already seized twenty-eight Italian, two German, and thirty-five Danish ships as well as the French liner, *Normandie*, in American harbors. Four days after Il Duce's speech on 14 June, all Axis funds in the United States were frozen. On the same day all German Consulate offices were ordered closed. On 7 July, United States Marines occupied Iceland, relieving badly needed British troops for duty elsewhere.

The Third Reich retaliated quickly. On 17 August, the American ship, *Sessa*, under Panamanian registry, was sunk near Greenland. On 4 September, the navy destroyer, *Greer*, was attacked near Ireland. On 7 September, the American freighter, *Steel Seafarer*, was bombed and sunk by a German plane in the Red Sea. Four days later the *USS Montana*, an American-owned cargo ship carrying lumber to Iceland, was torpedoed. Eleven lives were lost when the U.S. destroyer, *Kearney*, was attacked on 17 October, and one hundred crewmen died when another, the *Reuben James*, was sunk. All three U.S. Navy ships had been in Icelandic waters.

The foreign relations of the United States were not much better on the far side of the globe. On 24 July, the Secretary of State denounced Japan's moves into Indo-China. The following day all Japanese assets in the United States were frozen, resulting in a virtual embargo of trade between the two nations. Within a week the Nipponese answered by bombing the U.S. gunboat, *Tutuila*, at Chung-king, China. The United States then struck at the most vulnerable link in Japan's armor by forbidding, on 1 August, the future export of aviation fuel to the Imperial Empire.

The ban on oil hurt and this was indicated on 28 August, when the Japanese Premier, Prince Fumimaro Konoye, wrote President Roosevelt to the effect that Japan only desired "—to pursue courses of peace in harmony with the fundamental principles to which the people and government of the United States are committed."

On 15 November, Sabura Kurusu, who had signed the Tripartite Pact for Japan,[1] was named a special envoy to join with the Japanese Ambassador to the United States, Kichisaburo Nomura, in negotiating the differences between the two nations. His appointment was followed two days later by a statement of the new Premier, Hideki Tojo, that the Japanese foreign policy was aimed at peace in East Asia.

Not since Warren Harding's Arms Limitation Conference in 1922, had the United States been in a better position to negotiate with a foreign power. Under the code name of "Magic" the Jap-

[1] The Tripartite Pact was concluded with Germany and Italy in September, 1940. This treaty obtained from Japan's Axis partners recognition of the new order in Greater East Asia under Japanese leadership and the promise of assistance in the event of war with the United States.

anese diplomatic codes and ciphers had been broken, and the American government had the advantage of daily reading the messages between Japan and its envoys around the world. As a result, the State Department knew in advance every move of the Japanese negotiators. On occasion they saw messages from the Imperial Government before they were read by the Nipponese envoys. Unfortunately, restrictive security procedures limited this information to a very few top American officials.

The effectiveness of the oil embargo was again indicated by the conciliatory nature of the Japanese proposal presented to the American government on 20 November. Japan suggested: (1) Japan make no further armed advances in Asia or the South Pacific, except in that part of Indo-China where its troops were stationed; (2) Japan agree to withdraw these troops immediately after peace is restored between China and Japan, or upon the establishment of a general peace in the Pacific area; (3) both governments cooperate in obtaining those commodities they need from the Netherlands East Indies; (4) commercial relations between the two nations be restored and the United States supply Japan a required quantity of oil; and, finally, (5) the government of the United States refrain from any actions that would be prejudicial to a restoration of peace between Japan and China.

There were many in the U.S. State Department, as well as in the Army and Navy, who felt that the Japanese proposal represented a good starting point for negotiations, but Secretary of State Cordell Hull was later to characterize it as "—of so preposterous a character that no responsible American official could ever have dreamed of accepting."

Faced with what they thought was an inevitable war in Europe, both the Army and Navy hoped to avoid a conflict with Japan, or at least to delay hostilities until the nation was better prepared for war. Accordingly, they were willing to appease the Imperial Empire, if necessary.

Rather than answer the Japanese proposal point by point, Hull decided upon a counter-proposal, consisting of a three-month modus vivendi and a ten-point note listing America's long-range position.

This modus vivendi provided: (1) the two nations, hereafter,

6

adopt a policy directed toward lasting peace throughout the Pacific area, and that unless attacked, they make no advancements across international borders from points at which they now have military establishments; (2) that Japan remove her military forces from Southern Indo-China and reduce her northern forces there to 25,000 men; (3) both governments remove the restrictions they had imposed on the assets of each other; (4) the United States undertake to induce the British and Dutch governments on a reciprocal basis to remove similar freezing restrictions on Japanese assets; (5) the United States looks with favor upon negotiations between China and Japan toward a peaceful settlement of their differences and upon an armistice during such discussions; and, finally, (6) any agreement reached would not remain in effect for a period longer than three months unless mutually agreed upon.

The longer range ten-point note provided: (1) the United States and Japan would endeavor to conclude a multilateral non-aggression pact between the British Empire, China, Japan, the Netherlands, the Soviet Union, Thailand, and the United States; (2) both the United States and Japan would endeavor to conclude a treaty between themselves and Britain, China, the Netherlands, and Thailand, agreeing to respect the territorial integrity of French Indo-China and resist any threat to that territory, with each government agreeing not to accept or seek preferred commercial advantage in that area; (3) Japan to withdraw all military, naval, or police forces from French Indo-China and China; (4) the United States and Japan to support militarily, politically, and economically only the government of Chiang Kai-shek as the government of China; (5) both governments to give up all extraterritorial rights in China as well as obtain an agreement that all other governments do likewise; (6) the United States and Japan enter a trade agreement based on reciprocal most favored nations' treatment; (7) both nations to remove freezing restrictions on the funds of each other; (8) both nations to agree upon a plan for stabilizing the rate of the Dollar-Yen; (9) the United States and Japan to agree that no agreements which either has with any third power or powers shall be interpreted by it in such a way as to conflict with the purpose of establishing peace throughout the Pacific area; and, finally, (10) both governments to use their influence to cause other governments to adhere to and give practical application to the political and economic principles of such an agreement.

On 21 November, Secretary Cordell Hull presented a copy of the proposed modus vivendi to Admiral Harold R. Stark and General Leonard Townsend Gerow (acting for General George C. Marshall) and secured their approval. He was not successful with the Allied governments. China, and later Britain, opposed the terms of the modus vivendi as appeasement of the Japanese.

Either as a result of Chinese-British opposition, reports from British Intelligence that a Japanese convoy of troopships had been sighted traveling south in the area of Formosa, or the charges of appeasement in the public press, Secretary Hull with Roosevelt's approval, on the night of 25 November, decided to drop the modus vivendi and present only the ten points to the Japanese envoys. This Hull did the next day. At the same time a Japanese Task Force, steaming eastward, was already bound for Pearl Harbor from Yokohama and had been underway for more than twenty-four hours. The six carriers, two battleships, three cruisers, and twenty other ships, at this particular point in time, could still have been recalled.

In requiring the Japanese to withdraw from China and support the Nationalists (points 3 and 4) as well as terminate its Axis partnership (9) the American counter-proposal became an uncompromising statement of terms. With considerable justification, the U.S. terms were regarded by the Japanese and by American officials as an ultimatum.

The President, General Marshall, Admiral Stark and Secretaries Henry L. Stimson and Frank Knox so regarded the ten points at a meeting of the War Council on 25 November. The day before their dispatch to the Japanese, Roosevelt even suggested that the message could precipitate a Japanese attack on either the United States or on one of the Western belligerents, "perhaps next Monday, for the Japanese are notorious for making an attack without warning." The question, the President went on, "was how we should maneuver them into the position of firing the first shot without allowing too much danger to ourselves." Those present seemed in agreement.

In fairness, it should be noted that they all felt a war with Japan was inevitable. Roosevelt and Marshall were sincerely desirous of not placing the United States in the position of an aggressor but sought to unite the nation. Marshall and Stark agreed that should the Japanese attack, it would probably be against Thailand, Malaya or the Dutch East Indies—and not the Philippines. Pearl Harbor was not mentioned.

Nevertheless on 27 November, warning messages were dispatched to General Walter Short and to Admiral Husband E. Kimmel at Pearl Harbor. The Army message read: "Negotiations with Japan appear to be terminated to all practical purposes, with only the barest possibility that the Japanese government might come back and offer to continue."

Short interpreted the message as a warning of possible sabotage and so alerted his Army command.

The message to Kimmel was more specific: "This dispatch is to be considered a war warning. Negotiations with Japan toward stabilization of conditions in the Pacific have ceased."

Kimmel interpreted the warning as an order to prepare the Navy for long-range offensive action.

The messages of 27 November were not the only warnings received by the commanders at Pearl Harbor. There had been three previous alerts in Hawaii, all the result of extreme tension in Japanese-American relations. On 17 June, 1940, the French collapse, Britain's vulnerable position, and the loss of the French Fleet made a Japanese attack on the Panama Canal appear likely.

General D. Herron, then in command at Pearl Harbor, was advised of the danger. He immediately had all anti-aircraft posts manned with orders to fire on any foreign planes that flew over restricted areas.

In July, 1941, after Tokyo had served its ultimatum on the Vichy government demanding the use of air and naval bases in Indo-China and had subsequently, on 21 July, occupied these bases, the United States embargoed petroleum and cotton exports to Japan. Washington alerted both the Army and the Navy Commands, on the 25th, of the possibility of an attack.

Again on 16 October, 1941, with the fall of the moderate government of Prince Konoye in Japan, a strongly worded message went off to Short: "The resignation of the Japanese Cabinet has created a grave situation—hostilities between Japan and Russia are a strong possibility . . . . Since the U.S. and Britain are held responsible by Japan for her present desperate situation there is also a possibility that Japan may attack these two powers. . . ."

William Friedman had given the American diplomats in their dealings with the Japanese a commanding advantage. The principal Army cryptologist, Friedman, with the aid of an assistant, Harry Lawrence Clark, after eighteen frustrating months' work had, in late September, 1940, successfully devised a machine that broke the Japanese's most secret diplomatic code.

Friedman, a mathematical genius, was born in 1891 in Bessarabia, Russia, brought to the United States when he was two, and graduated from Cornell in 1912. His achievement in solving the Japanese encoded ciphers is probably the greatest breakthrough in the history of cryptology. Considered almost miraculous, the system Friedman and Clark had devised was given the dramatic code name of "Magic." Almost simultaneously with Friedman's achievement the Office of Naval Intelligence was successful in buying code books, from a Japanese traitor, that opened up other lower priority codes.

The days between 27 November and 7 December were uneasy times for Roosevelt and his advisers. The President had left for Warm Springs, Georgia, on the 29th but at Hull's suggestion he returned two days later. It was clear from "Magic" intercepts and troop build-ups in Formosa, Hainan, and Indo-China that something was about to happen but no one was quite sure what form the action would take or where the blow would fall.

The prevailing view was that the United States or its possessions would not be attacked—that the thrust would be directed toward Thailand, the Dutch West Indies, Singapore, or the Kra Isthmus with the ultimate objective Rangoon. The problem in the minds of the American leaders seemed to be, how could Congress be persuaded to enter the war if the Japanese attack was directed against Great Britain?

Stanley Hornbeck, Hull's Chief Adviser on Far Eastern Affairs, exemplified the position of the pro-China faction in the State Department and in Congress who had wanted a hard stand taken with Japan. This faction believed there would be no immediate war, and that if there was one it would end in an early and easy victory for the United States. The War and Navy Departments did not concur with this view.

Meanwhile, "Magic" intercepts revealed on 3 December, that the Japanese embassies in London, Hong Kong, Singapore, and Manila were directed to destroy their code books. An additional intercept of a message to Berlin from Tokyo advised that a war with the Anglo-Saxon nations would occur sooner than anyone expected.[2] On the same day Japanese consulates in the United States started burning secret documents.

Mrs. Dorothy Edgers was a newcomer to the Office of Naval Intelligence in Washington. She had spent thirty of her thirty-eight years in Japan and had taught in its elementary schools. Dorothy was given employment in the Department's translation section in late November, 1941. Her first two weeks had been busy ones as messages came in thick and fast, but the efficient bi-linguist found her work both interesting and rewarding.

On Saturday, 6 December, Mrs. Edgers was at her desk but there was little activity that morning. To pass away her time she selected several "Magic" messages from the "deferred" basket. "Magic" intercepts in this category were not considered important and might lie around for several weeks, but she set to work on their translations. Finishing several, all of which seemed important to her, she came to one—longer than the others—dated 3 December and originating from Hawaii.

As Mrs. Edgers recalled four years later before the Hewitt Inquiry, investigating the Pearl Harbor attack: "—it was a message saying how they [the Japs] were going to communicate from Honolulu—"

Inexperienced though she was in the field of Intelligence, Dorothy Edgers realized the telegram's importance. When Fred C. Woodrough, a co-worker, agreed with her she took the message, half-finished, to Chief Yeoman H. L. Bryant in charge of the office in the absence of Lieutenant Commander Alvin D. Kramer.

Bryant told her the message was interesting but could hold until

[2] Conversely, intercepted reports from the Japanese Ambassador in Berlin provided excellent reports on German military operations throughout World War II.

11

Monday because it was too long to be completed by noon. Mrs. Edgers returned to her desk and continued with her work, remaining after her colleagues had left for the weekend.

She had just finished the entire translation when Commander Kramer came in at three o'clock. When she showed him her work, she found her chief less than enthusiastic.

He curtly told her, "You just go home, Mrs. Edgers, we'll get back to this piece on Monday."

As she left the office, Dorothy Edgers must have felt like a novice golfer, who on one of her first days on a course makes a hole-in-one and discovers her drive was unobserved.

Actually the message she had so painstakingly translated was one of seventeen espionage "Magic" intercepts that had been sent from Honolulu to Tokyo and placed in the deferred category. Seven of these indicated the Japanese were on the verge of war with the United States and focused considerable attention on Pearl Harbor.

Mrs. Edgers had not been the only one whose advice had been disregarded that Saturday morning. Secretary Hull and the State Department had been opposed to Roosevelt's sending a personal message to the Emperor of Japan, asking him to bend every effort toward peace in the Pacific. Nevertheless, the President sent the message.

On Capitol Hill, Congress had recessed for the weekend with only a few Senators and Representatives remaining in their offices. Even the few who could be found seemed without apprehension, or any feeling that a time bomb was slowly ticking away. In fact, Conservative Senator Walter F. George told reporters "that the Japanese did not want to force the issue," and Liberal Senator George W. Norris of Nebraska suggested that "the Japs were ready to back down."

At 7:15 A.M. Saturday "Magic" had intercepted a pilot message from Tokyo to Japanese Ambassador Nomura advising him that a long fourteen-part message for delivery to the United States government was about to be sent. Thirteen of the fourteen parts of the communication that came through during the day proved to be a flat rejection of Hull's 26 November ten-point proposal.

Following dinner, Roosevelt was relaxing with his friend Harry

Hopkins in the oval study when he was given a copy of the first thirteen parts of the Japanese message. Both men agreed there would be war and Japan would strike first, probably in Indo-China. That neither of the two men mentioned Pearl Harbor is understandable. The President's Army and Navy advisers had never even suggested that an attack on Hawaii was within the realm of possibility. Specifically questioned, Admiral Stark had told the President that the U.S. fleet was at sea and that Pearl Harbor was not in danger. Nor had the President been given any of the espionage messages that had emanated from Honolulu. Actually he had only seen 64 out of the 1,800 "Magic" intercepts.

Sunday, December 7, dawned crisp and clear in Washington with the temperature hovering around fifty degrees. In the Victorian red brick Quarters No. 1, at Fort Myer, Virginia, General George Catlett Marshall, the Army Chief of Staff, arose at six thirty.

An aloof, austere man, the general was a creature of habit. Almost every Sunday morning, accompanied only by his Dalmatian, the general went horseback riding on his bay gelding, King Storm, along the Potomac River. On this particular morning, Marshall stayed on the Virginia side of the river, but unfortunately, he failed to tell one of his orderlies the route he planned to follow.

Even though it was Sunday, Colonel Rufus (Rufe or sometimes Tojo) Sumter Bratton, Chief of the Army's Military Intelligence Division, Far Eastern Section, was in his office in the Munitions Building by 9 A.M.

A South Carolinian, and a 1914 graduate of West Point, the 49-year-old Bratton had spent most of his military career in the Army's Intelligence branch. He would never become a general officer, but he was forthright, imaginative and, above all, responsible. Three tours of duty as a language student and as an attaché in Tokyo made Bratton "the right man in the right spot." Somewhat glum, even a Cassandra, Bratton had been of the opinion that war with Japan in the immediate future was inevitable. He even predicted that a Nipponese surprise attack would start the conflict. He prophesied the date as 29 November. When that date proved uneventful, Bratton received Bronx cheers from his colleagues.

As the War Department "Magic" custodian, Bratton was one of the few Army officers who had access to the decoded Japanese messages. Waiting for him in his office that morning was the missing fourteenth part of the long message plus several additional communications from Tokyo.

One instructed Nomura that, if possible, he submit the Japanese reply to the United States government at exactly 1 P.M. Washington time; the other stated that after the receipt of the current messages he (Nomura) "destroy at once the remaining cipher machine and all machine codes."

To Bratton, the messages, together, meant that war would start that day at 1 P.M.

He immediately telephoned Quarters 1 at Fort Myer and told Sergeant Aguirre, "Find General Marshall. Get assistance, if necessary. Tell him who I am, and ask him to go to the nearest telephone, that it is vitally important that I communicate with him at the earliest practicable moment."

However, because of the route the general had taken, Aguirre was unable to locate the general and the message went undelivered until Marshall returned from his ride.

When Marshall called Bratton at 10:25 A.M. to say that he would soon be at his office, the colonel was evidently unable to communicate to the general his feelings of urgency regarding the intercept. By the time Marshall completed his unhurried and meticulous ablutions, ordered his car from Washington and drove to his office, it was well past eleven thirty. Even then, the general refused to look at the messages that Colonel Bratton gave him until he had completely read the entire fourteenth part of the Japanese reply.

Finally, after examining the intercepts, Marshall was convinced of the gravity of the situation and prepared a note of warning to be sent to the commanders in the Pacific. Three precious hours had elapsed before General Marshall had taken positive action.

The warnings to Manila, the Canal Zone, and the Presidio in San Francisco, were immediately dispatched, but since 10:30 A.M. atmospheric conditions had prevented the Signal Corps from reaching Fort Shafter, which lies about six miles southeast of Pearl Harbor. The messages could have been sent by the Navy, whose channels with the AIEA Naval Radio Station were open, but Colonel Edward F. French, Chief of Traffic Operations, probably would not admit that Navy messages could get through when the

Army couldn't. Whatever his reasons, French elected to send the wire by commercial facilities. It was 12:17 when he gave the message to Western Union. Ten-and-a-half hours later, long after the last Japanese aircraft had returned to its carrier and the Nipponese fleet was homeward bound, the Marshall warning was delivered to General Short.[3]

General Marshall's Navy counterpart, Admiral Stark, was no more decisive. An erudite, progressive officer, he was at least in his office on that morning of crisis. Stark also had "Rufe" Bratton's "Magic" intercepts before him. Lifting up the telephone to call Admiral Kimmel, the thought of Navy protocol and doctrines he was violating stayed Stark's hand. After all, Kimmel was the commander in the field and it wasn't Washington's prerogative to tell him how to exercise command. The admiral decided he should tell the President of the intercepts. When advised that Roosevelt's extension was busy, he even gave up that attempt at action.

Pearl Harbor in all its tropical languor had never been lovelier than on the night of December 6, 1941. A light breeze ruffled the leaves of the coconut palms and the lights shining from the windows of the barracks seemed to shimmer in unison. The strains of dance music from the several officers' and enlisted men's clubs could be heard in the distance. Except for an occasional sentry or a couple looking for a secluded spot, there were few people on the streets and even they talked in hushed and subdued tones as if caught up in the magic of the tropical night.

Always cheerful, almost always smiling, New England-born Sergeant Charles Gallup had brought Helen, whom he had met only a short month before, to the dance at the NCO club. He had twice proposed to her and twice been rejected. Gallup detected a note of uncertainty in the second refusal and planned to try again that night.

He sensed that Helen loved him, but realized she thought he was

---

[3] The message from Marshall actually arrived at the Honolulu RCA terminal at 7:33 A.M. Honolulu time. The first Japanese plane attacked twenty-two minutes later. By the time the warning was delivered to the Signal Center and decoded, seven hours and three minutes had elapsed since the message had left Washington.

not serious enough to be a life companion. For days he pondered how he could convince her that he had ambition. Tonight he planned to tell her that he had been accepted for Officer Candidate School. Maybe that would do the trick. Gallup was to live through the next day only to die a captain three years later in a vineyard in Southern France. The daughter of Helen and Charles never saw her father.

Second Lieutenant Richard Noonan and his four-month-pregnant wife, Stella, had gone to the Schofield Barracks Officers' Open Mess for supper. It was a buffet to be followed by a benefit cabaret and dance. Noonan wanted to celebrate, but for what he wasn't quite sure. They were saving for the baby's arrival and watching their pennies. One night with Stella away from the dismal kitchen of their stuffy apartment would not ruin them financially.

Dick and Stella had married right after his graduation from V.M.I. He didn't regret their marriage, but somehow there hadn't been the glamour he anticipated. Nothing unusual occurred that night but Stella would always remember it as the night before Dick was killed. As he ran to his mobile battery, the ammunition for which was locked up more than six miles away, he was strafed by machine gun fire from a low-flying Japanese plane.

Lieutenant General and Mrs. Walter C. Short had also planned to be at the Schofield Officers Club but were delayed. Lieutenant Colonel William Buckell, a G2 on Short's staff, arrived just as they were leaving. Buckell reported an odd telephone call monitored by the FBI the previous day.

The call had presumably been placed by the Tokyo newspaper *Yomiuri Shinbun* to the husband of its Honolulu correspondent, Dr. Motokazu Mori, a dentist. The conversation had been about weather, planes, searchlights, and flowers. Was it in code? If so, why the open talk about planes, and anyhow spies seldom used the telephone. Neither Short, his G2, nor Lieutenant Colonel Kendall Fielders, who was also present, could make sense out of the message. They decided to let it wait until morning and the Shorts went on to the Club.

CINCPAC Admiral Husband E. Kimmel and his wife were attending a small dinner party given by Admiral and Mrs. Fairfax

Leary at the Halekulani Hotel. Kimmel was a tired and weary man that evening and not a very entertaining guest. His staff had assured him that there was no possibility of an attack on Pearl Harbor, but there was the nagging knowledge that talks between Japan and the United States had broken down in Washington. According to the FBI, the Nippon consulate staff in Honolulu was burning its code books and secret papers. He and Mrs. Kimmel left the hotel early, returned to their home and were in bed by ten o'clock.

Honolulu had begun to fill with enlisted men early that Saturday afternoon. The gaudy honky-tonk emporiums and bars, designed to extract the last penny from enlisted pay, were jammed with sailors and soldiers. There were more of the latter that weekend than usual. The crews of the mobile anti-aircraft batteries were not in the field simulating fire at friendly planes, as they had been doing the past months. Their conduct for youths in a foreign atmosphere was better than could have been reasonably expected. There were few fights and though the shore patrols and MPs did pick up a few drunks, most of the servicemen quietly played their pinball machines, watched the movies, or drank their beer.

By 3 A.M. Sunday morning, the brazen voices of the juke boxes were stilled, and the men had returned to their ships and barracks. The souvenirs that had been bought or won, all with the word Aloha, had been stowed awaiting delivery in the States.

As the officers and enlisted men on the ships and in the barracks were making ready for bed, a flotilla of six carriers, two battleships, three cruisers, and nine destroyers some four hundred miles to the north steamed quietly through the night toward the south.

Although the fleet's commander, Vice Admiral Chuichi Nagumo, was satisfied that he would achieve surprise, only shrouded binnacle lights broke the darkness, while the quiet was interrupted by the dull slap of the waves as the prows of the ships knifed through the warm waters.

Below decks on the carriers, many of the young pilots tried to sleep, but the excitement in anticipation of the morrow proved too much and they rolled and tossed. Others were writing home what they thought might be a last message (50 percent casualties in the

17

next day's operation had been anticipated). Often a lock of hair or a fingernail paring was included in the letter.

From the desk of the leading carrier several reconnaissance planes were launched to report back at dawn any ship movements at Pearl Harbor. When the fleet was about two hundred miles from its target, shortly after 3 A.M., the first combat planes started taking off and circling to get into formation. In two flights, spaced a half hour apart, two hundred and seventy fighters, dive-bombers, torpedo bombers, and attack craft took to the air.

After they were airborne, the pilots tuned in their radios to the Honolulu stations of KGU and KGMB. The usual programs were being broadcast. Obviously all was normal in Hawaii for there seemed to be no apprehension of danger on the part of the announcers.

At 3:42 A.M. on 7 December, Ensign R. C. McCloy on the small minesweeper *Condor* spotted what he thought was the wake of a submerged submarine. It was a thousand yards from the entrance to the harbor and in a restricted area. A quarter of an hour later by blinker the *Condor* signaled the destroyer *Ward* on patrol duty, "Sighted submerged submarine on westerly course, speed nine knots."

On the *Ward*, Captain William W. Outerbridge sounded the general quarters and for the next hour the destroyer searched vainly for the sub. At 6:30 A.M., Seaman H. E. Raenbig on the bridge of the *Ward* sighted a black object that was at first thought to be a buoy. The destroyer headed for the object, and determined it to be a small conning tower. General quarters was sounded again. A Navy PBY circling overhead also spotted the sub and the pilot, Ensign William Tanner, dropped two smoke pots to mark the sub's position. At 6:45, the first shot in the Pacific war was fired from the *Ward*. It was high but the second was a direct hit. Thereafter four depth charges were released from the stern of the destroyer, while Tanner dropped two from his PBY.

At 6:51 and at 6:53 Outerbridge dispatched messages to the Fourteenth Naval District Headquarters that he had "—fired on, depth-bombed and sunk submarine operating in defensive sea area." Only a few minutes later at 7:03, the *Ward* located another submarine on her sonar and dropped five more depth charges. A large black oil slick erupted some three hundred feet astern. Outer-bridge duly reported his actions to Headquarters.

It was 7:12 before the *Ward*'s 6:53 message had been decoded, typed, and placed in the hands of Commander Harold Kaminsky, the duty officer. It threw the headquarters into a dither. By the time all officers in the chain of command, including Admiral Kimmel, had been informed, it was 7:40. Concurrently, a message from Ensign Tanner that his PBY had sunk a submarine added to the confusion.

At the Army's radar station near Kahuku Point, Privates Joseph Lockard and George Elliott were about to go off duty. They had manned the post since 4 A.M. and it was now 7 A.M. These were the only hours General Short thought necessary or critical. The pickup truck that was to take them to breakfast had not arrived. Since they had nothing to do, they kept the radar set on.

At 7:02 a huge blip—the largest they had ever seen—appeared on the screen. Lockard at first thought there was something wrong with the set but, after checking, found it in working order, and decided it was a large flight of planes. Within a few minutes the position of the planes was established as 137 miles to the north, three degrees east.

Lockard realized the information should be sent on to someone but he was not sure to whom. He first tried calling the line to the spotters in the Information Center at Shafter, but found the line dead. He next tried the Army circuit and reached the switchboard operator, Private Joseph McDonald, who wrote down the message and took it to Lieutenant Kermit Tyler, a pilot, the only officer on duty in the Information Center.

Tyler was quite blasé about the matter and turned down McDonald's suggestion that they call back the plotters from breakfast. McDonald called back Lockard and found him quite excited—the flight was coming in fast. He asked to speak to Tyler, who assured him the blip was not important, saying, "don't worry about it." Lockard and Elliott followed the flight on the screen until 7:39 when they lost contact, turned off the set and were picked up for breakfast.

And then it happened!

At exactly 7:50, Honolulu time (1:20 P.M. in Washington) the first bomb exploded at Pearl Harbor. Within minutes the *USS Oklahoma* took five torpedoes, the *West Virginia* six, the *California* and *Utah*, two each, and the *Detroit*, *Raleigh*, and *Helena*, one. The backbone of the Pacific Fleet ceased to exist.

General Short's fear of sabotage had resulted in the Army planes at both Hickam and Wheeler fields being grouped together in neat rows. They were destroyed before their pilots could even reach them. When the last Japanese plane left at about ten o'clock, American naval power in the Pacific had been paralyzed. The Philippine Islands soon fell like a ripe plum into the orbit of the Greater East Asia Co-Prosperity Sphere.

Stanley D. Porteus in his book *And Blow Not the Trumpet* tells of a "professor who was spending Sunday morning at Waikiki with his newly acquired Scots wife. 'See my dear,' he said proudly, when the commotion was at its height over Pearl Harbor, 'that is the way we carry out maneuvers in America. Look at that smoke screen. See those anti-aircraft shells and the plane darting in and out. I'll guarantee you saw nothing as realistic as that in the European War all the time you were in Scotland.'" She agreed, she hadn't.

The cool bravery, the studied precision of civilians, enlisted men, and officers at Pearl Harbor, at Schofield, and at the airfields, is the stuff of which sagas are written and legends created. Somehow the guns of the burning and sinking ships went into action. The fixed anti-aircraft pieces opened up, and the mobile positions somehow obtained ammunition and began firing.

Dorie Miller, the twenty-two-year-old son of a Waco, Texas, Negro sharecropper, was waiting table in the junior officers' wardroom of the *USS West Virginia* when the call to battle stations was sounded. Running to the nearest ladder, Miller arrived topside when a cascade of bombs smashed the deck and mortally wounded the ship's commander.

Knocked down by the concussion of the explosion, Miller scrambled to his feet and carried the dying captain to cover. Under a hail of bullets from a strafing plane Miller then raced to an unmanned machine gun. He was untrained in the use of the weapon for, in the segregated Navy of that day, Negroes were restricted to messboy duties. Nevertheless, Miller was soon blasting away at the

20

Japanese planes. During the battle he shot down four enemy aircraft and won the highest Naval decoration—the Navy Cross. One of the authentic heroes of World War II, Miller died two years later, almost to the day, when the carrier *Liscombe Bay*, on which he was still serving as a messboy, was torpedoed and sunk in the Pacific.

Commander E. P. Kranzfelder was at the Moana Hotel in Honolulu when, at 8:20, the phone operator called to say an emergency necessitated an immediate return to his ship. Within ten minutes he was on the bridge of the *Maryland*. Receiving a frantic call for help from the nearby overturned *Oklahoma*, he was given permission to aid in the rescue work.

Fortunately he was able to lay his hands on a copy of the blueprints of the *Oklahoma*'s hull. On the overturned vessel he soon arranged for lines to be rigged from the bilge keel at intervals along the bottom and an air supply line from the *Maryland* as well as telephone communications.

Contact was made with two men trapped in the evaporator pump room. With information supplied by the imprisoned men and with the help of the plans, holes were cut in the ship's hull and the two men were extracted. It was a touchy business for practically the entire bottom of the *Oklahoma* consisted of oil tanks and a spark from the oxyacetylene torch could have started a serious fire.

In the harbor almost every craft was pressed into action. Tugs, lighters, and other small boats assisted in fighting the fires on the *West Virginia* and *Arizona* and rescuing personnel from the *Oklahoma*. The garbage lighter *YG 17* not only went alongside the *West Virginia* but for twenty-four hours directed streams of water on the battleship and on the edge of the burning fuel on the sea. A motor whaleboat from the *Honolulu* made constant trips along the edge of this burning oil in an effort to prevent its spreading. Time after time the boat would catch fire, but, after the flames were extinguished, would return to fight the burning oil.

Meanwhile, at Hickam Field just east of Pearl Harbor where, in accordance with General Short's sabotage order, the planes were lined up on the ground wing tip to wing tip, the base commander, Colonel William Farthing and members of his staff were in the control tower by 7:30 A.M. awaiting the arrival of twelve B17s from the mainland. That such a number of these new fantastic "Flying Fortresses" were to come in at one time made it quite an occasion. As they waited, they noticed a formation of planes diving on the naval installations and someone remarked that it was a "very realistic maneuver."[4] Their happy complacency was soon dispelled as the Jap planes began strafing the neat row of planes on their own field.

Unwarned, the B17s from the mainland received a peculiar type of welcome. Several of the "Flying Fortresses" had barely landed when they were attacked and destroyed.

While the control tower at Hickam calmly remained in operation during the Japanese attack, on the base itself there was general pandemonium. Both weapons and ammunition were under lock and key. Everyone wanted to do something, but didn't know what. Fortunately a bomb sheared off one end of the guardhouse releasing the prisoners and they seemed to be the first to realize that a war was on. Breaking into the storerooms, they were soon armed with rifles and .50 caliber machine guns and were firing away at the enemy planes.[5] At Wheeler the stockade was opened and all the prisoners released. The security of a lock and key meant nothing to the former guardhouse inmates and they soon had a series of machine gun positions manned, and in operation.

There wasn't quite as much confusion at Schofield Barracks. Bugler Frank Gobeo didn't know how to blow call to arms so he substituted pay call and found it quite effective. The men quickly broke into the supply rooms and were soon firing at the enemy planes. However, others were prevented from having weapons by a bureaucratic top sergeant who insisted that arms could not be released without permission from the adjutant.

At Pearl Harbor it was some time before many realized that they were actually under attack. It just could not be. The possibility had been talked about for so long. Now it was here and it just didn't

[4] Walter Lord, *Day of Infamy* (New York, Henry Holt and Company, 1957), p. 78.
[5] Often the troublesome peacetime soldier performs well in combat. See Robert Adleman and George Walton, *The Devil's Brigade* (Philadelphia, Chilton, 1966).

seem possible. Lieutenant Tyler at the Shafter Information Center was finally convinced the air raid was real and recalled his plotters from breakfast.

By ten o'clock, when the attack ended, eighteen ships, including the battleships *Arizona, Oklahoma, West Virginia, California, Tennessee, Maryland, Pennsylvania,* and *Nevada*; the target ship, *Utah*; the destroyers *Downes, Shaw,* and *Cassin*; the minelayer *Oglala*; the cruisers *Helena, Honolulu,* and *Raleigh*; the seaplane tender *Curtiss*; and the repair ship *Vestal,* were either sunk, beached, or badly damaged.[6] On the airfields 188 planes were destroyed and 159 damaged.

Even more important, when the Nipponese aircraft had made their way back to their carriers, 2,008 sailors had been killed and 710 wounded; 218 soldiers killed and 346 wounded; 109 marines killed and 69 wounded; 68 civilians killed and 35 wounded, for a total American casualty list of 3,581. For all this the Japanese Navy had paid with 29 planes, 1 large and 6 midget submarines, and the lives of 55 airmen, 9 midget sub crewmen, and an undetermined number of the crew of the large underwater craft.

There is no glib and easy explanation of the Pearl Harbor disaster. Rather, its causes are diverse and complex. Certainly, except for a few thoughtless remarks and equally careless actions, there has not been a shred of evidence produced to prove that any official of the United States government deliberately acted to provoke the attack to draw the nation into the war.

Within a matter of days, General Short and Admiral Kimmel were relieved and officially made scapegoats. Both men were deprived of critical information and the last messages they received were so ambiguous that Short interpreted his as a sabotage warning and Kimmel concluded that it was a directive for strategic planning. Nevertheless, within their respective commands, the two commanders cannot be excused from the charge of laxity.

With considerable justification, Admiral Stark was preoccupied with the danger of sabotage. He and his staff believed this posed a greater threat in the Hawaiian Islands than the remote possibility of attack. If there could be a Fifth Column in France, Norway, or

[6] Lord, *op. cit.,* p. 220.

Denmark, how much greater was the chance in Hawaii, where one-third of the population was of Japanese origin.

Many of the Asians boasted of the land of their ancestors. As late as 1939, it had been necessary for the Federal Securities and Exchange Commission to go into court and ask for an injunction to prevent the sale of Japanese War Bonds in the Islands.

In March, 1941, fifty tons of comfort for the Emperor's soldiers had been shipped from Honolulu to Japan by the Japanese Chamber of Commerce. These bags contained blankets, shoes, candy, and other items to gladden the hearts of the Jap GIs. Fifteen hundred tons of scrap iron for the Nipponese war effort also went by the same ship.[7]

Accordingly, when General Short and his staff received the warning of 27 November, they thought not in terms of attack, but rather of sabotage. A full-scale alert was not ordered, but the guard was doubled and the planes on the airfields were lined up wing to wing so that they might be more easily protected. That they made beautiful bombing and strafing targets never entered anyone's mind.

Nevertheless, neither Short nor Kimmel met the challenges of that "Day of Infamy." As commanders in the field, theirs was the primary responsibility to meet any contingency that threatened their commands. As Secretary Stimson was later to say: "The outpost commander is like a sentinel on duty in the face of the enemy. . . . He must assume that the enemy will attack at the time and in the way in which it will be most difficult to defeat him. It is (the commander's) duty to meet him at his post at any time and to make the best possible fight that can be made against him with the weapons with which he has been supplied."

A share of the responsibility for the complacency that existed at Pearl Harbor on the morning of 7 December, 1941, must also be accorded the respective staffs of General Short and Admiral Kimmel as well as the other officers of their commands. Not only did the staffs advise their commanders that an attack was not likely but, with alerts commonplace, the officers of the permanent party had become careless.

[7] Stanley D. Porteus, *And Blow Not the Trumpet* (Palo Alto, California, Pacific Books, 1947).

For some weeks prior to that Sunday morning, the mobile anti-aircraft batteries had been in the field every weekend, but without live ammunition, and it took hours to obtain the shells from Alia-mann Crater where they were stored. The Ordnance Department possessively objected to the ammunition being in the field where it might get muddy and have to be cleaned. When the Japanese struck, the batteries were not only out of position, but the am-munition was six miles away. By the time they were ready to go into action the attack was over. The fixed batteries did have their shells handy, but they were crated in boxes.

Nor was complacency confined to those in the military at Pearl Harbor. In Washington, even in hours of crisis, bureaucratic in-sistence on business as usual, regular hours, and the postponement of decisive problems that might interfere with a weekend prevailed. Commander Kramer's reaction to Mrs. Edger's concern over the message she had translated is a typical example of this mentality. Colonel Bratton was to say, after the war, when talking of the Edger incident, "If we had gotten that message (on December 6) the whole picture would have been different."[8]

In the months prior to 7 December, 1941, many officials in Wash-ington held a number of pre-conceived notions which they refused to abandon. Originally, in 1940, the State, War, and Navy De-partments agreed that any Japanese attack, if it came, would be directed toward the Russian Pacific Maritime provinces. This would have been a logical move on the part of Japan since the United States would have found it difficult to embargo oil and scrap to a nation fighting Communists, much less declare war.

In 1941, when Japanese movements were to the south, those in the Army and, particularly, the Navy War Plans Divisions con-cluded that any attack would be directed against the British or Dutch and not against territory of the United States. Because both Great Britain and the Netherlands were heavily committed else-where, they were vulnerable. Japan, they believed, was a carrion nation, a jackal, that would only attack an injured enemy. That the Japanese would be so illogical as to court disaster by attacking the powerful United States, they could not believe. Information sup-

[8] Ladislas Farago, *The Broken Seal* (London, Arthur Barker Ltd., 1967) p. 368.

plied by the Peruvian Embassy to Ambassador Joseph Grew in Tokyo in January, 1941, and his warnings, of 3 November that same year, of the possibility of an attack on the United States were dismissed as fantastic.

Navy officers, from Admiral Stark down, were firmly convinced that an attack on Pearl Harbor was outside the realm of possibility. The strength of that base went far beyond anything that could be thrown against it. Besides, the depth of its water was not sufficient for the use of torpedo bombers. According to U.S. naval experts, the effective use of torpedoes required a depth of at least 75 feet. At Pearl, outside the main ship channel, the water ran only 30 feet deep. The fact that the British had developed a torpedo that did not require such a depth was ignored. No one believed the Japs could possibly top this British achievement.

In 1941, those engaged in Intelligence work were not held in high esteem. Line officers did not aspire to spend their careers in Intelligence. The trade received little attention after World War I, and Intelligence officers were considered second rate or, even worse, eccentric. Secretary Stimson best expressed it when he remarked: "Gentlemen, don't read each other's mail."

Intelligence became a dead end street. An Intelligence expert might reach the rank of Army colonel or Navy captain but it was almost impossible to advance to general or flag grade.

There were, of course, in the Intelligence ranks many able and brilliant officers—men of the caliber of Colonel William F. Friedman, who broke the Japanese code and who was responsible for "Magic;" and Colonel Bratton. But because of the persistent and prevailing tendency to downgrade Intelligence work, Army and Navy Intelligence estimates and analyses were often greeted with suspicion and the conclusions reached by its practitioners met with indifference.

This was not the whole story of the breakdown in Intelligence prior to Pearl Harbor. There must be added what today would be called an "information handling problem." "Magic" intercepts were, for security reasons, circulated only to a select group of officers and officials. Rigid handling instructions required their immediate return. It was impossible to consider an intercept in relation to a previous message. There were sufficient Intelligence indications of intentions, prior to 7 December, to have arrived at the conclusion that an attack on Pearl Harbor was both possible and probable—but they were locked in steel safes in the old Munitions Building.

Pearl Harbor was a perfect example of the military doctrine of "strategic surprise." Within living memory the United States has been the victim of this military principle in at least three instances. The first was Pearl Harbor. The Battle of the Bulge, or the Ardennes offensive, fell into this category because Hitler's objective was strategic—a second Dunkirk. The third example of "strategic surprise" was the Chinese attack across the Yalu River and the defeat of the Eighth Army in the Korean War. All three of these events occurred when the United States Intelligence community failed to properly interpret information it possessed. There was adequate intelligence, but the experts had developed a set mind. Today another "strategic surprise" may well be in the making in the Near East.

The intellectuals, the Far Eastern experts, the university professors, without exception, argued that war with Japan was most unlikely. They insisted that she was so bogged down in China that it was impossible for her to conduct a full scale war; that the Imperial Empire was close to economic collapse if not social revolution.

In 1940, Owen Lattimore wrote: "This collapse [of Japan]—an intricate matter of combined military prostration, financial strain, and industrial inadequacy—can be realistically expected."

Almost on the eve of the attack on Pearl Harbor, the professors still argued that Japan was bluffing. On 26 November, following the dispatch of Hull's ten points, Dr. Stanley Hornbeck, a Far Eastern expert who had spent many years in China, wrote a memorandum for Secretary Hull in which he said:

> In the opinion of the undersigned, the Japanese government does not desire or intend or expect to have forthwith armed conflict with the United States. So far as relations directly between the United States and Japan are concerned, there is less reason today than there was a week ago for the United States to be apprehensive lest Japan make "war" on this country.
>
> Were it a matter of placing bets—the undersigned would give odds of five to one that the United States and Japan will not be

at "war" on or before December 15—would wager three to one that the United States and Japan will not be at "war" on or before the 15th of January—would wager even money that the United States and Japan will not be at "war" on or before March 1—.

Stated briefly, the undersigned does not believe this country is now on the immediate verge of "war" in the Pacific.[9]

The illogical belief—racism, if you please—that the little myopic yellow man of Japan could never make his country a first rate power was also to contribute to our "comeuppance." Stemming from Victorian days when the Nipponese were the favorite comedians in the musicals of Gilbert and Sullivan, this conception reached its peak with the exclusion and discrimination against the Japanese in California. Pearl Harbor and the subsequent war in the Pacific soon ended this misconception. Today, we may not love the Japanese, but they are accorded our respect.

That the Pacific fleet should have been at San Diego rather than at Pearl Harbor is now generally agreed. It had been originally sent to the Islands on maneuvers in the spring of 1940. However, on the theory that its presence was a deterrent to Japanese ambitions, it was allowed to remain there indefinitely. Roosevelt and his naval advisers committed an error of judgment in considering the Pacific fleet a threat to Japan, rather than a target.

As the bombs rained down on Pearl Harbor this nation exchanged a decade of economic stagnation and nationwide poverty for the horrors of war and an industrial development of unprecedented magnitude. The affluence of today, that allows our youth the luxury of tearing the nation apart, had its birth at Pearl Harbor. Our fantastic commercial growth, increasing for over three decades, came into being as the first Japanese pilot started his bomb-run.

The economic depression that plagued the nation in the late thirties began to disappear when the little Austrian paperhanger unleashed his legions on September 1, 1939. The last vestiges of that industrial paralysis died that Sunday morning at Pearl Harbor. In spite of the examples of World War I, Tojo, Hitler, and Mussolini all underestimated the economic might of America.

[9] *Ibid.*, pp. 284-285.

28

Now that we were in the shooting war, the nation's industries were able to accomplish miracles. The saga of General Motors and its conversion from "guns and butter" to just "guns" is typical. In the days following December 7, its peacetime production lines ground to a halt. New factories were built, new men trained, and other workers re-trained. Machines were replaced or re-tooled, new assembly lines established. Within months the corporation was turning out the materials of war.

During the next four years General Motors produced items ranging from tiny ball bearings to thirty-ton tanks. It made .30 and .50 caliber machine guns, the M-1 carbine, the Oerlikon 20mm anti-aircraft cannon, the 40mm Bofors cannon, the 75mm cannon, the 20mm cannon that was used in the noses of war planes, and the big 90mm anti-aircraft cannon. Other branches of GM turned out blockbuster fuses, aerial torpedoes, ambulances, trucks, weapon carriers, tanks, and aerial items including the liquid-cooled Allison engine, the Pratt and Whitney radial engine, and the Hamilton-Standard propeller.

More than 12,000 independent companies sub-contracted for General Motors during the war years. Altogether during this period the company produced military equipment with a dollar value of more than $12¼ billion. At its peak it ran as high as $12 million per day. It produced one-fourth of all airplane engines, tanks, and armored cars and one-half of all machine guns and carbines, two-thirds of all heavy trucks, and three-fourths of all Diesel engines used by the Navy.

The war stories of the other industrial giants of America are equally fabulous. Westinghouse, General Electric, RCA, and Ford all turned in records of accomplishment that are almost beyond comprehension. Pearl Harbor had seen the birth of the military-industrial complex.

American industrial might was not the only achievement to emerge from the holocaust. Medical research advanced further in the war years that followed Pearl Harbor than in all the ages of its history. A preventive for polio, influenza, and a host of vaccines and antibiotics, as well as new life-saving surgical techniques, were discovered. These medical miracles created the population explosion which a later discovery, "The Pill," may help to correct. A bio-medical revolution began on that day of battle.

Although inter-related, the social changes in the national fabric that were to follow may be even more important than the industrial, medical, and scientific developments. Certainly the family structure was never to be the same again.

With full employment and often with the wife or mother an additional wage earner, the income of the average blue-collar family soon rose to an unprecedented peak. Those who had struggled for generations, economically, reached the middle class. Having arrived, there came the desire for the luxuries of life. The buying spree, mostly on credit, that came after World War II and continues to this day, logically catapulted a large segment of our population into a different, more affluent social category.

Material possessions were not the only desires of this newly elevated class. Dreams of better living conditions, of a cleaner environment with fresh air, were realized by a massive exodus from urban areas. Levittowns soon dotted the landscape.

As with all who have advanced a few rungs on the social ladder, children soon became a new obsession. Largely neglected in their former urban environment, they were placed on a pedestal, after 1945, as status symbols. Allowed to run at will during the war when Mother had been employed, it was now much easier to raise them under the new permissive theories of the child psychologists. Mentally capable or not, they must receive the college education that their fathers and mothers had been denied. Thousands of little colleges with few admission requirements sprang up all over the land. Ultimately, with standards necessarily lowered, we were to see a rapid decline in the quality of higher education.

While segregation in the armed forces continued through World War II, the end of that conflict spelled trouble in the area of race relations. The Negro who served in Europe, Africa, and the South Pacific and was almost treated like a human being was not willing to return to America as a third-rate citizen. As long as the nation continued to be blind to racial unrest, conflict and excesses were inevitable, but Pearl Harbor hastened their arrival.

Another overall effect not to be overlooked is that the moment Japan precipitated the war in the Pacific it set the stage for the development of an entirely different China. Had Japan not elected to go to war, China might not have emerged as it did—a powerful, lumbering giant, Communist-oriented, and an unstable influence in

Far Eastern affairs. Actually, the Pacific hostilities that ensued brought about the decline of the Dutch and British as colonial powers in the area and, though Japan later emerged as an important global power in the 1960s, China itself had by this time undergone many changes. In its own way, it had become a colossus beyond our control and Russia's, with whom it shared a form of its ideology.

The Japanese attack also thrust America into the leadership of the Free World. That we were ill-prepared, or that a democracy is not the best vehicle for such a role, is beside the point. A leadership vacuum existed and we had no other alternative than to assume the responsibility. We did our best, and some of our efforts were good and some were bad. The Truman Doctrine, the Marshall Plan, the Berlin Airlift, the military assistance throughout the world, the Korean War, the Dominican crisis, and the conflict in Vietnam today were all reactions to what we considered a global responsibility. We were to learn, as had England and France, that a democracy cannot fight a prolonged and limited war of the magnitude of that in Vietnam.

The end of innocence, of isolationism, and the assumption of world leadership by the United States, were not the only products of the Japanese attack. Pearl Harbor marked both the beginning of American militarism, and her great military-industrial complex. On the world scene, it set in motion events that would ultimately lead to an end of colonialism.

Pearl Harbor was a turning point in history, perhaps equal to the Fall of Carthage, Constantinople, the Battle of Hastings, or the Russian Revolution.

There are few of us who were over ten that day who do not remember just where we were and what we were doing when we heard the news of the Japanese attack. Thereafter, adult Americans divided their lives into two periods, before and after Pearl Harbor.

Later that Sunday afternoon, still in a state of shock, as we hovered over our radios avid for news, we had little conception of the impact of the events in those distant isles. All that we could then grasp, was that the concept of "Fortress" America had been a gigantic illusion and that our lives would never again be quite the same.

2.

THE BOOB
TUBE—
TELEVISION

The invention of television is not isolated in the sense of Pearl Harbor or even Hiroshima. It did not occur in a relatively short period of time, but was the result of the work of many generations of men over a period of almost a century and a half.

It began, perhaps, 153 years ago, in 1817, when a Swedish scientist by the name of Professor Jons Berzelius discovered that a sulphur substance, selenium, could conduct electricity. Sixty years later an Irish telegrapher, Andrew May, found that by using selenium he could electrically transmit light.

The first television set was constructed by Paul Nipkow, a German, in 1884. By means of a scanning disc that picked up the picture through peepholes and etched them on a light-sensitive tube, he was able to produce crude reproductions. In 1890, Julius Eister and Hans Geitel, both Germans, produced the photo-electric cells which were to make the TV camera possible.

Following the dawn of the twentieth century, in 1907, A.A. Campbell Swinton, an Englishman, and Boris Rosing, a Russian, working separately and not knowing of the existence of the other, developed a tube that would store light for the TV camera.

Thereafter, scientists continued their efforts in this field, but not until the 1920s were there any considerable breakthroughs. In 1923, Charles Francis Jenkins in the United States and James Logie Baird in London, using the Nipkow scanning discs, were successful in transmitting shadows by radio. Other scientists, particularly Drs. Philo T. Farnsworth and Vladimir K. Zworykin, tried scanning pictures with an electric beam. Zworykin, working in the laboratories of General Electric, used the Swinton principle to develop the iconoscope. By the middle 1930s, American industry had spent $10 million on television research.

The decades between 1920 and 1940 were periods of television experimentation and conjecture. Would the new medium follow the course of radio? Would it be used in conjunction with the telephone? Would it find a use in retail merchandising? Would it be used in theaters, or would there be a combination of uses?

Dr. Zworykin had a profound influence on the solution of this problem when he transferred his allegiance from General Electric to the Radio Corporation of America. Had he continued with General Electric it is possible that the motion picture industry would have taken over the new medium and its form today might be quite different. Because the Russian scientist joined RCA, television developed into the image of radio.

The first commercial use of television was made in 1924 by the William Morris Agency of New York. A bulky and heavy set was constructed from which pictures were transmitted from one side of a stage to the other. Audiences were not only interested, but delighted. Unfortunately, the set was so heavy that it fell through the floor of a stage in a Baltimore theater and crashed into the basement. The set was never rebuilt.

The first closed circuit television broadcast was made over the wires of the American Telephone and Telegraph Company on April 7, 1927. In New York, selected guests of AT&T saw and heard Herbert Hoover, then Secretary of Commerce, speak from Washington.

In 1931, the H. and H. Corset Company of New York, using the lines of AT&T, conducted a modeling show of its products for the benefit of a buyer from Franklin Simon. The models were at the Bell Laboratory in lower Manhattan and the viewers were two miles north. It was just a stunt, but it suggested another possible use for the new medium.

The year 1928 saw the first use of TV as we now know it. From its laboratory in Schenectady, General Electric broadcast a one-act play, *The Queen's Messenger.* TV hams reported receiving the program although the picture on their tubes was only 3 by 3 inches. Because of this handicap, only closeups of the actors or props could be seen. It was, however, a long step forward.

Meanwhile, progress was also being made in Great Britain. The British Broadcasting Company, already established in 1927, broadcast the Coronation of George VI, and while it had only been received on a comparatively few home-made ham sets, it represented a major accomplishment. In 1936, BBC began the first regular scheduled broadcasts for three hours a day. At first, British television programs were received on home-made contraptions, but by 1938 English manufacturers were marketing sets that sold for $300. Unfortunately, due to a skeptical public, only 3,000 of these machines were purchased in the first two years.

On April 30, 1939, the speech of Franklin Delano Roosevelt, opening the New York World's Fair, was broadcast over the National Broadcasting Company's station WZXBS. This speech inaugurated the first regularly scheduled program to be telecast in the United States. Simultaneously with this pioneer effort, RCA offered the public its first television sets at prices that ranged from $199 to $600. Like their British counterparts, the New York public was wary and in the first five months only five hundred sets were sold. Commercial programs were inaugurated on July 1, 1941 by NBC's station WZXBS, renamed WNBT, and Columbia Broadcasting System's WCBW. The Bulova Watch Company sponsored the first commercial NBC broadcast—a Brooklyn Dodgers–Philadelphia Phillies baseball game.

The indescribable hardships under which the early television actors and mechanics worked in those days almost beggar description. The heat generated by camera lights often produced temperatures in excess of 100° in the studios. In July, 1940, during the Republican National Convention in Philadelphia that NBC experimentally covered, the heat became so intense that the sweltering delegates asked that the broadcast be discontinued (air conditioning was still to be born).

During World War II television experimentation was discontinued but military innovations in communication were to contribute to the advance of the practical home set. During this wartime period, the industry remained in a fairly dormant state. Broadcasting stations only operated in New York, Philadelphia, Chicago, Schenectady, and Los Angeles. At the end of the war there were only 7,000 home sets in operation in the United States. All but 1,500 were in the New York metropolitan area. The public, however, was no longer skeptical about the practicality of TV, and waited eagerly to buy sets as fast as they could be produced. Starting in 1947, the industry was turning out 15,000 sets a month, and they were quickly grabbed up by the buying public. Within three years there were one hundred local stations in the country beaming programs to four million homes.

In the past decade, television has reached into almost every home in America. Today, 95 percent of the households in the nation have one or more sets. The average family spends two to three hours before their tube, more time than is consumed in any other leisure activity.

Newton N. Minow has called television "a vast wasteland" but most of us feel, I think, there are many oases scattered throughout that desert and, more times than not, they are our favorite programs.

A young man I know never speaks of the television other than to refer to it as the "Boob Tube." He looks with considerable disdain on my liking for *Gunsmoke* yet spends Saturday afternoons with his eyes glued to the screen to watch a baseball or football game. I am certain that if there were three games on three channels he would be happy to have three sets operating simultaneously.

A midwestern millionaire, who has made great contributions to American industry, will stop almost anything he is doing so that he does not miss the *FBI* program. And I know of a distinguished lawyer who will interrupt a dinner party to watch *Hogan's Heroes*.

Certainly there is no dearth of criticism of the programming of the television medium. The charge is made that network programs are vulgar, lacking in culture, errant escapism, and so preoccupied with violence that they are chiefly responsible for the crime and rioting that plagues the nation today.

That many of the programs and certainly a number of commercials are vulgar, no one can deny. Deodorants, laxatives, toilet paper, and diapers admittedly are all necessary articles, but there must be some better way of calling our attention to such products than on a screen in our living room. A new high in vulgarity was reached when the nuptials of Tiny Tim were viewed on the *Johnny Carson Show*.

However, just as long as the networks are operated as commercial enterprises under our much-vaunted free enterprise system, television will remain on a cultural level matching that of the vast majority of Americans. I have heard many complaints from those whose pet programs have been pre-empted by a presidential address, a documentary, a particularly outstanding presentation by *Hallmark* or the *Kraft Hour*, or one sponsored by AT&T. The majority of viewers want entertainment, not uplift. Unless we are willing to accept government-operated television similar to that of BBC, without commercially sponsored programs, ours will remain the wasteland it is charged with being. Actually, more people will view *Bonanza* during the course of a season than will attend the Kennedy Center for the Performing Arts during the next century.

Television programs have not been as bad as charged. Certainly most have been superior to the stories in the pulp magazines and confession periodicals of a generation ago. Even *Peyton Place* and the daytime soap operas are a notch better than the tales that appeared in *True Confessions* and the articles of *Screen Play*.

Only an intellectual snob will object to a reasonable amount of escapism in the life of the average American. Groucho Marx has said, "I don't need tranquilizers, I watch television."

Living a fiercely competitive life there is real need for relaxation —for divorcing the mind from the everyday problems of a hectic existence. How better could that be done than in the company of one's family watching a show that comes into your own home? The lives of the pre-television generation were considerably more physical than that of their counterpart today and there was much less need for diversion. But, even they had *The Saturday Evening Post* and *Collier's*. Who can say that *The Virginian* is inferior to the tales of the late Clarence Budington Kelland or Harold Bell Wright.

Unquestionably there has been too much violence on TV, but to claim it has corrupted our youth and is responsible for the problems of our city streets has not been proven. However, on September 24, 1969, the President's Commission on Violence, chaired by Dr. Milton Eisenhower, released an eleven-page statement that said in part:

> We believe it is reasonable to conclude that a constant diet of violent behavior on television has an adverse effect on human character and attitudes. Violence on television encourages violent forms of behavior, and fosters moral and social values about violence in daily life which are unacceptable in a civilized society. . . .
>
> There is reason to believe that repeated exposure to media violence may have the effect not only of dulling the audience's emotional reaction to fictional violence but may also desensitize viewers to violence in real life and thus, make them more willing to engage in aggressive actions when provoking circumstances arise.

This is, of course, pure tommy-rot. There is nothing on television today even comparable with the early motion picture serials, *The Perils of Pauline* or *The Clutching Hand*. Nor was the succeeding generation's fare of Lon Chaney any less violent. As Schramm, Lyle, and Parker put it: "What television is bringing to children—is not essentially different from what radio and movies brought them; but what children bring to television and the other mass media is infinitely varied."[1] Certainly children's books such as Robert Louis Stevenson's *Treasure Island* and the works of G. A. Henty are not without their violent passages. Granted this new medium gives a steadier diet of carnage, but much more depends on the home life of a boy or girl—on family and environmental behavior patterns than on the fantasy they may view on the tube.

Beginning in 1958, Wilbur Schramm, Director of the Institute for Communication Research of Stanford University; Jack Lyle, Assistant Professor in the Graduate School of Journalism of the University of California (Los Angeles); and Edwin B. Parker, Assistant Professor in the Institute of Communication Research of the University of Illinois, made an exhaustive study of the effect

[1] Wilbur Schramm, Jack Lyle, and Edwin B. Parker, *Television in the Lives of Our Children* (Stanford, California, Stanford University Press, 1961).

38

of television upon the lives of our children. Their findings were published in 1961. They concluded:

The effects of television may not be so potent as they have sometimes been pictured. This is the fact that television always enters into a pattern of influences that already exist. Actually television may bulk rather small beside those other influences, for they come from the home, the peer group, the school, the church, and other culturals generally.

In any case it is seldom that we can point to any behavior of a child and say that this is due solely to television, television contributes to it, or catalyzes it, or gives it a particular shape. For example, a child commits a burglary and says that he learned to do it from television. Even without questioning the truth of his statement, we must then ask why did this particular child learn to commit a burglary when other children did not?

A little reflection will suggest that many other forces and influences were active in determining his particular behavior. The child who came to television and, therefore, learned to commit and did commit a burglary was different in some important ways from other children who came to television. And these differences grew out of experiences and qualities other than television. It is seldom that the causes of any complex behavior in human beings are simple or single causes, and it is well to keep that in mind.[2]

Nevertheless, there are many who sincerely believe the new medium is corrupting our children. Walter Lippmann writes:

There can be no doubt that the movies and television and the comic books are purveying violence and lust to a vicious and intolerable degree. There can be no real doubt that public exhibitors of sadism tend to excite sadistic desires. Nor can there be any real doubt that there is a close connection between suddenness in the increase in sadistic crime and the new vogue of sadism among the mass media of entertainment.

[2] *Ibid.*

Senator John O. Pastore of Rhode Island has recently demanded that the Public Health Service study the possible pathological effect of the exposure of children to the sex and violence of television. Dr. William H. Stewart, the Surgeon General,[3] has accordingly announced the appointment of a Committee on Television and Social Behavior. This panel is restricted to scientific findings from works already published.

Actually, I am much more concerned with the effect on teen–age girls and adolescent boys of programs similar to *Peyton Place*, the soap operas, and the distorted view they give of adult life. A very large share of children's television viewing is centered on adult programs. Unfortunately, the picture they see of their elders is of sexy women, philandering men, inadequate fathers, and crooked or stupid judges and policemen. Youth absorbs an erroneous picture of adult life which may later require hard adjustments. It also may cause premature aging. Joseph Klapper has said that adult programs:

> . . . deal almost exclusively . . . with adults in conflict situations . . . continued exposure to such fare might unnaturally accelerate the impact of the adult environment on the child and force him into a kind of premature maturity, marked by bewilderment, distrust of adults, and a superficial approach to adult problems or even an unwillingness to become an adult.[4]

Perhaps our generation gap is a product of the tube, and, just perhaps, the children's crusade, the moratoriums, the college riots, the demand for complete sexual promiscuity, the twenty-four-year-old college men who speak of their fellow students as "kids," and the fad for long and dirty hair, are all the results of the impact of a distorted picture of adult life upon immature minds.

Certainly television has radically changed the lives of our children. How much it is probably too early to determine. We do know that the modern child stays up just a little later at night, and

---

[3] Dr. Stewart has since been succeeded as Surgeon General by Dr. Jesse L. Steinfeld.
[4] Joseph Klapper, *The Effects of Mass Communication* (New York, Columbia University Bureau of Applied Research, 1959).

that his reading is more selective than that of his predecessors. We are still, however, in the dark as to the impact television has made on his total adjustment to life. Needless to say, we are apprehensive.

It is, however, possible to draw certain conclusions as to how politics has been affected by television. First and foremost, TV brought into being the "Pretty Boy" age of American politics. No matter how weak or even nonexistent the legislative record of a Congressman or Senator might have been, if he is young, photogenic, and appeals to the motherly or fatherly instincts of his middle-age viewers, he has a tremendous advantage over a less personable opponent who may have a distinguished record and years of experience behind him. Although they were not all without ability, the late John F. Kennedy and his brother Robert, John Lindsay, Mark Hatfield, Charles Percy, and a host of other attractive young men fit into this category.

It is doubtful that John Kennedy, with his questionable Senate record, could have defeated Hubert H. Humphrey in the 1960 presidential primaries or Richard M. Nixon in the general election had it not been for his shining personality. Certainly the contrast between the personalities of Kennedy and Nixon in their famous 1960 debates profoundly affected the outcome of that year's presidential election.

Nor are the middle-aged the only ones influenced by television's charisma. Eugene McCarthy and Robert Kennedy, both with negative programs but with charming personalities and a handsome appearance, in 1968 were able to rally the young on what almost amounted to a political crusade. Before Kennedy's unfortunate assassination the contest between these two ideological brothers had taken on the dimensions of a Mr. America Beauty Contest. Charles Percy could not have taken his Senate seat from the distinguished Paul Douglas unless he had been young, photogenic, and handsome. Certainly an older, less attractive President would not have so readily been forgiven for the hesitancy that caused the Bay of Pigs fiasco.

The political importance of the Madison Avenue–type public relations operator and the advertising agencies are also phenomena of the television age of politics. As Joe McGinnis has pointed out in his interesting book, *The Selling of the President 1968*, candidates are now put on the market like a new detergent or a brand of cigarettes. It is phony, yet it is the only recourse for a less personable candidate like Richard Nixon. When, however, "Barkus" is handsome, has been nurtured by public relations experts, and has an able advertising agency behind him, as was the case of Ronald Reagan and George Murphy in California, the appeal to the public seems irresistible. Robert MacNeil writes:

> The ideal candidate for television campaigning may not be a man with any original insights to offer his country, he may not be capable of grasping the immensities of the office he aspires to. What he must be is articulate and expressive in ways acceptable and expressive on television. He needs to be able to stress the appearance of competence rather than the fact of it. He needs an ability to appear assured and confident, because that is the impression he will leave with viewers long after his words and picture have faded out.[5]

It may well be that the time will come when a majority of the television viewing, voting public will not make their choice as if they were the judges in a Mr. America contest. Already there are signs that a resistance to the purely photogenic in politics may be developing. Certainly Nixon and Humphrey, of necessity, rested their case on experience, ability, and their views. Among the Democratic crop of hopefuls for 1972, there are few under consideration who rely solely on a "pretty face with naught behind."

More dangerous to the political life of America is the vast power over the dissemination of news held by the wire services and their subsidiaries. Newspapers, with the possible exception of *The New York Times*, are regional in reporting and circulation. The publishers of the *Washington Post* with their ownership of *Newsweek*, television and radio stations, have only a fraction of the power of those who present the news over the networks. *The New York Times* has a circulation of 800,000. Each night for years Huntley-Brinkley reached twenty-one million Americans, while Walter Cronkite talks to twenty-six million viewers.

[5] Robert MacNeil, *The People Machine* (New York, Harper & Row, 1968), p. 138.

For millions of Americans, the daily news broadcasts are the only opportunity they have to learn what is happening in the nation and the world. Chet Huntley, David Brinkley, and Walter Cronkite have, on the whole, been unbiased and objective, but there have been instances when their reports have given the nation a slanted or biased view. Not for a moment do I think this to have been a conscious effort. Rather it has risen from two factors. First, startling and violent events make more interesting news. Spiro Agnew has said, "One minute of Eldridge Cleaver is worth ten minutes of Roy Wilkins." Secondly, no man can be completely objective, and this is more true with the spoken than the written word.

Probably the most glaring example of television news distortion was in the reporting of the National Democratic Convention of 1968. Although the protesters in the streets of Chicago were unquestionably out to provoke violence on the part of the police, and although more officers landed in the hospital than did demonstrators, the edited film that reached the public pictured the Chicago cops as sadistic "storm troopers" brutally assaulting idealistic American kids.

Quite the contrary was true. According to a report[6] made by a staff member of the House of Representatives Commerce Committee, the network personnel "deliberately sought out to interview those with known biased feelings against the conduct of the convention and the city government" and ". . . deliberately withheld from the air, film and video tape which would have been derogatory to the demonstrators."

CBS reel-5, according to Anderson's summary, showed the beginning of the conflict between the police and the hippies. One of the announcers declared, "They are assaulting the police lines." When the material was presented over the air, "the report states, 'no reference was made to the above quoted remark, nor was any scene of such an assault visible. Shots of material raining down from the Hilton Hotel on to the heads of the police and news camera crews was also available but not broadcast.' "

In one sequence a crew chief is heard instructing, "Stand by for trouble, otherwise we don't start." The report continues, "While

[6] The report is confidential. This account is from Jack Anderson, *Washington Post*, November 5, 1969.

many of the major commentators spoke at length concerning the shock they felt concerning what was happening to the young demonstrators downtown, little or no comment was made concerning profanity, obscene signs and gestures, and physical abuse employed by the demonstrators to provoke the police."

There are many who believe the Chicago demonstrations or riots, as they were reported to the American people, were responsible for the defeat of Hubert Humphrey. Subconsciously, the viewers of the distorted scenes blamed the successful nominee of the convention and his supporter, Mayor Richard Daley. It was months before the Democratic candidate could recover from this biased reporting. Only during the last weeks of the campaign did Humphrey begin to overcome this handicap. By then it was too late.

Back in 1967, the networks had given an equally biased presentation of Mailer's *Armies of the Night* assault on the Pentagon. The TV cameramen obligingly waited until rioters doused their bandages with red paint, and had torn paper dresses to shreds before aiming their cameras.

On Monday evening, November 3, 1969, President Richard M. Nixon delivered a speech over a nationwide network on the subject of his policy for ending the Vietnam War. The address had been widely publicized for weeks. There were few Americans, hawk or dove, not seated before a television set that night. Seventy million viewers were said to have tuned in. While there was some question of the propriety of delivering what should have been a non-partisan talk on the night before several important elections in the country, the President was legitimately appealing for support of the program he had developed.

There was little in the speech that was not already known, but Nixon did reveal that he had made a number of informal attempts to approach the enemy, including his writing a personal letter to Ho Chi Minh. Ho's reply, received three days prior to Ho's death, was said by the President to have been as intransigent and unyielding as any position previously taken by the North Vietnamese government. A copy of Ho's letter was released simultaneously with the speech, and it confirmed the President's conclusion.

President Nixon had barely finished speaking when the instant analysts—political commentators, including the former chief of the

Paris negotiators, Averell Harriman—appeared on the screen and, without exception, took a critical position on the speech.

Marvin Kalb of CBS disputed Nixon's statement that Ho Chi Minh's letter was intransigent. It "contained," said he, "some of the softest, most accommodating language found in a communist document concerning the war in Vietnam in recent years." (As a matter of fact it did no such thing.) ABC's Bill Lawrence questioned the President's "abilities as a politician," and Bill Downs, also ABC, charged Nixon with following the Pentagon line (some in the military would prefer a harder line).

The choice of Harriman at ABC to answer Nixon instantly was, as *Time* later said, "—biased in a sense; it clearly indicated that ABC meant to criticize the President," and, it should be added, intended to do so long before the contents of the speech became known. Although I have never been a Nixon rooter, I recall having been annoyed that night at the bitterness of the newsmen and their complete failure to present anything in the nature of constructive criticism. Frankly, the networks seemed out to get Nixon.

Ten days later, Vice President Spiro Agnew delivered an address in Des Moines, Iowa. Agnew, since the day of his selection as a candidate, has been the pet whipping boy of the newspapers, the networks, and the liberal establishment. His slightest boo-boo was hailed with delight by the commentators and magnified out of all proportion. Actually, while his language is sometimes intemperate, his is a healthy influence. Agnew bluntly speaks his mind and calls the shots as he sees them.

That night, Agnew accused the television networks of presenting a biased and distorted picture of national events to the viewing public. He also charged that "a little group of men not only enjoy a right of instant rebuttal to every Presidential address, but more, wield a free hand in selecting, interpreting, and presenting the great issues of our nation." Agnew was careful to point out that he was not asking "for government censorship or any kind of censorship."

For Agnew, the speech was quite temperate. He merely presented a problem and gave no glib answers. That he had struck home, and, indeed, had touched a pulsating nerve, was soon evident from the vitriolic responses of the TV industry. By the next morning the network heads had all issued statements attacking Agnew and agonizing over the imminent threat of governmental repression.

Frank Stanton, President of CBS, in a formal statement said, "Apparently the Vice President embarked upon a campaign, despite his rhetoric to the contrary, to intimidate and discredit the news media into reporting only what he wants to hear." ABC's President, Leonard H. Goldenson, was even more bitter in his release: "—an attempt to intimidate and discredit not only TV news reporting but other major news media." NBC's President Julian Goodman called Agnew's speech "an appeal to prejudice."

Chet Huntley sourly added, "I hesitate to get into the gutter with this guy [the Vice President of the United States] but this speech is obviously not off the top of Spiro Agnew's head. We've known that the White House has been very unhappy about the remarks after Nixon's speech. This is a concerted drive on the part of the administration. It could be very vicious and very bloody." ABC's Edward Morgan held Agnew's speech to be "sinister."

The "hate Agnew" liberal establishment was also quick to rush to attack this threat to freedom of speech. To a man they jumped on the speech as ill-advised, divisive, and an attempted blackmail of the networks. That the original instant reply of the commentators was ill-advised and divisive was conveniently ignored. Unquestionably, the most ingenious of these onslaughts was that of the *Washington Post*'s Nicholas von Hoffman. Hoffman, in one column, was able to vent his spleen at the Vice President and, at the same time, take to task the networks for not having fairly presented a true picture of the vast crowds at the Washington Monument moratorium rally. In his column of November 17, headlined "TV Blackout" he wrote:

> The television networks can broadcast live and in color from the moon but not from the base of the Washington Monument, NBC had one, mind you, one live camera to photograph the largest political meeting in the history of the United States. It was broadcast three times for a total of five minutes, and that was all the live coverage there was on American television; the other networks had none. . . .
>
> A lot blame this disaster on Slugger Agnew. Slugger's all

right. Don't pick on him because he's one of the few elected officials we've got who shows himself for what he is. If he feels his boss isn't getting adulation from Alpo Dog Food salesmen who read the Associated Press wire copy on the air, Slugger muscles himself some airtime to threaten the network executives. He needn't have bothered; it appears from asking around that the decision to blackout the enormous rally in favor of "The Archie Comedy Hour" and "Wacky Races" (CBS, the both of 'em) was made before Slugger opened America's biggest mouth. And that's the pity of it. They don't need to be threatened with censorship. They'll castrate themselves and call it "sound news judgment."

If I may be permitted a cliché, "it all depends on whose ox is being gored." It is interesting to note that those who most deplore Agnew's rhetoric make use of the most violent language. Nevertheless, Herr von Hoffman may well have a point.

The *Washington Star* said in an editorial:

> There has been a vast amount of nonsense in the response of some news executives to Mr. Agnew's attacks. An editor or a television commentator thinks nothing at all of lambasting every politician in sight. Let one of them talk back, however —let him voice an effective suggestion that the critics are biased or uninformed—and the screams of editorial anguish can be heard in Timbuktu. Suddenly we are all to be intimidated into regimented silence.

Agnew presented a problem that had long worried many thoughtful Americans and he did it without rancor. He stated facts that no one could or has denied. Rather than stop to consider for a moment that there might be some truth to the criticism, that a certain amount of reform might be in order, TV executives and commentators violently denied any possibility that their presentation of the news might be less than objective.

There are many who at least partially agree with the Vice President. This was indicated by two recent reports. On 12 October, 1969, a study of the performance of television stations in the District of Columbia, Virginia, West Virginia, and Maryland was released by the Institute for Policy Studies, a Washington–based institution. The study was privately financed by the Stern Family Fund.

The 336-page report, in words stronger than Vice President Agnew's, charged that the networks are "doing no less than preparing the people for tyranny." They recommended that control over television stations be placed in the hands of the public, in the form of local groups and communities, and also charged the Federal Communications Commission with negligence in monitoring the air waves.

"It is time," the study read, "to call a halt to the rapacious plundering of our mental life unloosed by the Federal Communications Commission and unchallenged by Congress. Neither the FCC, nor Congress nor the licensees own the airways. The public owns them."

Just a week before the Vice President's speech, a committee supported by the Alfred I. DuPont Foundation and Columbia University—consisting of Sir William Haley, the former Director General of the British Broadcasting Company; authors Marya Mannes and Michael Arlen; Richard Baker, the acting Dean of the Columbia Graduate School of Journalism; and his predecessor Edward Barrett—issued a 130-page study of news reporting. The critique concluded that during 1968–69, "documentary programming hit a new low, that television reporting of the 1968 election campaign did not adequately inform the viewers. That broadcasters' greed, rather than a desire for public service was the chief cause of the crisis in broadcasting."

Perhaps even more important for the future of America than news distortion, has been the effect of graphically depicting the scenes from the battlefields of distant Vietnam on a screen within our homes. Not since the Civil War has there been carnage within the borders of the United States and only those who have been in combat can know its horrors.

Television has changed this. Almost nightly we see the waste, the nightmare, the utter senselessness of war. There are those—the Quakers, for example—who would say that this is good, but it could result in America's refusal to accept its role of world leadership, a reversion to an isolationism more stringent than any we have known in the past, and an absolute refusal of Americans to even defend themselves. In the world in which we live that would be national suicide.

Joseph Kraft, writing in the *Washington Post* on the floods of emotion behind the moratorium demonstrations, said:

> There was heightened sensitivity to a remote event. What might have been a mere border war, well below the level of intense public consciousness, was brought into every living room by television. Even when the drama declined, when battles ceased, and casualties fell off, the TV left a hangover effect. Little episodes, like the affair of the Green Berets, seemed to trigger a kind of total recall—a general feeling of something badly wrong in Vietnam.

There are, in addition to the changes that television has made in the lives of our children, and in the political structure of the nation, a number of marked dissimilarities between now and when the tube entered our homes. Superficial though they may be, together they may ultimately represent a great change in a way of life.

The buying habits of the American consumer are entirely different from those days in the late forties when TV was introduced. By the adroit use of commercials we have been taught to ask for name brands. Today we go to our huge super markets to specifically buy Pee Wee Bouquet, not just soap; or My Lady hand lotion, not plain cold cream. Often we receive over-priced shoddy merchandise in spite of the fancy names they bear.

The hucksters of NASA have also conned us into a national program that is of dubious scientific value and one that the nation can ill-afford.

Book reading has definitely increased, but despite the increase only a disappointingly small fraction of the population can be said to read books regularly. Newspapers are still dutifully scanned, but are no longer as important in our lives as heretofore and they are often read to obtain more information on a subject we first learned about sitting before our TV sets. Magazines are fast fading into limbo. Those that remain are half their former size. Popular family periodicals like *Collier's*, *Woman's Home Companion*, and *The Saturday Evening Post*, which once reached millions, are only pleasant memories.

The sprightly conversations at the evening dinner table are only a memory. We sit with little TV trays before us, munching TV dinners, listening to TV drivel, and are inadequately fed in mind and stomach. We stay up later in the evening and, while many of us are physically together with our families, any attempt at communication is firmly shushed.

In the early days of television there were high hopes that there would be great cultural and educational dividends from the new medium. That closed circuit TV in our schools would add a new dimension to instruction, that adult courses beamed into our homes would raise the level of knowledge, that ballet, operas, symphony concerts would all have a cultural impact on the nation. To date these goals have only been partially achieved.

The closed circuit television within our school systems has little advantage over the motion pictures of the past, and has so far proven to be little more than a gadget. We of the twentieth century have always inclined toward the easy way, particularly in the field of learning, but there are no shortcuts to knowledge. There is no painless pedagogical process. Mark Hopkins on one end of a log is not in danger of being supplemented by television.

When the programs of commercial television proved so sterile and inane we were told the answer was non-commercial channels. While these educational stations have hardly lived up to their original billing, they do broadcast a number of sound adult educational programs, including some good foreign language programs. The non-commercial channels do also, on occasion, present cultural programs that are above average. *The Andersonville Trial* and *The Forsyte Saga* series are recent examples of such efforts. Unfortunately, a number of the educational stations, in an effort to fill time, have broadcast repeats of some of the most puerile of the commercial programs.

While they are not as numerous as might be hoped for, there have been, from time to time, programs on the major commercial channels that have been outstanding. Plays, symphony concerts, serious documentaries sponsored by our more responsible corporations, have often been a delight. Perhaps in time the Madison

Avenue hucksters will realize that outstanding programs sponsored by their clients create a good public image.

While most children's programs are sickening twaddle, there have also been a few outstanding achievements in this field. *Sesame Street* and programs for handicapped children are examples of what can be achieved. When Madison Avenue finally comes to realize that all our children are not stupid, there will be more *Sesame Streets*.

No amount of nostalgia will bring back a past irrevocably gone —killed by the tube. We have TV, and we had better learn to live with it.

The USS *West Virginia* and *Tennessee* in flames and sinking in the waters of Pearl Harbor after the Japanese attack on December 7, 1941.
(U.S. Army Photo)

Demolished planes and wrecked hangar at Wheeler Field in Hawaii after Japanese air assault.
(U.S. Army Photo)

The USS *Arizona* burning after the Japanese attack.
(U.S. Army Photo)

The first television broadcast from Washington, D.C., held at the Capitol. Photo shows Senator White of Maine looking into the television camera, and Marshall Diskin, CBS operator. *(Washington Star Photo)*

Man looking at an early television receiver.
(Photo by Keystone View Company—from the Library of Congress)

(Above) The devastated city of Stalingrad as it looked in January, 1943, after the long, bloody siege. Photo from seized German records.

(National Archives)

(Right) A muddy road behind the German front at Stalingrad in fall, 1942. Photo from seized German records.   *(National Archives)*

(Below) Symbol of Nazi defeat: a crude German cemetery on the outskirts of Stalingrad in December, 1942. Photo from seized German records.   *(National Archives)*

Dr. Jonas E. Salk (right) with Dr. P. L. Bazely, an assistant. *(National Archives)*

3.

THE RAT WAR— STALINGRAD

The fall of 1942 marked the high-water mark of the Third Reich. From the Rhine to the Channel and south to the Mediterranean the Axis powers held sway. In twelve violent days Crete had fallen to the greatest airborne assault that history had ever known. Rommel, flushed with victory, stood at the gateway to Cairo and the Suez. German troops deep within Russia were holding a front of 2,300 miles. The Wehrmacht had conquered lands inhabited by 60 million Russians or over one-third of the Soviet population. Almost thirty-two thousand industrial plants employing four million workers had been destroyed. Germany had taken by conquest more than fifty percent of the coal, iron, steel, and wheat areas of the USSR. Almost three million Red Army soldiers had surrendered to the Axis and their dead were numbered in the hundreds of thousands. The invincibility of Hitler's legions had become a legend that had not been dissipated by Leningrad or Moscow.

Nevertheless, there were clouds on the horizon for men to see if they would—clouds no larger than a man's hand. Britain had achieved the seemingly impossible and still survived. With an assist from the Japanese at Pearl Harbor, the United States, with its vast industrial might and no longer divided, had entered the conflict. Russia still held Kiev, Leningrad, and Moscow. She had made Germany pay a stiff price for her Soviet victories, Nazi casualties having passed the million and a half mark.

Hitler, personally assuming command of the German Armies on

December 19, 1942, had determined that for the 1942 campaign the Wehrmacht would strike for the rich oil fields of the Caucasus. The campaign, the Führer decided, would not only deprive the Russians of vitally needed oil but would secure those resources for Germany. Gasoline in the Third Reich had become a scarce commodity. If the war were to continue it was required not only for the armies on the Eastern front, but also for industrial use at home.

Military experts, and retired generals with the advantage of hindsight, agree that Hitler's decision to strike for the Caucasus was a mistake, that at best the campaign "was a gamble with only remote chances of success."[1] If, instead, the Wehrmacht had first captured Moscow, its reduction and the subsequent disruption of the Russian railroad system would have created as much economic chaos for the USSR as the loss of its oil fields. The fall of Moscow might well have brought about the collapse of the Soviet Government, or, at the very least, been a vital blow to an already tottering government.

General Anders notes that in the Caucasus, "the Wehrmacht . . . was too weak to carry out such a deep drive, or to hold the conquered territory until lack of fuel paralyzed the enemy."

Certainly, in formulating his decision Hitler dispersed his strength, and added the problem of a long, dangerous, and tenuous line of supply. He also lost sight of the military principles of the concentration of his forces at the decisive point, and he failed to move toward a clearly defined objective.

Hitler's plan called for Army Group North and Army Group Center on the Leningrad-Moscow fronts to conduct an active defense, continuing attempts to seize Leningrad and to link up with the Finns. On the southern front Field Marshal Wilhelm W. List's Army Group A—consisting of General Paul von Kleist's First Panzer Army, and Colonel General Richard Ruoff's Seventeenth Army— was to strike toward the Caucasus. Field Marshall Fedor von Bock's Army Group B—consisting of General Maximilian Freiherr von Weich's Second Army, General Herman Hoth's Fourth Panzer Army, and General Friedrich von Paulus's Sixth Army—was to advance to the Volga River to cover the main thrust to the Cau-

---

[1] General Wladyslaw Anders, *Hitler's Defeat in Russia* (Chicago, Henry Regnery, 1953).

casus.[2] The operation, code named *Blau* (Blue), had in reserve the Second Hungarian Army, the Eighth Italian Army and the Third Rumanian Army. The satellite forces were also to protect the flanks of the primary mission.

Supporting the ground troops were between seven hundred and a thousand aircraft, the bulk of them assigned to Army Group A. In the two Army groups and in reserve there were a total of about sixty German divisions of which ten were armored and six motorized. The German division units were understrength. The Rumanian, Hungarian, Slovak, and Italian soldiers were poorly equipped and handicapped by low morale. In fact, the Rumanian troops were said to be almost worthless.

Opposing Army Groups A and B in this southern sector was Russian Marshal Semyon Timoshenko with about 140 divisions. The Soviet Army of 1942 was mostly composed of Asiatics. As the late General J. F. C. Fuller noted:

> The tough Hunnish people of Central Asia who centuries before had followed Attila and Genghis Khan . . . although of low intelligence and almost wholly illiterate . . . possessed immense natural tenacity and endurance. They not only replenished their supplies from regions through which they advanced, but also their numbers, all able bodied men found en route were conscripted straight into the front line units.[3]

Field Marshal Fritz von Mannstein says, "The dynamics of the Red Army were the same as that of the Revolutionary Armies of France, a combination of fanaticism, and terror;" while General Kurt Dittmar, another German, considered the Russians' chief asset was "the soulless indifference of the troops" which was "something more than fatalism."

Hitler's plan envisioned that the Fourth Panzer Army and the Sixth Army would advance toward Voronezh, wheeling southeast down the right bank of the Don River in the direction of Stalingrad. As the two armies advanced, the river line would be taken

[2] Later, on July 13, because of a delay that irritated Hitler, von Bock was relieved of his command and replaced by von Weich. General Hans von Salmuth was given the Second Army.
[3] Major General J. F. C. Fuller, *Decisive Battles of the Western World*, Vol. III (London, Eyre & Spottiswoode, 1956), p. 520.

over by the Second German, Eighth Italian, Second Hungarian, and Third Rumanian armies. Simultaneously Army Group A would attack from the area between Taganrog and Izyum toward the lower Don. The First Panzer Army was to lead the assault and after it had crossed the Don, the Seventeenth Army was to be committed.

The Führer had hoped that the operation would be underway by early May, but his timetable was thrown off by both the foul weather and the Russians, who struck first. On May 9, Timoshenko launched a large scale offensive in the Kharkov area and made serious penetrations into the Nazi line. The initial Russian success, however, was soon reversed. When counterattacked by the German First Panzer, Seventeenth, and Sixth Armies, the Soviets could not withdraw from Izyum and, on 26 May, they were surrounded and forced to capitulate. Twenty-two Russian divisions and five hundred aircraft were destroyed; 240,000 prisoners were taken; and 2,025 guns and 1,300 tanks were captured or destroyed. It was, however, a Pyrrhic victory. Hitler's main offensive was delayed by almost two months and the Russians had gained time—time they desperately needed.

The German Sixth Army, which had taken a decisive role in the defeat of the Russian troops in May of 1942, was a veteran unit, the cream of the Wehrmacht. In the summer of 1940, the Sixth had smashed through Belgium and the Netherlands. Under the command of General Walter von Reichenau (later Field Marshal), the Sixth had entered Paris and subsequently seen combat both in Yugoslavia and Greece.

The Sixth Army's commander on the Eastern front, the dignified General Friedrich von Paulus, was an able if unimaginative officer. As a dapper field grade officer he had been known as "The Lord" and "The Major with sex appeal." The charge that he lacked boldness and moral courage was probably true, for he was a "do it by the book" type soldier. Unfortunately, he also sincerely believed that the highest and first duty of an officer was blind obedience to superiors.

Operation *Blau* was finally underway on 28 June when Army Group B's Fourth Panzer and Second Army attacked in the Kursk area. The Russians, not expecting an assault at this point, were caught off balance, and the Panzers soon penetrated deep into the

Red lines. Von Paulus started his offensive with his Sixth Army on 30 June and made good progress.

Voronezh was reached by the Second and Fourth Panzer armies on 5 July and Hitler ordered the Fourth Panzer to wheel southward down the Don while the Sixth Army was to advance southeast toward Rossosh. On 9 July, the First Panzer Army, advancing down the northern bank of the Donetz, captured Kamensk-Shaktinski. On the 10th, the Fourth Army occupied Kantemirovka. The Russians withdrew from Voroshilovgrad and, on the 17th, they retreated toward the southeast, pursued by the German Seventeenth Army. Almost at the same time, the First Panzer Army crossed the Donetz near Kamensk. West of the Donetz, the Fourth Panzer Army, advancing down the Don with the Sixth Army on its western flank, met little or no opposition.

Once again Hitler's legions seemed invincible and the disorganized Russians were unable to stop the advancing armor and infantry. Blitzkriegs that had torn apart the armies of France, Britain, Russia, and a host of smaller nations, were being repeated. With some justification during those first three weeks of July, 1942, in his temporary headquarters at Vinnitsa in the Ukraine, Hitler concluded that the Wehrmacht could not be stopped, that the summer campaign would not fail in its objective, and "that Russian resistance was at an end." In this mood on 17 July, the Führer made what Hanson Baldwin has called "a fatal error";[4] and Major General J. F. C. Fuller described it as "a step that went far to ruin the campaign."[5]

Apprehensive that von Kleist would have difficulty crossing the lower Don, Hitler transferred the Fourth Panzer from Army Group B to Army Group A. The Sixth Army, which had been making progress toward Stalingrad, now forced to operate without its Panzer support, was soon stopped cold.

In other sectors, however, the advance continued. On the 19th, the Fourth Panzer Army of General Hoth crossed the Don at Tsimlyanskaya and, on the 23rd, Rostov fell and the Seventeenth Army established four bridgeheads across the Don.

Fanning out from Rostov, Army Group A advanced into the

[4] Hanson W. Baldwin, *Battles Lost and Won* (New York, Harper & Row, 1966), p. 161.
[5] Fuller, *op. cit.*, p. 524.

Caucasus and Hitler began detaching troops. He directed the Fourth Panzer Army to shift its attack toward Stalingrad rather than the Caucasus and returned the Fourth Panzer Army to Group B control.

The entire month of August witnessed the continued eastward thrust of the Nazi hordes. The Fourteenth and Twenty-fourth Panzer and Eleventh and Fifty-first Infantry Corps captured nine divisions and nine brigades. Von Paulus's Sixth Army crossed the Don and continued its attack toward the Volga. The Maikop oil fields were overrun and on August 23 the Sixth Army reached the Volga on the outskirts of Stalingrad. August was the low-water mark of Russian resistance to the German armies in World War II.

Stalingrad, a long narrow ribbon of a city stretching for twenty miles along the high west bank of the Volga, 580 miles east of Moscow, was the third most important industrial city in Russia. A curious combination of factories, modern office buildings, and log houses filling its winding streets, it had an odd patchwork appearance. Between the city and the advancing Wehrmacht were open steppes with only an occasional low-lying hill to break the horizon. Should Stalingrad fall, control of the lower Volga, Russia's greatest communications artery, would fall with it. The city also produced more than a quarter of all Russian tanks and trucks.

Stalingrad's capture had originally been conceived as a by-product of the German campaign for the Caucasus. Fortunately for Russia and her allies, the city was to ultimately become the primary objective of the 1942 German offensive.

Hitler's detachment of the Fourth Panzer Army from Group B had delayed the advance of the Sixth Army and given the Russians time to fortify Stalingrad. By September it was strongly garrisoned by the Russian Sixty-second and Sixty-fourth Armies consisting of a total of sixteen divisions under the command of General Vasili Chuikov, an able and experienced officer.

Son of an illiterate peasant, Chuikov had joined the Red Army as a youth in 1918, and served during the Revolutionary period. Graduating from the Soviet Military Academy in 1925, he had been assigned to the Artillery. In 1940 he became Chief of the Russian Military Mission to China. When the mission was withdrawn in 1941, he returned to Russia and in 1942, was given the Sixty-second Army which was conducting a delaying action against the German advance to the Volga. In Stalingrad, Chuikov maintained his command post in a deep bunker along the northern bank of the Tsaritsa River.

Hitler now had two alternatives open to him in planning the assault on Stalingrad. He could force a crossing of the two and a half mile Volga either north or south of the city, stop boat traffic on the river, and lay siege to Stalingrad, then wait for starvation to force its capitulation. He also could storm the city by direct attack. He chose the latter.

To avoid any chance that the frontal attack on Stalingrad might fail, Hitler next strengthened his Sixth Army. Most of the German divisions on his exposed northern flank were transferred to Stalingrad, and the line along the Don, from Voronezh to Kletskaya, was held by the Rumanian Third, Hungarian Second, and the Italian Eighth Armies—probably the poorest of all Axis troops.

South of Stalingrad, the line across the Kalmyk Steppe was held by only a single motorized German division that patrolled a front of hundreds of miles.

Establishing his supply dumps and airfields between the Don and Stalingrad, General von Paulus opened his attack on September 15. Dive bombers soon set fire to or collapsed many of the buildings, and the burning oil tanks along the river sent long columns of fire and smoke into the sky. Stalingrad had become an inferno.

The flaming oil from the wrecked storage tanks slowly seeped down the bank into the river and the Volga was soon a mass of flames. On a small river barge that the fire had not yet reached, an old man, Andrei Parfenov, was trying to fix the engine that had stopped when a bomb had exploded near the boat. The barge, which was almost as old as Andrei, had been his livelihood since he had been a young man, but he had willingly brought it to Stalingrad when he learned that the city was threatened, and that he could be of help in ferrying children and the elderly, as well as supplies, across the Volga.

His helper, a young boy named Matsve, called down from the deck, "The river's on fire," and the old man could hardly believe his eyes when he stuck his head above the hatchway.

Knowing that he could not get the engine started, Andrei suggested that the boy swim ashore and come back with a dinghy. Although he had spent all his life on the river, the old man could not swim and, besides, he held vague hopes that they might be able to tow the barge to safety. Matsve stripped and dove into the river. As the old man waited, he prayed for the boy's return not so much for himself but for Mother Russia who he knew would need even an old man's hands in the days ahead.

Matsve was finally successful in finding a boat as well as a fifteen-year-old girl to help him row. They made an odd picture as they rowed toward the barge, the girl in a colorful peasant dress and the boy stark naked. They were just in time, for the river flames were starting to lick at the boat's hull. With the old man aboard they drew back and watched the flames consume the old paint-encrusted timbers.

After they reached the shore, Andrei and Matsve crossed the river by ferry and went into Stalingrad to see if there was any way in which they might help. They found the city in shambles but finally located a Russian CP where they were issued arm bands and rifles and given a post to man.[6]

As von Paulus's troops entered the city, they met terrific opposition not only from the Russian soldiers but from the civilian population. Both male and female factory workers deserted their benches, took up arms and helped man the barricades and defense positions. Tanks were driven directly from the factory assembly lines into combat.[7]

Within a week the German troops had penetrated to the city's center. On the 28th they succeeded in reaching the factory district to the north, but were dislodged the following day by a counter attack. Hitler now began to detach troops from his defensive lines and send them to the Sixth Army. With these reinforcements von Paulus, supported by large numbers of tanks and dive bombers, renewed the assault on October 4. The days that followed were to see some of the most ferocious fighting of World War II. Block by block, building by building, the German troops pressed forward.

In his original concept of the campaign, in substituting economic goals for military objectives, in stretching his already overloaded

[6] Ronald Seth, *Stalingrad: Point of No Return* (London, Victor Gollancz Ltd., 1959).
[7] Fuller, *op. cit.*, p. 163.

lines of supply, in extending his front for over more than two thousand miles, in transferring the Fourth Panzer Army that had ended the Sixth Army's push for an undefended Stalingrad and weakening his defensive lines, Hitler by this time had committed every error in the book. He now was guilty of his final folly—he ordered the attack by direct assault to cease so that Stalingrad could be devastated by artillery fire and aerial bombardment.

As Allied troops of the American Fifth Army were later to learn at Cassino, this substitutes debris for buildings and bomb craters for streets and thus makes the defense of a restricted area much easier. It also prevents the effective use of tanks. The battle was soon back in the hands of the infantry which began calling it the "Rattenkrieg" or "Rat War."

During October and early November there was more hand-to-hand combat in Stalingrad than during any other period in World War II. Yard by yard the German troops inched forward while the losses of men on both sides kept rising. Corpses literally paved the ruins of the city. As an example, "Some 3,500 wounded Russians, casualties in one day's fighting, were transported across the Volga the night of October 14."[8] By the first of November about nine-tenths of Stalingrad was held by the German Sixth Army.

Almost every night during this period a number of small-scale actions occurred in which Wehrmacht infantry units, supported by tanks, tried to drive the Russians out of a group of houses. In such close fighting there was no opportunity for maneuvering and the German troops would crawl forward and dig into rubble. Soviet machine guns and rifles would open up from windows and apertures in the buildings and the Germans would lob grenades into the openings. Tanks at point-blank range would blast the beleaguered garrison. In such a constricted area the din of the exploding shells and grenades, as well as the machine gun and small arms fire, interspersed with the screams of wounded or dying men became almost intolerable.

Finally the attackers would slowly advance to the house, leaving their dead and dying in the streets, and the Russians would be

[8] Baldwin, *op. cit.*, p. 168.

blasted room by room. The neighborhood would again grow quiet. Such actions often resulted in casualties of two-thirds of the attacking force and all of the defenders.

In other theaters of the war things were not going so well for the Wehrmacht, and these events affected the battle at Stalingrad. On 5 November, in distant North Africa, General Erwin Rommel was defeated by General Bernard Montgomery's forces in the battle of El Alamein and, on 8 November, Morocco and Algeria were invaded by British and American units. Thereafter, reinforcements from Germany were sent to Tunisia rather than to the Russian front. It also became necessary to transfer a number of aircraft from the eastern front to the Mediterranean.

With the arrival of four battalions of specially trained street-fighting units, the Germans began their last push on the night of 9 November. The Russian forces were then compressed into a six square mile area, shaped somewhat like a tennis racket and comprising the center city and the factory area.

The new German force made small gains here and there and actually reached the Volga at several points, but the bulk of the Russian troops, from their rubble pillboxes, their cellars, roofs, and crater foxholes, held and broke the attack.

Since July, under the leadership of the "savior" of Moscow, General Georgi Zhukov; the Chief of the General Staff, General Alexander M. Vasilevski; and General Nikolai N. Voronov, the Russians had been planning a counteroffensive. During the months that the fighting in Stalingrad had continued, over half a million Red troops, as well as fifteen hundred tanks and thirteen thousand artillery pieces and mortars, had been concentrated to the north along the Don.

Three new Soviet armies were created north of Stalingrad. The Voronezh, commanded by General Filipp I. Golikov; the southwest, commanded by General Nikolai F. Vatutin; and the Don commanded by General Konstantin Rokossovski. They faced the left wing of the German Sixth, the Third Rumanian, the Italian Eighth and the Second Hungarian armies. From Stalingrad to the south, the Russian troops were commanded by General Andrei Yeremenko.

The Russians hoped that by concentrating their attack against German weak spots—the fronts held by Germany's vulnerable satellite forces—the Sixth Army might be trapped within Stalingrad and just possibly Rostov might be recaptured and parts of Army Group A isolated in the Caucasus.

Weatherwise, the timing was perfect for the hardy Red troops. Stalingrad lies on the edge of a weather zone where the warm air of the Caspian Sea meets the cold Siberian winds from the steppes. From November until late April there are violent storms and blizzards with the temperatures seldom rising above zero. The Luftwaffe was grounded, German armored vehicles and tanks needed spare parts and fuel, and the troops were exhausted from summer and fall operations.

On 19 November, Rokossovski began the attack with his three tank corps, three cavalry corps, and twenty-one infantry divisions. He broke through the thinly held one-hundred-mile front of the Third Rumanian Army. Thousands of infantry troops, supported by tanks, followed a seven-and-a-half-hour artillery barrage and the battle soon become a rout with a fifty-mile gap torn in the Axis ranks. Thousands of Rumanian troops died, fled, or were captured. While Rokossovski's right wing, supported by Vatutin's left, pursued the enemy toward the Chir River, his center advanced toward Kalach.

The following day General Yeremenko, with two corps and nine infantry divisions, penetrated the lines of the Fourth Rumanian Army in the Ergeni hills, and with his right wing advanced toward Kalach.

The Russian pincer movement was successful on 23 November when Rokossovski lined up with Yeremenko near Kalach. More than 200,000 soldiers of the Sixth Army, elements of the Fourth Panzer Army, two Rumanian divisions, a Croat regiment, and Luftwaffe units were surrounded.

Von Paulus during the first ten days following the encirclement could probably have cut himself out of the trap, but Hitler back at his headquarters, after being assured by Goering that the Luftwaffe could supply von Paulus by air with fifty tons of supplies a day, insisted that the Sixth Army remain in Stalingrad. Announcing that hereafter the beleaguered Army should be known as "Fortress Stalingrad," the Führer turned to the problem of how it could be relieved.

Hitler's first step was a good one. He named Field Marshal

Fritz Erich von Mannstein, probably the ablest of all World War II German generals, as commander of the newly named Army Group Don which included the Sixth Army, Fourth Panzer Army, and the Third and Fourth Rumanian armies. Von Mannstein's task was to defeat the Russian forces encircling the Sixth Army and re-establish the Stalingrad front.

However, with the limited forces available, it was an impossible assignment. Von Mannstein took command on 27 November and was ready to launch his counteroffensive by 12 December. Hoth's Fourth Panzer Army was to advance up the Stalingrad-Kotelnikoro railroad against the forces of General Yeremenko and then to wheel and hit General Rokossovski's right flank, while von Paulus struck it from Stalingrad.

Von Mannstein's offensive made good progress at first and, by 21 December, was within thirty miles of Stalingrad. But the Russian attacks continued and the fate of the Sixth Army was sealed when Vatutin crossed the Don on the 19th and sent the Italian Eighth Army reeling back in panic. With his entire front disintegrating, his troops tired and worn after fighting in sub-zero weather, von Mannstein decided to defy Hitler and, on 21 December, ordered von Paulus to break out of his encirclement and join him within twenty-four hours. The literal-minded Sixth Army general did not have the moral courage to ignore the Führer's orders, and he replied that he had only enough fuel to go twenty miles. Actually he had only sixty tanks left and these he could easily have abandoned.

The situation on the German front continued to deteriorate and von Mannstein was hard put to extricate two armies of Army Group A that had continued to hold their position in the Caucasus, while the Don flank behind them collapsed. He was successful in keeping open a corridor at Rostov and Kleist while conducting a brilliant retreat of his two armies.

Von Paulus needed a minimum of seven hundred tons of ammunition, fuel, and food a day for his troops and would require even more when his reserves were dissipated. His supply line had been precarious and a problem even before the railroad line had been severed by the encirclement. It had now become impossible for the boastful Goering's aircraft to deliver more than eighty tons a day. This trickle stopped when, on 25 January, the Russians captured the last remaining German airfield. The entrapped German troops were soon close to starvation. Artillery ammunition began to fail; medical supplies were exhausted; dysentery and typhus ran rampant.

Even before the capture of the Sixth Army's airfields, the daily ration of its soldiers had been reduced to half a pound of bread a day. During December 280 transport aircraft were destroyed. Thereafter, many pilots refused to land. Instead they had their crews drop the cargo out of the doors. Most of such supplies were lost. By December 26 the daily ration had been reduced to four ounces. Horses, dogs, cats, rats, and mice began to become a scarcity within the city of Stalingrad.

Without fuel and with the thermometer hovering at 20° below zero, the men of the Sixth Army lived through days of horror in their craters and cellars. Their enclave, littered with frozen dead, was about twenty miles long by thirty miles wide. Subjected to steady shelling and constant attacks, General Georgi Zhukov wrote: "I would not have believed such an inferno could open up on this earth. Men died, but they did not retreat."

On 8 January, Rokossovski sent a surrender ultimatum to von Paulus which was rejected. On 10 January a Russian assault followed a barrage of five thousand guns and mortars. The German lines were compressed, but held. Attack after attack followed by the middle of January. "Fortress Stalingrad" had now been reduced to an area fifteen miles long by nine miles wide. Von Paulus and the remnants of his troops were taking Hitler's orders literally—that they should fight to the last man.

Typical of the fighting that took place was that described by a Soviet Army correspondent:

> The Fascists had taken up strong positions in a tall, many storied building. They had even got a gun in there. From behind a corner we could observe the course of the battle. Two of our tanks drove up quite close to the house and opened fire on the spot from where the German tommy-gunners were firing. The gunners brought the gun to bear and taking careful aim, began to batter at the loopholes.
>
> Now the barrel of a tommy-gun gleamed in one of them. Unhurriedly the gun-layer began to direct his gun on to this

loophole while the Red Army men in cover behind the ruins egged him on. "Come on, mate. Let him have it."

The gun fired and the loophole was immediately transformed into a mass of fire and dense smoke. Done for. But almost instantly little flashes dart from the next floor, the Germans have climbed up there. Firing shell after shell, as if he were hammering a nail, our gunner chased the Germans higher and higher up. Already one tiny human figure could be seen on the roof.

A shell bit a slice out of the edge of the roof and everything was wreathed in smoke. Our men jumped out from behind their cover and rushed the house. The gunner switched his fire to the next house. It was getting dark and tracers screamed through the air like fiery needles.[9]

The conditions of the sick and wounded in the final days of the battle of Stalingrad can only be described as horrible. Heinz Schroter, a German Army correspondent, reported:

There were no beds and no bandages, and no help. Sixteen doctors fought a hopeless fight, stretcher bearers and medical orderlies worked till they dropped but the maelstrom of chaos was too much for them.

Newcomers were constantly arriving. They crawled over the heaps of men lying in the halls and corridors and pushed down into the cellars or up the staircases. And there they stayed. Without a bed or a word of encouragement, without any help or even the hope of help. They asked for water and food, but neither was given them; they called for a priest, a doctor, an orderly, for morphia, bandages and writing paper, for their friends, mothers, wife or child and some asked for a revolver.

Sometimes they were handed a revolver, and then their place was free for another to occupy. . . .

In the cellar under Simonovich's warehouse eight hundred men lay pressed against the walls and all over the damp and dirty floor. Their bodies littered the stairs and blocked the passages. All men were equal here; rank and class had been shared as the dead leaves fall from the November trees. In the

[9] Soviet Army Correspondents, *The Epic Story of Stalingrad* (London, Hutchinson and Co. Ltd., N.D.).

Simonovich's cellars they had reached the end of life's journey, and if there were any distinction to be drawn between them it was only in the severity of their wounds or in the number of the days that they still had to live. There was also one other difference, namely the way in which each man met his death.

A man lay on the steps dying of diphtheria, and beside him lay three others who had been dead for days, but no one had moved them because it was dark and they had not been noticed. Behind them a sergeant, whose tongue hung from his mouth like a piece of red hot iron, and whose feet had rotted off up to the ankles, screamed with thirst and pain.

On the wall in the middle of the cellar a foul smelling wick burned in an old tin. It stank of paraffin, but also of fetid blood and gangrenous flesh and suppurating pus, and over all was the sickly smell of decaying bodies and iodine and sweat and excrement and filth.

The air was well nigh unbreathable, lungs and throat were parched and eyes streamed tears.[10]

Methodically, and at terrific cost, the Russians slowly compressed the German enclave. By 24 January they had split the pocket in two, and von Paulus sent off his last message to Hitler: "Troops without ammunition or food—effective command no longer possible—further defense senseless, collapse inevitable, Army requests immediate permission to surrender in order to save lives of remaining troops." Hitler's reply read: "Capitulation is impossible. The Sixth Army will do its historic duty at Stalingrad until the last man."

Like a punch-drunk boxer who battles after all consciousness has left him, the remnants of the Sixth Army continued to resist. As late as 30 January, the 295th Infantry Division counterattacked and recaptured a group of battered buildings and rubble. It was no longer a contest, but a series of small localized fire-fights.

On January 30, 1943, Hitler named von Paulus a field marshal, but the end had come. The following day he became the first German field marshal to ever have surrendered. It took two more days to clean up the remaining pockets of resistance, where Nazi fanatics fought to "the last man."

Louis L. Snyder in his history of World War II writes:

[10] Heinz Schroter, *Stalingrad* (New York, E. P. Dutton, 1958), p. 340.

Never before in Germany's history had so great a body of troops come to so humiliating an end. Hitler had not wanted a second Verdun, but in many ways Stalingrad had the same elemental fury, the same blind conflict of wills as that earlier blood bath. A wave of German flesh and blood had smashed against a wall of Russian steel, only to be shattered and thrust back, leaving the soil of Russia covered with bodies, still and grotesque in death, of the flower of the Wehrmacht. It was as terrible a collapse as that of Napoleon's Grande Armee in 1812.[11]

Axis troops captured at Stalingrad included 24 generals, 2,500 officers, more than 90,000 enlisted men, and an unknown quantity of Rumanian auxiliaries. German casualties totaled something like 100,000 killed, starved, or dead from illness; while the wounded, many of whom died later, made up another 100,000.[12]

Russian casualties are not known but have been estimated to total half a million. It had been a great, but costly victory for the Soviets.

Even with the advantage of hindsight it is almost impossible to understand what moved Hitler's paranoiac mind to wager so much on that campaign.

Stalingrad was unquestionably the decisive battle of World War II. It was one of the definitive turning points of the conflict and made an eventual Allied victory inevitable. It ended the specter that haunted the waking hours of both Churchill and Roosevelt, that the USSR might make a separate peace with Hitler. It also ended the possibility that the Communist government of Russia might collapse and a pro-Fascist regime take its place. Without Russia, the Allies could not have won the war. Had Hitler been able to hurl the troops engaged on the eastern front at the Normandy invaders, there can be little doubt as to the ultimate outcome.

Almost as important is the influence of Stalingrad on subsequent postwar history. From the Russo-Japanese War, through World War I, to the confrontation with little Finland, the Russian had earned worldwide contempt as a soldier. At Stalingrad he stood up

[11] Louis L. Snyder, *The War, A Concise History, 1939-1945* (New York, Julian Messner, Inc., 1960), p. 307.
[12] A large number of those wounded had been air evacuated.

to the best troops that the world could offer and came off victorious. Without the confidence acquired on the banks of the Volga, and the knowledge that Russian troops, properly equipped and led, were equal to the best, it is doubtful that the Soviet political and military accomplishments of the last twenty-eight years would have been realized. Russia, thereafter, became a major military power whose thrust and influence would range from Eastern Europe to the Middle and Far East.

> Stalingrad was the turning point of the Kremlin's policy in the direction of Russo-Soviet imperialism, pursued from then on without disguise and quite often with brutal and cynical frankness.[13]

As Fuller summarized it: "Into the minds of a hundred million Moscovites flashed the myth of Soviet invincibility, and it forged them into the Turks of the north."[14]

Stalingrad brought victory to the Allies in 1945, but it also let a genie out of a bottle.

[13] Anders, *op. cit.*, p. 153.
[14] Fuller, *op. cit.*, p. 538.

4.

JONAS SALK—
POLIO VACCINE

When Jonas Salk stood before the television camera on a memorable March evening in 1953, he was truly a man of the twentieth century. A curious combination of dedicated scientist, Madison Avenue promoter, and ambitious empire builder had led Salk into an accomplishment that by any standards was fantastic. He was destined to defeat a crippling and life-destroying disease and put an end to the nagging fear of the approach of summer and the annual polio season.

Although Salk didn't realize it at the time, like Charles Lindbergh of an earlier generation, he was to become an authentic people's saint. Unlike the "Lone Eagle," there were to be any number of devil's advocates during his canonization rites.

Salk was introduced on television that evening in 1953 by Daniel Basil O'Connor who, in turn, became an integral part of the Salk legend. "Doc" O'Connor, the Taunton, Massachusetts-born son of an Irish Catholic laborer, had worked his way through Dartmouth College by playing the violin in local dance bands. His tuition to Harvard Law School had been paid by a wealthy lawyer impressed with his debating skill.

By the mid-twenties, O'Connor was a well-to-do corporate lawyer. Intrigued with a suggestion of one of his clients, John B. Shearer, O'Connor formed a legal partnership with Franklin Delano Roosevelt who had been Democratic candidate for Vice

President in 1920, and had been stricken with crippling polio the following year.

Roosevelt was not much of a lawyer and could only bring sterling Brahmin and WASP connections into the firm. Nevertheless, O'Connor was astute enough to recognize that the Roosevelt family background was what his law practice needed. Even without a·law degree, Roosevelt's association with the ambitious and active young Irishman changed FDR's image from that of a dilettante.

Roosevelt became interested in the Meriwether Inn at Warm Springs, Georgia, believing the waters of the pool were helping him to regain partial use of his paralyzed legs. In 1926, Roosevelt, together with friends, purchased the Inn, the pool, and 1,260 adjoining pine-studded acres. The property was thereafter transferred to a charitable foundation that in its early days encountered many operating difficulties. By the time Roosevelt had been elected Governor of New York in 1928, the venture had accumulated a pile of debts.

When Roosevelt was elected President in 1932, Warm Springs' continued existence seemed questionable because sources of charitable gifts were drying up following the stock market crash in 1929. After his inauguration, Roosevelt asked O'Connor to assume management of the foundation and the Irish lawyer accepted. It was literally the gift of a headache.

Late in 1933, Carl Byoir, a public relations expert, suggested to O'Connor that the foundation should hold nationwide annual Presidential birthday parties. The proceeds would go to the Warm Springs Foundation. O'Connor was delighted with the idea and the first series of balls brought in more than a million dollars.

When Roosevelt's popularity dwindled among those financially able to support the project, annual receipts from the yearly drives began to decline. In 1936, less than $600,000 was received. Roosevelt determined, as far as possible, to disassociate himself from the anti-polio movement. Accordingly, in September, 1937, he announced the formation of a new organization ". . . to lead, direct, and unify the fight on every phase of this sickness." The National Foundation for Infantile Paralysis became the nation's leader in the fight against the dreaded scourge.

Although belonging to another ethnic group, Jonas Salk's background was not far different from that of Basil O'Connor. Both were the products of self-respecting but economically deprived parents—O'Connor an Irish Catholic, Salk an Orthodox Jew. Salk was born in New York City on October 28, 1914; his father worked in the garment district and the family lived in a succession of tenements on the Lower East Side, Harlem, and the Bronx. Despite the environment, the Salks were not culturally deprived. Nor was there any lack of ambition on the part of Dolly Salk for her sons. She never allowed anyone to question the necessity of her boys going to college and thereafter to either medical or law school.

Small and thin, inept at games and play, Jonas Salk had few friends as a boy. At twelve years of age he was accepted by Townsend Harris High School where a select group of bright boys might complete their secondary education. Jonas graduated within three years and entered City College, determined to become a lawyer. His plans soon changed when he discovered science. From that day forward any desire for the law died. He wanted only to be a scientist—engaged in the pursuit of pure truth.

At nineteen, Salk received his bachelor's degree. In the autumn of 1934 he enrolled in the New York University College of Medicine. However, Jonas did not plan to practice. From the start of his graduate work, Salk was bent on the field of medical research.

When Salk entered medical school, Dr. Maurice Brodie, an assistant professor of bacteriology at N.Y.U., had just developed a crude polio vaccine. Brodie's discovery, as well as a similar one by Dr. John Kolmer of Temple University in Philadelphia, was believed to hold the key to the end of the dreaded disease. Salk could not know that both vaccines, through premature use, would ultimately bring heartbreak and tragedy. Rather, he must have been thrilled by this apparent dramatic advance in his chosen field. Between the vaccines of Brodie and Kolmer there started a controversy over the efficacy of live and killed virus. This ultimately affected the work and career of Jonas Salk.

During his last year in medical school, Salk came under the influence of Dr. Thomas Francis, professor of bacteriology at New York University. Francis put the young man to work in his laboratory on a study of the inactivation of influenza virus with ultra-violet light. They discovered that it was possible to kill the virus without destroying its ability to produce antibodies. As an indication of the older man's regard for his young protégé, Francis allowed the name of Jonas Salk to appear as the senior author of the report subsequently published on the subject.

After graduating from medical school in June, 1939, Salk obtained a fellowship. He remained nine more months, continuing to work under Dr. Francis. Before starting his internship, Jonas met and married Donna Lindsay, a Smith College graduate and social worker.

In 1942, Salk received a fellowship grant from O'Connor's National Foundation for Infantile Paralysis. Concurrently, he followed Dr. Francis to the University of Michigan where his preceptor had become Professor of Epidemiology. At Ann Arbor, Salk worked with Francis on field testing an influenza vaccine for the Army, and because of the essential nature of his work was granted a deferment by his local draft board.

Dr. Francis was distinguished from most of the scientists in the vaccine field. He firmly believed in the use of killed virus rather than live virus. Francis concluded that, after its injection in the body, killed virus could still stimulate the buildup of antibodies in the bloodstream and protect the patient from the disease.

Those engaged in vaccine research of the live virus were in the majority. These scientists argued that the best way to produce a real immunity to an infectious disease was by injecting the patient with a mild dose of the disease. They contended that when killed virus was injected, it did not cause an infection, antibodies were only produced against the particles injected and, therefore, a temporary low level of immunity was the best that could be hoped for. This school of thought could also point to the successful use of "live" smallpox and yellow fever vaccines.

The problem of the killed vaccine faction became the development of a vaccine that, with properly spaced injections, would produce a booster effect to produce lasting immunity. The scientists hoped to do this through adjuvants; the best of these seemed to be mineral oil as the fluid suspension instead of water. The oil forms a deposit in the body releasing the virus very slowly into the bloodstream thus prolonging stimulus for the development of antibodies.[1]

Influenced by Dr. Francis early in his career, Jonas became an

[1] The best lay description of the two schools of thought is to be found in Greer Williams, *Virus Hunters* (New York, Alfred A. Knopf, 1959).

advocate of the use of killed virus. He remained with Francis at Michigan for five years and became an assistant professor of epidemiology.

By 1947, Dr. Salk, at thirty-three, was ready to move on. He wanted his own laboratory or department, and he began to look around for an opening. His accomplishments in the development of the Army flu vaccine were recognized. He had even been sent to Germany by the government to set up diagnostic influenza laboratories. His name had appeared on learned articles in medical journals—not always as the senior author, much to his annoyance. He had high hopes of securing a position commensurate with this background. While there were openings at the University of California, Western Reserve in Cleveland, and Mount Sinai Hospital, none were offered to him, and Salk began to despair that he would ever find an appropriate base for his work. At this point an opportunity presented itself at the University of Pittsburgh School of Medicine.

Among the medical schools of the country, Pittsburgh's stood at the bottom of the totem pole. Overshadowed in the state by the prestigious University of Pennsylvania and Jefferson Medical College, Pitt's faculty consisted mostly of practicing physicians who gave part of their spare time to teaching. Consequently, the school lacked any significant program of basic research. In 1947, Pitt's entire program was a grant of $1,800 for the study of high blood pressure.

Dr. William S. McEllroy, Dean of Pitt's Medical School, hoping to improve the school's standing, was endeavoring to recruit full-time faculty members capable of carrying on research that could result in large grants from foundations.

Hearing of Salk, the dean asked him to come in for an interview. After the visit, the young scientist, wanting independence and an end to being second-fiddle, could see nothing but opportunity in McEllroy's offer. Salk had become increasingly estranged from Dr. Francis, who viewed Jonas' move to Pitt as a mistake. Francis finally agreed to release him with his blessings.

As Dr. Francis anticipated, Salk found the arrangements not as ideal as he had hoped. His administrative superior, Dr. Max A. Lauffer, was a biophysicist with little knowledge of medical research. Even space for his laboratory presented a problem. Never easily discouraged, Salk masked his disappointment and went to work. He soon found his opportunity in the field of polio vaccine research.

Poliomyelitis is probably as old as the human race. Egyptian mummies have been found with one leg shorter than the other, with limbs withered as if from the disease. The first recorded epidemic of polio was not until 1835 when the hamlet of Worksop, England, had four cases of stricken children. Cases were also reported on the island of St. Helena. A similar visitation of the disease occurred in Louisiana in 1841.

Given the name of "spinal infantile paralysis" in 1850 by Dr. Jako Heine, a German orthopedist, the disease seemed to grow in virulence as the living conditions of the world improved. In the last half of the nineteenth century, epidemics were reported in Lyons, Oslo, Boston, Stockholm, and Otter Creek, Vermont. Thereafter, particularly in America, the incidence of the disease rose rapidly.

The author vividly recalls as a boy, the epidemic of 1916 when 27,363 cases, including 7,197 deaths, were reported. Together with my sister, I was taken to the New Jersey coast for it was popularly believed that there was less chance of contracting the disease near the sea. On the trip we were required to carry papers certified by our home physician that we had not been exposed to anyone with polio. At each town through which we passed, the papers were inspected by public health officials. The theory—probably of lay origin—that proximity to the ocean gave a child a better chance of not contracting the disease persisted as late as 1939. I recall during that year's epidemic my two sons were kept at the seashore until November.

As early as 1908, Doctors Karl Landsteiner and Erwin Popper in Vienna reported they had produced polio in monkeys by inoculating the simians with tissue taken from a human who had died from the disease. The following year Doctors Simon Flexner and P. A. Lewis passed a human polio virus from monkey to monkey. By 1910, the possibility of the development of a vaccine became obvious when it was proven that the blood of monkeys recovering from the disease contained a new blood fraction, later to be identified as antibodies, that destroyed the living virus when mixed with it in the laboratory.

76

In the years that followed, particularly after the epidemic of 1916, it was learned that polio was transmitted through secretions or droplets from the nose and mouth, and in fecal matter. The virus established itself in the intestines and moved from there through the bloodstream to the spinal cord or brain. Polio infections usually occurred in infancy, a period of life when paralysis is rare. Once having had the disease, the child was immune for life. Accordingly, in less advanced nations where hygiene and indoor plumbing are not found, the disease was endemic and epidemics in older children were unknown.

In the more advanced nations of Scandinavia and North America, some children were protected from the virus until they reached a stage in life where they were susceptible to paralysis. In the cities of the more affluent countries, swimming pools, a ready source of infection, were increasing yearly. At the beaches where swimming was done in the broad ocean there was less chance of contracting the disease.

In 1931, Dr. MacFarlane Burnet of Australia discovered that there was probably more than one strain of polio. He reported that his studies indicated animals immune to one strain were not immune to another. Burnet's findings were confirmed two years later by Drs. James Trask and John Paul of Yale.

Harry Weaver, Research Director of the National Foundation, realized a successful polio vaccine would have to give immunity to all strains of virus. Unfortunately, no one was certain how many types there might be, and the formidable task of classifying all strains might take years and cost millions. Nevertheless, Weaver, supported by O'Connor, decided to go ahead with the project. The program eventually cost $1,370,000 and 30,000 monkeys.

Weaver knew of Salk and invited him to join in the work and become a member of the National Foundation Committee on typing strains. With Salk were his former preceptor, Dr. Francis, who discovered the Mahoney Type I; Dr. Charles Armstrong of the United States Public Health Service who isolated the Lansing Type II strain; Dr. John F. Kassel who found the Leon Type III strain; as well as Dr. David Bodian of Johns Hopkins University; Dr. Albert Sabin of Rockefeller Institute; Dr. Louis P. Gerhardt of the University of Utah; Dr. W. Lloyd Aycock of Harvard; Dr. Herbert A. Wenner of the University of Kansas; and Dr. Weaver.

Classifying the virus strains was a dull, laborious process but the yearly grant of $200,000 from the National Foundation enabled Salk to equip a large laboratory in the nearby Municipal Hospital for Contagious Diseases and assemble a competent staff of fifty. The study was finished in 1951, when it was finally established they knew there were only three types of polio virus.

Named Research Professor of Bacteriology and Director of the Virus Research Laboratory of the University of Pittsburgh, Salk now undertook the more adventurous and rewarding task of finding a polio vaccine. Any qualified scientist was eligible to apply for a grant from the National Foundation, and Salk was only one of a number, including Dr. Sabin, who filed applications which were approved.

For the three types of polio virus strains he would use, Salk selected the Mahoney strain, the strongest of all for Type I; from a Middle East victim of MEF I Bulbar Polio, Salk obtained Type II; for Type III he chose the Saukett strain which he isolated in 1950 from a boy with paralytic polio.

The first problem was to assure the safety of the vaccine he was ultimately to produce. The virus had to be destroyed so that it could neither kill nor paralyze children. At the same time, its ability to stimulate the growth of antibodies had to be preserved. To do this Salk resorted to a process known as "cooking."

He determined that virus fluid cultures should be cooked at a ratio of 4,000 to 1 of formaldehyde at body temperature. Adding a safety factor, Salk concluded that the cooking process should be carried on for a period of nine days. The virus at the end of that period should be as he was later to remark, "safe, and it cannot be safer than safe."[2] Subsequent happenings supported Salk's conclusions.

The next big problem involved the increase of antibodies after inoculation. Now, man's friend, the monkey, had to be abandoned and the experiments conducted on man. Monkeys, rodents, and men do not always react in the same way in their resistance to disease. Killed virus increased the antibodies in monkeys, but would it act the same in man?

The determination of the number of antibodies in a human is

[2] *Ibid.*, p. 287.

difficult.[3] The patient's blood is injected with the killed virus and enough time is allowed for antibodies to develop. Then the serum is injected into an animal or live tissue culture along with the infecting virus. The serum is diluted and the process is repeated until the process of dilution makes the concentration of antibodies so weak that the animal or tissue finally becomes infected. The degree of dilution is called the "titer"[4] of the serum tested.

Salk decided his safest course was to experiment with children who had previously suffered from polio. In May, 1952, he went to the D. T. Watson Home for Crippled Children at Leetsdale, Pennsylvania, and saw Dr. Jesse Wright, Medical Director; Harry F. Stambaugh, Chairman of the Board of Directors; and Lucille Cochran, R.N., Administrator. They gave their wholehearted consent for the experiment.

On June 12, Salk took blood from the children and found that sixty out of sixty-nine had antibodies for the most common polio strain Type I. On July 2, he returned to the Home and administered his vaccine, part of which was suspended in water and the rest in mineral oil.

The results of the D. T. Watson Home experiments were a complete success! There were no adverse reactions of any kind among the child subjects. From a titer of four for Type I, before vaccination, the number shot up to 3,264,128 and even higher.

> Some of the vaccine given to children whose blood contained antibody prior to inoculation had produced far higher levels of antibody—an impressive booster effect. And some of the subjects whose blood contained no detectable antibody before inoculation were now giving samples of blood replete with antibody. The levels of antibody were high enough to destroy living polio viruses. Salk saw it under his microscope. Blood samples taken from the vaccinated were deposited in tissue culture that contained virulent polio virus. If the virus remained alive, it would destroy the tissue cells. But in these cultures the tissue cells continued to grow. The antibody produced by vaccination had killed the virus.[5]

[3] It is now a very exact science.
[4] The reciprocal of the highest dilution of the solution showing specific activity.
[5] Richard Carter, *Breakthrough* (New York, Trident Press, 1966), p. 139.

Jonas Salk and his associates had apparently discovered a safe and effective "killed" polio vaccine.

Experimentation, however, continued. Following his success at the D. T. Watson Home, Salk extended his tests to those with no prior history of polio. In October, sixty-three mentally retarded patients at the Polk State School at Polk, Pennsylvania, were inoculated. Again the results were a complete success.

Salk spent the next several months preparing a report of his findings for an article to appear in the 28 March, 1953, issue of the *Journal of the American Medical Association.* In January, he attended a meeting of the Immunization Committee of the National Foundation where he summarized the conclusions of his study. Leaving New York in a light mood, Salk was upset upon his return to Pittsburgh when he learned that Earl Wilson, the Broadway columnist, had jumped the gun and reported the discovery of a new polio vaccine. Since a March of Dimes Fund Campaign was underway, Salk assumed an overzealous National Foundation public relations officer had leaked his findings to Wilson. Furious, Salk immediately returned to New York and saw O'Connor. His subsequent television appearance of 26 March, 1953 was the outcome of the conference.

After an introduction by O'Connor, Salk outlined the historical background of the drive against polio. He told of the 1909 immunization of monkeys; of the 1939 discovery of more than one strain of virus; of the premature effort during two previous decades to find a vaccine, and of the painstaking work that followed to develop a safe but effective immunization program. While Salk admitted that there was cause for optimism, he stressed the need for caution and patience:

> However, this objective will be achieved if we move cautiously, and with understanding, step by step. Certain things cannot be made without establishing first the wisdom of the one before. We are now faced with facts and not merely with theories. With this new enlightenment we can now move forward more rapidly and with more confidence.

From a popular standpoint, Salk's speech was a tremendous success. He had spoken with restraint, with caution, but his assurance that there would be a vaccine—that all the effort had not been in vain—gave parents new hope. Professionally, his talk was not well received. His fellow scientists felt that such an address to laymen before he had even reported his findings to his colleagues was a degrading spectacle—an example of self-seeking publicity. Physicians were of the opinion that they should have been given his conclusions before he had talked to the public. The speech eventually caused Salk many heartaches.

Because there were still a number of unresolved problems, the experiments continued at the Pittsburgh laboratory during the spring of 1953. These difficulties centered around the merits of oil or water as a suspension body, and the most effective way of killing the virus.

In May, Salk vaccinated himself and his family as well as five hundred school children in the well-to-do Pittsburgh suburbs of Sewickley and Leetsdale. Salk also discussed with O'Connor the possibility of a mass trial of the vaccine, for he could see the continuous growth of antibodies in those he had vaccinated the previous year.

In late November, 1953, O'Connor made the announcement Salk had been anxiously awaiting. A mass test inoculation of between 500,000 and 1,000,000 children would take place prior to the polio season of 1954.

Dampening the good news of O'Connor's release was a statement made the same day by Dr. Albert Milzer of the Michael Reese Hospital in Chicago, who reported that he had been unsuccessful in killing polio virus with formaldehyde.

Dr. Hart E. Van Riper, the Medical Director of the National Foundation, felt it necessary to reply to Milzer's statement. Van Riper assured the public that "No human being has been or ever will, in any field trials, be inoculated with any material that has the remotest suspicion attached to it."

Unfortunately, Milzer was not the only medical scientist with doubts about the safety of the Salk serum. Many thought the polio program was getting out of hand, that it was proceeding too rapidly, and that there had not been a thorough evaluation of Salk's claims.

Nevertheless, plans for the massive field test went forward under the direction of Van Riper. Vaccination of second grade children would take place in two hundred selected counties, with the work carried out under the supervision of volunteer physicians. For each child inoculated, written permission was required from parent or guardian.

The National Foundation originally planned to contrast the incidence of polio among the vaccinated second graders with those of the non-inoculated first and third graders in the same community. This concept was viewed as a non-scientific procedure by most of the epidemiologists. They favored a plan whereby doses of vaccine and of a dummy vaccine (placebo) would be packaged alike, with the virulent and the placebo given to alternate children, the physician being unaware of which he was administering. The incidence of polio among those who had received the vaccine and those who had received the placebo would then have real meaning.

In late November, the National Foundation capitulated to the epidemiologists and Van Riper telephoned Salk's former preceptor, Dr. Francis, who was on sabbatical leave in London, and asked him to direct the field trial. Francis did not immediately agree, but after his return to the States in December, he took over the task with the understanding that he could design the test and there would be matched controls.

On 26 April, 1954, the program of vaccination began. When it had been completed, 1,829,916 children of the first, second, and third grades had taken part in the study. Francis had divided the program into two parts. In the so-called placebo areas, 209,229 children received the Salk vaccine while 201,229 received the dummy injection, and 338,778 received neither. In the observed areas 231,900 children were vaccinated and 775,160 were not.

Dr. Francis had insisted when he took over that the findings from the test remain secret until his report was completed. This put O'Connor in a dilemma. If he waited until the report proved the efficacy of the Salk vaccine, it would be too late to order sufficient vaccine from the pharmaceutical companies to mount a massive attack on polio in 1955. If, on the other hand, he ordered the production of the vaccine and the tests proved ineffective, he would have squandered millions of dollars of the Foundation's money on a useless vaccine. O'Connor took a calculated risk. He contracted to buy twenty-seven million doses of Salk vaccine at a cost of $9 million.

Dr. Francis read his report on the tenth anniversary of the death of Franklin Delano Roosevelt, at ten-thirty in the morning of April 12, 1955, in almost a Hollywood atmosphere, before an audience of five hundred assembled in the large auditorium of the University of Michigan. As the television cameras ground, he told the nation that the Salk vaccine was "safe, effective, and potent," that it was "80-90 percent effective against paralytic poliomyelitis; 60-70 percent effective against disease caused by Type I virus; and 90 percent or more effective against that of Type II and Type III virus."

Even before Dr. Francis had finished speaking, paeans rose throughout the nation. Church bells rang in many towns, people entered church to give thanks to God for Jonas Salk, courts interrupted their proceedings for a moment of silent thanks, and a huge burden was lifted from the hearts of parents. The drama was not, however, finished.

Cutter Laboratories of Berkeley, California, in 1955 produced a batch of defective serum resulting in the death or crippling of a number of children and another spate of criticism followed. But the incidence of polio in the ensuing years spoke for itself.

In 1954, there had been 38,694 cases in the United States. By 1957, after more than half of all Americans under forty had received at least one shot of the Salk vaccine, the total number of cases in the nation had fallen to 5,787. In 1960, 3,190 cases were reported; in 1961, the incidence of the disease had been reduced to 1,312 cases, and in 1962, the number dropped to 910. The Public Health Service during the year 1964 reported only 94 cases of paralytic polio in the United States and a record low of 40 cases in 1967. Polio had been unequivocally defeated.

The short and forceful Dr. Albert B. Sabin had become interested in polio research as far back as 1946 but had done little about it until 1953. A Russian Jew, born in 1906 in Bialystok, he had been, from 1924 to 1926, a dental student at New York University. Switching to medicine after he became a naturalized American citizen, he earned his M.D. degree in 1931.

An advocate of live virus, he felt that the killed-virus vaccines were unpractical as they would, he thought, "require multiple doses and yearly re-inoculations." A critic of Jonas Salk and of his accomplishments, his live vaccine was ultimately to almost supersede Salk's discovery, although its merits were still to cause considerable controversy.

In the years between 1953 and 1961 the National Foundation supported Sabin's polio vaccine program to the tune of $1,120,000. The Foundation was, however, more conservative than Sabin felt necessary. It contended that, since Salk's vaccine was a success, there should be no large human experiments until Sabin's vaccine was demonstrated to be as safe. Sabin tested his vaccine on the prisoners at the federal reformatory in Chillicothe, Ohio, in 1955. The results were successful, but the Foundation still persisted in its cautious stand.

The vaccine that he ultimately developed had the distinct advantages that it required no needle but could be administered orally on lumps of sugar and, after taking three doses, you were presumably immune for life.

The idea of nonmedical personnel passing out candy from door to door had great appeal to Russian public health officials. Accordingly, in 1959, the Soviet authorities inoculated about 75 million people with Sabin vaccine without—they claimed—severe reactions.

Mrs. Dorothy M. Horstmann of Yale University was, however, later to investigate the Russian inoculation program. She found that in Karagand in the Central Asian Republic of Kazakhstan where 171,000 children had been inoculated, twenty-two cases of paralytic polio had occurred among children recently given Sabin vaccine. Of the children not vaccinated only eighteen cases had occurred.

From 1959 on, the U.S. Public Health Service was under great pressure to license the Sabin vaccine. It was not, however, until 1962 that the Sabin strains were given the go-ahead. In that same year Great Britain accepted the Sabin vaccine. Both vaccines are now used in the Western countries with Sabin's used exclusively behind the Iron Curtain.

Today the more convenient Sabin vaccine has all but superseded that developed by Jonas Salk. The controversy as to the merits of the two vaccines, although somewhat muted, continues.

Walking along the streets of the average American suburban town two decades ago, one would have seen at least a few crippled children. Today the sight is a rarity. The despair experienced when

84

one learned a child had been stricken with polio is now only a memory of an older generation. The lives that the Salk and Sabin vaccines have saved, the living deaths of crippled misery they have prevented, the hours of anguish parents have been spared—these are just a part of their gift to the world.

Today there are few who recall the fear that, in the pre-Salk days, gripped the hearts of parents as the annual polio season approached. Other than pray that the plague would pass our doors there was little that we could do, for not much seemed to be known about the disease. We tried to keep our children out of crowds, keep them from swimming pools and, if we could afford it, get them to the seashore. But we all knew of other parents who had done all that, and their children still wore braces.

Daily we saw mute evidence of the crippling effect of the dreaded scourge. Parents went about their daily work not only with this fear but with a nagging frustration that arose from our inability to protect those for whom we were responsible. The jubilation and the hysteria that greeted Jonas Salk's discovery was but a small manifestation of the deep-seated relief that all of us felt for our deliverance.

There are also many less important spin-offs, by-products of the Salk and Sabin vaccines. Modern parents, unlike their fathers and mothers, can plan summer months without considering the threat that polio once posed. Through a combination of affluence and the vaccines, the average American family has been put on wheels during the summer. As a result, there has been a phenomenal growth in the tourist industry. There are more motels, more vacation spots, more campers and campsites, more leisure and pleasure than would have been possible were it not for the dedicated genius of Jonas Salk and Albert Sabin—and parents can feel free to avail themselves of leisure activities without risking the health of their children.

The breakthrough in polio, and, in particular, the flamboyant and dramatic manner in which it was accomplished, may result in an earlier defeat of cancer and a host of other diseases. There were many vaccines developed before those of Salk and Sabin, but these never struck the hearts and feelings of the American public in quite the dramatic fashion that marked the reaction to the polio medication. Salk's discovery gave the nation confidence in its ability to

85

conquer other plagues. Contributing to various fund drives dedicated to the conquest of disease, the individual has the feeling that not only will the gift be well spent, but that he, too, is taking part in healing research.

Those of us who reached middle age in the thirties and forties can be proud that we belonged to a generation that included Jonas Salk, Albert Sabin, Basil O'Connor, and their dedicated colleagues.

5.

A SMALLER
WORLD—
JET AIRCRAFT

On a clear, crisp October day of 1942, in a classroom of the Army Air Corps Intelligence School at Harrisburg, Pennsylvania, Captain William Massey paused in his lecture. Already familiar with "Aircraft of the World," the subject of Massey's talk, the student officers slumped and dozed in their seats or gazed out the wide windows.

Massey's next words, "this is top secret information," brought the students out of their lethargy. Their faces revealed more and more concern as the captain continued: "The Italians have developed a jet-propelled aircraft. This is probably the secret weapon Mussolini boasts of, for it could considerably change the balance of air power between the Axis and the Allies. Jet aircraft traveling at speeds unknown today will be invulnerable to anti-aircraft fire, and propeller driven planes will be sitting ducks. Fortunately, because of British research in this field, we are not too far behind the enemy."

Most of the students in Massey's class spent that evening in the school library reading the little information that was available on jet propulsion. They learned the basic principles of the jet engine are that "fuel is burned with previously compressed air in combustion chambers. From these chambers the hot gases from the burnt fuel pass to a circular chamber, open to the air and facing the rear. A turbine is housed near the rear of the unit, and before passing outside the gases spin this turbine. By means of a long shaft, the turbine drives a compressor at the front of the engine to provoke compressed air for burning with the fuel."

They learned that the difference in the operation of a turbo jet engine compared to a reciprocating engine with a propeller lay in the mass and velocity of the air and gases affected.

"The propeller hurls a comparatively large volume of air rearward at a relatively slow velocity, while the turbo jet engine takes in a smaller volume or mass of air, expands it with burning fuel, and blasts it to the rear at a very high velocity. The larger the mass of air, and the more it is accelerated, the greater will be the thrust."[1]

Several of the student officers were disabused of their previously held belief that a jet engine gains its power from the backward thrust of the hot gases against the outside air pressure. Rather, the thrust is against the front of the unit.

"The drive is obtained through the unbalanced pressure inside the jet exhaust pipe. If the exhaust pipe were closed, the hot gases forced into the jet pipe would exert pressure all around the inside of the pipe. With the port open, the pressure is unequal, and the greatest reaction to the outgoing gases takes place at the point opposite the opening. Since the pressure inside the pipe is many times greater than that of the atmosphere, and the greatest effect of that pressure is against the front end of the pipe, forward speed is gained."

Before World War II, all aircraft engines were powered by piston type reciprocating engines. The discovery of the principle of jet propulsion is, however, shrouded in antiquity. In 150 B.C., the priests of Egypt, who wished to amaze their worshippers with supernatural illusions, commissioned Hero of Alexandria to design a device whereby the temple doors would be opened without visible aid. His efforts on behalf of his ecclesiastical clients produced the aeolipile, a machine whose energy was supplied by the burning of fuel that converted water into steam. Attached to the head of the boiler were two tubular uprights that formed trunnions for a hollow sphere. Projecting from the sphere were two nozzles which discharged the steam at right angles to the axis of rotation.[2]

[1] Jack V. Casamassa and Ralph D. Bent, *Jet Aircraft Power Systems* (New York, McGraw-Hill, 1957).
[2] *Ibid.*, p. 1.

It is doubtful that the aeolipile aided the priests in opening their temple doors, but Hero's ingenious contraption is the first known use of jet propulsion.

Solid fuel rockets, a form of jet propulsion, were in use in China as early as 1232 A.D. Employed as a weapon, they were fueled by gunpowder.

Giovanni Branca, an Italian, used a turbine to drive a stamp mill in 1629. Branca forced steam through a jet to impinge upon buckets around the periphery of a wheel, causing the wheel to rotate.

Fifty-one years later, Sir Isaac Newton designed a steam-driven horseless carriage, but it is doubtful that it was ever built or operated. Newton planned to have a long nozzle extending to the rear of a boiler from which escaping steam presumably would cause a reaction and propel the carriage forward. It is questionable that the thrust would have been sufficient to move the vehicle.

A year before Orville and Wilbur Wright made the first controlled, power driven, sustained flight at Kitty Hawk, North Carolina, on December 17, 1903, Stanford A. Moss at Cornell University designed the first gas turbine built in the United States. In 1918, while working for the General Electric Company, Dr. Moss supervised the development of the earliest application of the gas turbine for driving a supercharger for reciprocating engines.

Monsieur L. Lorin is generally regarded as the father of jet propulsion. In 1908, he proposed the use of a reciprocating engine and the exhaust jet. Lorin suggested that after performing its normal operation of suction, compression, and ignition, each engine cylinder allow the combustion gases to exhaust down a funnel into the atmosphere.[3]

Another French engineer, Monsieur G. Marconnet, in 1909 wrote of jet reactions in which compression was affected by a Rootes blower. In 1917, a British scientist, Harris, invented a jet engine that used a centrifugal blower with forward-facing intake driven by a small twin-cylinder piston engine.

During 1926 Great Britain began to make strides in jet propulsion

---

[3] O. E. Lancaster, ed., *Jet Propulsion Engines* (Princeton, N. J., Princeton University Press, 1959).

research. In that year, Dr. A. A. Griffith of the British Royal Aircraft Establishment developed a theory of turbine design based upon flow past airfoils rather than through passages. His plan favorably impressed the Royal Air Ministry.

In 1930, Sir Frank Whittle, a student at the Royal Air Force College, applied for the patent of an engine that used a compressor burner and turbine to produce jet thrust. Whittle's work in the field of jet propulsion was later to be the base from which American research proceeded, after the start of World War II.

On August 27, 1939, the first jet-propelled flight was made in Germany. The plane, a Heinkel 179, was purely experimental. In Great Britain a similar jet plane was flown on May 14, 1941, but the Germans and the Italians remained substantially ahead of the Allies in jet propulsion research during the entire period of the Second World War.

In the closing months of the war in Europe, American troops were often told, after being strafed and bombed by the Axis jets, that the Allies would soon have similar aircraft in the air. However, VE Day came and went without a sign of a single American or British combat jet plane over Europe. Unfortunately for Hitler, his jet engines, produced with inferior materials, had a life span of only ten hours in flight.

During the war years, Allied research on jet military aircraft continued. The first Whittle engine was brought to the United States on October 1, 1941, and one year later a fighter built by Bell Aircraft Corporation, with a General Electric GEI-A turbo jet engine, made a successful test flight. Considering time limitations and complexities of the problems involved, the development of this aircraft was one of the outstanding engineering feats of the war.

After VJ Day, American experimentation with gas turbine aviation engines continued. The first operational military jet was the Bell F-80. In the Korean War, the North American F-86 Sabre jet fighter gave good service but the limitations of the jet as a military weapon became apparent. Traveling at great speed, neither its strafing nor bombing was as accurate as the slower propeller-driven aircraft. Also, high fuel consumption sharply limited the amount of time a jet aircraft could stay aloft.

The commercial jet planes designed and produced during the

years since World War II are the descendants of those military aircraft developed but never used during that conflict. The birth of jet-propelled commercial aircraft was inevitable, but the ingenious feats accomplished during wartime unquestionably reduced the necessary period of experimentation by at least several decades.

Continued progress in commercial jet-propelled aircraft research has led to the huge Boeing 747 that will be dotting the skies during the 1970s. This 335-ton super–jet, with a length of 231 feet, is longer than the distance of the first flight of the Wright brothers in 1903. More comfortable and commodious than any of its predecessors, its greater passenger capacity may eventually bring lowered fares. The 747's 20-foot-wide cabin can accommodate 490 passengers, and flight time between New York and London has been reduced to about five and a quarter hours. How much additional pollution the plane will release into our sky has not yet been revealed.

Each of these super-jets cost $25 million. For the thirty or more 747s expected to be operative by summer, 1970, the airlines will pay more than $4 billion. Greater jet capacity will also project giant problems for our already over-expanded airfields. Few terminals are adequately equipped to handle an increased volume of passengers with the necessary car parking spaces, ground transportation, and baggage facilities.

It is also estimated that the airlines will be required to advance as much as $2 billion in the next four years for the purchase of fifty-four-ton tractors to tow the planes on the ground, and new boarding ramps designed to lift passengers seventeen feet from the ground to the aircraft. Huge and fast as these super-jets may be, the future holds even larger and speedier planes. The point of diminishing return in the field of jet aircraft is still far distant.

The drastic reduction by jet aircraft of travel time between American cities has increased the living pace of the nation's business executives and has had a profound influence on the lives of us all. It has, in fact, brought about a complete revolution in air travel and communication. Perhaps the most important effect of this time-space shrinkage has been its acceleration of the existing trend of Americans to become a nomadic people. Today, when a young man is offered employment in another part of the nation he is rarely concerned with those he may be leaving. He knows that, within hours, they can be together again.

The frequent cutting of domestic roots has developed a different type of American family. With grown children and grandchildren scattered over the length and breadth of the land, the older generation has considerably less influence on their descendants than had their fathers and mothers. Mobility, combined with the new permissiveness, the decline of organized religion, and a constantly rising incidence of divorce, has not only produced a more independent generation of children and young adults, but one that neither cares nor knows about the lessons that can be learned from the past.

There are, of course, other changes that fast transportation has brought about. The American people are becoming more homogeneous. The average middle-class American family, not living in the area of its birth, or having friends and neighbors who come from other parts of the country, is less provincial and has less sectional bias. No longer do we think of the "Solid South," the isolationist Midwest, or the radical Far West. The American melting pot has been bubbling more merrily since the development of the jet (and the automobile) than it did during the previous two centuries. Ultimately, should we survive, we may become a cohesive society in which the origin of our grandparents, our race, our religion, or our sectional prejudices will play little part.

Ease of travel plus television has given America a uniform language. Sectional accents are disappearing. Colloquialisms are seldom heard except when used by an older person. Strangers are no longer identified as a southerner, a damn Yankee, or a Brooklynite. Certainly no one wants all Americans to look or think alike, but an end to the barriers of sectional antagonisms is welcome.

The speed and ease of air travel has allowed American industry to decentralize its operations. No longer is it necessary, for supervisory reasons, to locate offices and plants within a narrowly restricted area. An executive of an American corporation can leave his New York office in the morning, visit a plant in South Carolina, and be back at home on Long Island that evening. The old New England factory, with the home of the president on a nearby hill, and the other officers of the company living within shouting distance, has become an anachronism. During the past decade decentralization of industry has proceeded at such a pace that there are now corporations with dozens of plants scattered all over the continental United States and throughout the world.

The impact of the greater speed of the jet on our railroads has, however, not been as favorable as on other American industries. Already affected by the competition of the low-fare bus lines, the arrival of commercial jets gave the final coup de grâce to railroad travel, and has had a particularly deleterious effect on long-distance passenger trains.

Oddly enough, down through the years the railroads haven't done much to arrest the downhill glide of passenger service and equipment. They had forgotten they had been given the right of eminent domain and other privileges as a consideration for providing passenger services. Instead of trying to upgrade service, they discouraged passenger travel by every means possible including outmoded dirty cars, minimal service, frequent unnecessary delays, and poor terminal accommodations. Unfortunately, the railroad industry in the last century has been taken over by profit-conscious bankers instead of the imaginative adventurers of earlier years. Perhaps our railroads could, with profit, study the operations of Japanese trains.

Today these same executives run to the I.C.C. and with dubious statistics, ask permission to discontinue the operation of this or that passenger train. That it is their entire profit picture, rather than the specific loss in the operation of a single train, is not discussed—but all that is another story. What remains is that railroad passenger service is dead—finally killed by the jet.

Ever-increasing jet travel between nations should also be noted on the positive side of the ledger. Prior to World War II, an American who had been abroad was considered unique—a man or woman "of the world." Today, a good proportion of our citizens have enjoyed foreign travel. The advent of package air travel plans, nonscheduled airlines with their group tour rates, has made it increasingly easy and attractive to travel abroad. And more and more Americans are availing themselves of the opportunity. This includes young married couples (European, Asian, and Caribbean honeymoons via jet planes are commonplace), business executives, secretaries, clerks, college and high school students.

This is also true of the nationals of other Western nations. Only in the Communist countries are citizens denied tours that leave their homeland. Less than fifty years ago, except for the immigrant, one rarely met a foreigner in the United States. Today tourists from abroad are an everyday occurrence.

The result of this communication between nationals can only be beneficial. We now know that all foreigners do not have horns, that all Frenchmen do not think like Charles de Gaulle, that all Japanese are not replicas of Tojo. Today it would be impossible for a William Hale ("Big Bill") Thompson, of the 1920s, to be elected mayor of Chicago on a platform that he intended to poke the Queen of England in the nose. That is certainly progress!

The pride that enveloped the American people on their TVs when they saw Neil Armstrong step out on the moon, as well as the joy of the Russians when the first Sputnik was launched on October 4, 1957, are both the results of jet propulsion research. The wisdom and practical benefits of the Apollo program may be questionable, but it nevertheless remains a magnificent achievement of the American people, its scientists and engineers.

While the intervention of the United States in Southeast Asia might have been possible without the jet transport and freight carrier, it has certainly been facilitated by the use of these aircraft. With the airports of Vietnam only eight hours' flight time from our West Coast, it is possible to shuttle troops back and forth at will, and priority material can be delivered within a few days.

The ease of travel is also responsible for the steady flow of visiting politicians to the war zone. With eyes on the headlines, they can leave their Senate offices in the morning and be in Vietnam that evening. Perhaps when historians consider, point by point, the factors that have brought us to our present dilemma in that far country, the speed and comfort with which the computerized Secretary of Defense, Robert McNamara, could commute to Saigon and influence the course of battle will not play an inconspicuous role.

The sailing ship, the steamboat, the transoceanic cable, the wireless, and the airplane all, in turn, broke down the barriers between nations, but ultimately the jet will do more to reduce the importance of international boundaries than all the other methods of communications combined. With hour distances between nations drastically reduced, no country can, in the years ahead, continue to remain isolated. Statesmen, whether they be dictators or elected presidents, will not be able to contain their constituents as prisoners within their respective homelands. Neither a Berlin Wall nor Chinese bridge guards will eternally hold back the curious. For this we may thank the jet—born in the furnace of war, but with the possibility of bringing peace and, certainly, more understanding throughout the world.

6.

END OF
AN AGE—
HIROSHIMA

Sitting on the screened porch of his beachfront vacation home on Peconic Bay, Long Island, clad only in a T-shirt and a pair of soiled, rolled-up trousers, Albert Einstein was drafting a letter. Because he believed it to be of vital importance, he had spent most of the Sunday afternoon of July 30, 1939, composing it.

He had returned from sailing in the nearby cove that morning to find the two Hungarian-born physicists, Drs. Eugene P. Wigner of Princeton and Leo Szilard of Columbia, waiting for him. Both men—they had driven from Princeton, New Jersey, that morning— were gravely concerned about the progress of German nuclear research. They feared the possibility that Hitler might develop a nuclear fission bomb before the United States, and use the super-weapon in his quest for world domination. They urged Einstein to write a letter to President Franklin D. Roosevelt expressing this fear.

When Wigner and Szilard left they took with them the substance of the message. Two days later, with Dr. Edward Teller, Professor of Physics at George Washington University, Szilard returned to Long Island with the typed letter. After several small changes Einstein signed it. It read in part:

> Sir:
> Some recent work by E. Fermi and L. Szilard, which has been communicated to me in manuscript, leads me to expect

that the element uranium may be turned into a new and important source of energy in the immediate future. Certain aspects of the situation which have arisen seem to call for watchfulness and, if necessary, quick action on the part of the Administration. I believe, therefore, that it is my duty to bring to your attention the following facts and recommendations:

In the course of the last four months it has been made probable—through the work of Joliot in France as well as Fermi and Szilard in America—that it may become possible to set up a nuclear chain reaction in a large mass of uranium, by which vast amounts of power and large quantities of new radium-like elements would be generated. Now it appears almost certain that this could be achieved in the immediate future.

This new phenomenon would also lead to the construction of bombs, and it is conceivable—though much less certain—that extremely powerful bombs of a new type may thus be constructed. A single bomb of this type, carried by boat and exploded in a port, might very well destroy the whole port together with some of the surrounding territory. However, such bombs might very well prove too heavy for transportation by air.

The United States has only very poor ores of uranium in moderate quantities. There is some good ore in Canada and the former Czechoslovakia, while the most important source of uranium is the Belgian Congo.

I understand that Germany has actually stopped the sale of uranium from the Czechoslovakian mines which she has taken over. That she should have taken such early action might perhaps be understood on the ground that the son of the German Under-Secretary of State, von Weizacker, is attached to the Kaiser-Wilhelm-Institut in Berlin where some of the American work on uranium is now being repeated.

The letter was to be hand-carried to the President by Alexander Sachs, a friend of Szilard. A Russian by birth, Sachs was a Vice President of the Lehman Corporation and an occasional consultant to Roosevelt, but he was unable to obtain an appointment with the Chief Executive until October 11. Something of an amateur scientist, Sachs took with him, in addition to the letter, a collection of technical documents and a memorandum prepared by Szilard.

He would have probably accomplished more in less time, had he just presented Einstein's letter to the President, for after Sachs had read all the memoranda and documents Roosevelt appeared bored with the matter. However, he did ask Sachs to return the next morning.

At the second conference Roosevelt made the query, "Alex, what you are after is to see that the Nazis don't blow us up?"

"Precisely," replied Sachs.

The President thereupon sent for his military aide, Major General Edwin M. ("Pa") Watson, and turned the matter over to him with the words, "This requires action."

Watson, in turn, formed an Advisory Committee on Uranium, with Dr. Lyman J. Briggs as chairman. Other members of the group included Army Lieutenant Colonel Keith F. Adamson, Navy Commander Gilbert C. Hoover, as well as Szilard, Teller, and Wigner.

At the first meeting of the committee on October 21, Adamson, an unimaginative ordnance officer, made no effort to conceal his opinion that the whole thing was ridiculous. Nevertheless, the committee finally agreed to appropriate $6,000 for uranium research. The physicists wanted the money to purchase graphite for Dr. Enrico Fermi's experiments on chain reaction. The program that was to develop from this original investment eventually cost the United States $2 billion.

During 1940 and 1941, a total of $300,000 of government money was spent on atomic research. In spite of the work that was being done, the decision to go ahead and manufacture the bomb was not made until the day before the Japanese attacked Pearl Harbor. The British were well ahead in the nuclear field and agreed to pool their knowledge with the Americans.

Under Brigadier General Leslie Groves, who supervised the building of the Pentagon, the program was code-named the Manhattan Engineering District Project. Oak Ridge, in the Tennessee mountains, became a veritable city as did Los Alamos Laboratory, north of Albuquerque, New Mexico. Research was also carried on in a number of universities.

Dr. J. Robert Oppenheimer directed the scientists at Los Alamos. He was a brilliant scholar, poet, and bi-linguist and chiefly responsible for the eventual development of the atom bomb. Republics are notoriously ungrateful, but the subsequent humiliation of this man was to be something apart. The ordeal Oppenheimer endured was probably the most unfair ever imposed on an American citizen.

Collaborating with this brilliant scientist were Drs. Fermi, an Italian; Wigner and Teller; a native Russian, George Kistiakowsky; two Germans, Hans Bethe and James Frank; and from Denmark, Niels Bohr. American scientists working on the project included James Bryant Conant, President of Harvard; Karl Compton, MIT's President; Arthur Holly Compton; Dr. Ralph E. Lapp, prominent American physicist; Ernest Orlando Lawrence of the University of California's Radiation Laboratory; Vannevar Bush of Carnegie Institute; Commander Frederick L. Ashworth, USN; Captain William S. Parsons, USN; and a host of other distinguished scientists.

General Groves's deputy was Brigadier General Thomas F. Farrell, a World War I hero. Groves, Farrell, and other military men were well liked and respected by the scientists at both Oak Ridge and Los Alamos, and good relations continued during the entire project. However, some resentment developed toward the military police and counter-Intelligence personnel. The professors did not seem to understand the necessity for restrictive security regulations, and on occasion refused to cooperate with what they felt were infringements on their personal rights.

When a conflict arose between the two groups, counter-Intelligence usually came out on top. That the latter did a masterful job is indicated by the fact that when the bomb was perfected and dropped it proved to have been the best kept secret in the history of the United States.

Unfortunately, tight security measures did not keep two Russian spies, David Greenglass and Dr. Emil Joseph Klaus Fuchs, out of the program. Greenglass, an Army enlisted technician, was one of thousands who worked on the program and somehow he missed detection. Fuchs, a brilliant German physicist who had been granted asylum from the Nazis in England, came to the United States with the British group and was not investigated. Fuchs and Greenglass, who were convicted and sentenced to fourteen and fifteen years respectively, will probably go down as the greatest spies in all history. Their efforts were no doubt responsible for the Russians' detonating a nuclear device as early as August, 1949.

On 17 December, 1944, the United States Air Force activated a new unit, the 509th Composite Group. It was a unique outfit. While the 509th was attached for administration to the 21st Bomber Command of the 20th Air Force, it received its orders from the President of the United States—through channels that included the Secretary of War, Henry L. Stimson; General George C. Marshall, the Army Chief of Staff; and General Henry ("Hap") Arnold, Chief of Army Air; and General Groves.

The 509th had a strength of 1,767 officers and men, plus a number of scientists and technicians. It was composed of the 390th Air Support Group; the 603rd Air Engineering Squadron; the 1017th Materiel Squadron; the 320th Troop Carrier Squadron; the 1395th Military Police Company; the 1st Ordnance Squadron; Special Aviation; the 1st Technical Detachment; and War Department Miscellaneous. Its combat element, the 393rd Bombardment Group, had fifteen B29s from which the armor and guns had been removed, with the exception of two twin .50-caliber machine guns in the tail section. The forward bomb bays had also been considerably increased to accommodate a larger bomb.

Colonel Paul W. Tibbets, Jr., was anything but the typical flamboyant air corps flyer of the 1940s. Reserved, scholarly, and quiet, the pipe-smoking officer had just passed his thirtieth birthday.

Tibbets had been born in Quincy, Illinois, but was raised in Des Moines, Iowa, and Miami, Florida. Sent back to Illinois for his preparatory education, he graduated from Western Military Academy in Alton in 1933. Planning to study medicine, Tibbets attended the Universities of Florida and Cincinnati.

In 1937, he determined to become a flyer and enlisted in the Air Corps Cadet Program. Tibbets found his niche in the Army Air Corps. At the right time and place, he rose rapidly in rank and responsibility. From England Tibbets led his outfit, the 97th Bombardment Group, on its first mission against Nazi–occupied France. He flew General Mark Clark from England to Gibraltar for the general's pre-invasion submarine trip, and General Eisenhower to the Mediterranean to assume control of "Torch."

Tibbets later led a number of the first heavy bomber strikes on Italy and Germany from North African bases. In 1944, the 97th Group returned to the States. After a period of test flying of the then secret B29s at Alamogordo Air Field in New Mexico, Tibbets was selected to command and organize the 509th.

At Wendover Field, Utah, Tibbets assembled his command. Wendover was a desert post, 120 miles west of Salt Lake City. Its isolation made it ideal for the organization of a super-secret unit.

After a short training period, crews from the 509th were sent to the Martin plant in Omaha to pick up the fifteen B29s required by the outfit. Among the planes brought back to Wendover was one carrying the number 82. Later Tibbets christened this aircraft the *Enola Gay* after his mother. Modified for its special mission, and with all the newest scientific equipment, the plane was piloted only by Tibbets or Captain Bob Lewis.

The training was completed at Wendover by April, 1945, and Tinian in the Marianas was selected as the combat base of the 509th. The island had been wrested from the Japanese in July, 1944, and on it the Seabees had constructed the world's largest airfield.

The ground echelon of the 509th sailed on the *SS Cape Victory* from Seattle for Tinian on May 6, arriving at their new lush tropical home on May 29. The B29s started to arrive on June 11 and, needless to say, security forces greeted both the ground personnel and the combat crews.

Training during June and July consisted, in the main, of actual flights of several planes dropping a single bomb filled with conventional explosives from a height of 30,000 feet on a Japanese city, then banking and turning at an angle of 155 degrees. The turn had to be executed flying at 200 miles an hour in less than thirty seconds. "No one had to tell a pilot the object of that maneuver—to get the hell away from there fast."

At 2:45 A.M., on August 6, 1945, the huge but graceful aircraft, *Enola Gay*, gradually picked up speed as it moved down the two-mile runway at Tinian. With only a few feet of the long strip to spare, the nose of the aircraft lifted and the ship became airborne. She was followed down the runway at two-minute intervals by two similar planes, the *Great Artiste* and the *91*, both carrying scientists, their instruments, and photographic equipment.

As the *Enola Gay* rose into the night sky and leveled off at 4,700 feet, the tension that had built up within the aircraft gradually subsided. Captain Lewis, nominal commander of the plane, although flying as co-pilot, signaled to Colonel Tibbets that he would take over.

The colonel had not slept well the night before and had hoped to get at least a two-hour catnap before Iwo Jima, but his mind refused to relax. This mission was, after all, the culmination of months of planning and hard work, not only by himself but by thousands of others.

A total of 539,000 men and women had been involved in one way or another in the manufacture of that bomb back in the bay. All their efforts, billions of dollars, and perhaps an early end to the war were dependent on this flight. It was now out of his hands—success or failure rested on the performance of the others aboard the aircraft. They were good men, however, and why not? He had selected all but the naval Captain William S. Parsons. Had he known Parsons and been given the opportunity to request him, "Deak" also would have been his choice.

Now that they were airborne, the duties assigned the quiet, thoughtful naval officer were probably more important than those of any other crew member. A 1922 graduate of Annapolis, the forty-four-year-old Parsons was the oldest man aboard the *Enola Gay*. He had spent five years as gunnery and fire control officer on the *USS Idaho*, and attended Ordnance School at Annapolis and the Washington Navy Yard. He was an expert and a recognized scientist and had been named Deputy Director of Los Alamos.

Parsons was one of the very few men who understood and knew the functions of the gun-type fission bomb in its entirety. It had been decided that arming the bomb before take-off would be too dangerous; a mistake or a mishap on the runway might blow Tinian off the map. It became Captain Parsons's job to arm the monster in flight.

Assisting in this dangerous task was an Air Force officer and fellow scientist, Morris Jeppson, a Mormon from Carson City, Nevada.

Perhaps the only other person aboard the *Enola Gay* that morning who could be characterized as a pure scientist, was twenty-four-year-old Lieutenant Jacob Beser, AC, the electronic counter-measures officer. The son of a Baltimore lawyer, Beser was studying engineering at Johns Hopkins at the time of the Pearl Harbor attack and next day enlisted in the Army. During his training period he was a student in the Aviation Cadet Program at Scott Field, Illinois; the Radar School at Boca Raton, Florida; and the Air Corps School of Applied Tactics at Orlando.

In charge of all electronic equipment, navigation, and radar countermeasures for all of the aircraft of the 509th, Beser had an additional duty on his present mission. The bomb's proximity fuses were the last of a series of steps that would trigger the bomb's detonation. None of this series would start until fifteen seconds after the bomb left the bay. Not until the air pressure indicated the bomb was within two thousand feet of the earth would it explode. At a given point the bomb would send off radio signals that would bounce back off the earth. On the nineteenth bounce the last fusing switch would close. It was Beser's task to see that the Japanese were not using a wavelength too near the one previously selected for the bomb, and cause a premature detonation.

Iwo came into view at the exact time the plane's navigator, Lieutenant Theodore Jerome Van Kirk, had estimated. A Pennsylvanian, born at Northumberland on 27 February, 1921, Van Kirk attended public school and then studied chemical engineering at nearby Susquehanna University. Enlisting in the Air Cadet program in September, 1941, he graduated from navigation school at Kelly Field, Texas.

Sent to England as a casual,[1] he had been assigned to the 97th Bombardment Group where he became Colonel Tibbets's navigator. Van Kirk had plotted the flights of Generals Mark Clark and Eisenhower prior to the North African landing. After his return from Europe and prior to his joining Tibbets, he had been an instructor at a navigation school in Louisiana.

Lieutenant Van Kirk worked closely with Staff Sergeant Joe Stiborik, the radar operator. The thirty-year-old son of a Czech emigrant, Joe had been raised in Taylor, Texas, where he graduated from high school. A bookkeeper with a cotton firm, Stiborik enlisted in the Air Corps in June of 1942 and was assigned to glider training. Later he was sent to radar school and thereafter studied electronics. In flight, one of his primary duties was to pass on information to the navigator that the radar disclosed.

Radio operator Richard Nelson was also charged with giving

---

[1] A military term referring to an officer sent to a theater of war without an assignment.

Van Kirk data. Twenty-year-old Dick Nelson was the youngest of the twelve-man crew, and officially the "low man on the totem pole," not yet having made Pfc. Born and raised in Los Angeles, he had been a business administration student at the University of Southern California when he had enlisted at eighteen.

Washed out of the Air Cadet Program because of an eye deficiency, he was sent to radio school. Why he had been selected for the 509th or the *Enola Gay* was a mystery to many. His grades in radio school had been above average but they had not been outstanding. Nevertheless, young and enthusiastic, he was a welcome addition to the crew. He had a happy disposition and was well liked.

Staff Sgt. George Robert Caron, tail gunner, Staff Sgt. Wyatt E. Duzenbury, flight engineer, and Sgt. Bob Shumard made up the balance of the enlisted personnel aboard the *Enola Gay*. Caron, twenty-six years old, Brooklyn born, had graduated from a technical high school and then worked as a draftsman for a number of engineering firms. Joining the Air Corps in 1942, he had studied power turrets. At thirty-two, he was the oldest airman on the plane. Caron first met Tibbets at Alamogordo when the colonel was testing the B29s. Called "Dad" by most of his enlisted men, he seemed interested only in machinery and sports. Duzenbury had also met Tibbets at Alamogordo where the colonel had been impressed with the young mechanic's steadiness under pressure. Fellow crewmen knew little of Duzenbury's background or where he came from, but they were aware that he knew his business and that no one was allowed to put a wrench to the *Enola Gay* except under his supervision.

If anyone aboard the *Enola Gay* was along for the ride, it was twenty-five-year-old "Bob" Shumard who was charged with watching for any signs of trouble with the engines. He also had enlisted in the Air Corps in 1942 and had been trained as a gunner. At this point, however, he was without a gun.

At an airspeed that varied between 197 and 227 miles an hour, and at an altitude of 30,700 feet, the engines of the *Enola Gay* droned on as dawn caught up with the huge ship speeding toward the Imperial Empire. At eight-thirty the first of the Japanese Islands could be seen, and shortly thereafter Honshu, then to the southeast, the city of Hiroshima.

As the aircraft started on its bomb run, Major Tom Ferebee, the bombardier, took over. Ferebee, a North Carolinian born in Mocksville, a small town in the central part of the state, had been with Tibbets in Europe. A sports enthusiast, he had been proficient at baseball, and before the war had dreamed of a career in the big leagues.

Like a football placekicker who is sent into a game for one sole purpose, Ferebee's work occupied only a few seconds of a flight—but the success or failure of a mission was dependent on his split-second timing. Cool, collected, unflappable, Ferebee was the ideal bombardier.

The crew had been warned they were not to look at the detonation without their special Polaroid goggles. The duties of Ferebee, however, made him the only one on the *Enola Gay* unable to pull down his glasses as the aircraft approached the target.

At exactly 09:15:17, as the sprawling city of Hiroshima appeared below, Ferebee triggered the bomb shackle releases and the five-ton atom bomb started its downward descent. The *Enola Gay* immediately made a sharp 155 degree turn to the right, dropped a thousand feet, and increased speed. In the words of one of the enlisted men, "We got the hell out."

As the plane sped away, there was a blinding purple flash and, almost immediately thereafter, a huge, ugly mushroom-shaped cloud began to form over the target area.

Hiroshima was the headquarters of the Imperial Second Army Corps and an important industrial center with aluminum, nitrogen fertilizer, and oil plants. A provincial city with a population of 250,000, it was almost entirely surrounded by hills and mountains. Built on a delta of the Ota river, on a bay of the Seto Inland Sea, its waterfront docks, wharves, and piers made it a city of considerable maritime significance.

While American planes were a daily sight, and sometimes disturbed the inhabitants' sleep, Hiroshima had been spared the saturation bombings and fire raids that had been the lot of most Japanese cities. Almost every night formations of the big bombers would fly over, but they had not disgorged their lethal loads. In the morning a weather plane or two would generally cause an alert, but when it was not followed by a formation of bombers, the all-clear quickly sounded.

All sorts of fantastic explanations were advanced for its good fortune, including the story that the son of a prominent American was being held prisoner-of-war in the city and the father had exercised pressure for the removal of Hiroshima from the target list. Despite this talk, the citizens could not conceal their apprehension that next time it would be their turn.

There were also other significant worries that bothered the people of Hiroshima. Days of celebrating the feats of arms and victories of the Imperial troops were long since past. Communiqués that spoke of "planned withdrawals" were not fooling the Japanese people. They knew that, of the former Axis powers, they now stood alone. The preparations the military were making to meet the expected invasion of the home islands could not be kept a secret. Even on the outskirts of Hiroshima, soldiers were building defensive positions and tank traps. Many Japanese correctly suspected that their leaders planned to offer them up in a last, vast Kamikaze defense of the home islands.

August 6, 1945, bid fair to be a hot sultry day in Hiroshima. It started as any other day in that long summer of discontent. Shortly after seven, an alert was sounded but it turned out to be the usual morning weather plane. Around eight, the siren sounded again. This time three high-flying planes were observed heading for the city. Since no large fleet of bombers followed, observers concluded that the three aircraft were on a reconnaissance flight. The "all-clear" sounded and the people of Hiroshima resumed their daily affairs.

Then it came. A blinding, searing flash of light. Those within six hundred feet of a point directly below the bomb were instantly vaporized, leaving no trace other than perhaps a shadow imprinted on a stone wall. Bricks and tiles simply dissolved and vanished.

There was no sound of an explosion, but seconds after the flash there was a crushing impact of a massive shock wave and fires broke out all over the city. People more than two and a half miles away from ground zero were burned on their bared skin. Invisible, lethal radiation—by-products of the fission process—attacked unprotected

Japanese in the target area. The effects of "hot" alpha, beta, and gamma particles caused a delayed death or permanent disfigurement for thousands. The horrors of the sights of the survivors are beyond description.

Father John A. Siemes, a German and Professor of Modern Philosophy at Tokyo's Catholic University, was staying at a mission on the side of a mountain about two kilometers from Hiroshima on the morning of August 6. He was sitting in his room when the whole valley was filled by a great light which he said resembled the magnesium light used in photography. The flash was followed by a wave of heat and the entire window and frame exploded into the room.

Sprayed with particles of glass but not otherwise hurt, Father Siemes rushed into the hall to find the building in shambles. All the windows and doors had been blown in, and the building was severely damaged. Believing that a bomb had landed nearby, the priest, on going outside, was unable to find a crater. Looking toward the city, he saw several homes were burning and the woods across the valley were aflame.

The city itself was obscured by a thick ball of smoke and it began to rain large black drops. A long procession of people began to stream up from the valley. Many were seriously injured and pleaded for help and the priests helped them into the chapel and gave them first aid. Medical supplies were soon exhausted, but the parade from the stricken city went on. As Father Siemes describes it:

> More and more of the injured come to us. The least injured drag the more seriously wounded. There are wounded soldiers, and mothers carrying burned children in their arms. From the houses of the farmers in the valley comes word: "Our houses are full of wounded and dying. Can you help, at least by taking the worst cases?"
>
> The wounded come from the sections at the edge of the city. They saw the bright light, their houses collapsed and burned the inmates in their rooms. Those that were in the open suffered instantaneous burns, particularly on the lightly clothed or unclothed parts of the body. Numerous fires sprang up which soon consumed the entire district.[2]

[2] Fr. John A. Siemes, eyewitness account in *The Atomic Bombings of Hiroshima and Nagasaki* (U. S. Army, The Manhattan Engineer District, N. D.).

In the late afternoon Father Siemes and six of his fellow priests went into the city in an attempt to rescue Father Superior LaSalle and Father Schiffer who, they learned, had been seriously injured and were in Asano Park on the river bank. Father Siemes continues his narrative:

The houses at the edge of the city are all severely damaged. Many have collapsed or burned down. Further on, almost all of the dwellings have been damaged by fire. Where the city stood, there is a gigantic burned-out scar. We make our way along the street on the river bank among the burning and smoking ruins. Twice we are forced into the river itself by the heat and smoke at street level.

Frightfully burned people beckon to us. Along the way there are many dead and dying. On the Misasi bridge, which leads into the inner city, we are met by a long procession of soldiers who have suffered burns. They drag themselves along with the help of staves or are carried by their less severely injured comrades.

Father Siemes and his party finally rescued Fathers LaSalle and Schiffer. Of a later return to the city that day he wrote:

Beneath the wreckage of the houses along the way many had been trapped and they scream to be rescued from the on-coming flames. They must be left to their fate.

Before nightfall, thousands of those alive in Hiroshima that morning were dead. It is not accurately known how many Japanese men, women, and children perished from the bomb and its lethal aftereffects. Some estimates run as high as 200,000.

The *Enola Gay* returned to Tinian without incident. Three days later a second atom bomb, this time the implosion—"Big Boy" using the plutonium rather than uranium—was dropped on Nagasaki. "Big Boy" killed from 40,000 to 80,000 Japanese civilians. On August 9, Russia declared war on Japan and her armies moved into Manchuria, with little opposition. Five days later, the Imperial Japanese Government capitulated and the following day, at noon, the Emperor broadcast to a stunned nation that they must "endure the unendurable."

Japan and the world did not know that when the bomb was dropped at Nagasaki we had used up our small arsenal. While one, and perhaps two additional bombs, could have been manufactured within days or weeks, it would have been months before an appreciable number could have been produced.

In August of 1945, having spent the previous three years in combat duty in Africa, Sicily, Italy, France, and Germany, the author was a student at an Army school in Meridian, Mississippi, awaiting orders for the Pacific. When he heard President Truman's announcement of the dropping of the atom bomb, like millions of other Americans he wanted to return as soon as possible to his family and what he considered a normal way of life.

Any question of the moral justification of the use of the bomb never entered his mind. If the war had been shortened by even a week, the action taken had been proper. There were few at the time who would have disagreed. Certainly those of us who were to invade the Japanese home islands were in accord with the President's action. Only with the passage of time are we afforded the luxury of moral indignation at Truman's decision to unleash the bomb.

Plans were already underway for "Olympia," the code name for the landing on southern Kyushu, which would be followed in March by "Coronet," the landing on the Tokyo plains. Estimates of American losses, based on the 41,000 American casualties suffered on Okinawa, ran between 250,000 and 1,000,000, while Japanese losses would be considerably greater. It is argued that the war with Japan had already been won and that, before the time of the invasion had arrived, Japan would have capitulated.

It is true that Tokyo had made some tentative peace overtures, but an unconditional surrender would never have been allowed by the Japanese military caste. Realizing that Japan could not win, they wanted the nation to die in a fiery suicidal Samurai defense of the homeland. The use of the atom bombs gave the Emperor and Japanese liberals a face-saving excuse for surrender. According to John J. McCloy, former American High Commissioner for Germany, "We didn't need the bomb to win, but we needed it to save American lives."

Perhaps, it might have been different had we not clung to the phrase—"Unconditional Surrender"—and sent word to the Japanese that, even after capitulation, they could keep their Emperor.

"Yet no man can ever be sure about the 'might have been.' Not the statistics of defeat, but the human imponderables—the code of Bushido, the vestiges of the age of feudalism, the profound Japanese belief that death in battle means life in heaven—hung in the balance as the *Enola Gay* made her bombing run."[3]

Even more interesting speculation involves the atom bomb and the post World War II period. Had the scientists of the Manhattan project failed to produce the bomb, the shape of the world today would be quite different. The slogan, "bring the boys home," that resulted in a rapid demobilization following both World War I and II, left the United States virtually defenseless in 1946. Russia, faced with no such internal demand, retained her wartime conventional forces. There can be no doubt that following World War II, Russian troops could and would have swept over western Europe had it not been for Soviet fear of retaliation by the atomic bomb.

The development of the atom bomb not only gave the United States a tremendous leverage in global affairs, but was principally responsible for the United States being thrust forward into leadership of the free world. Until the atom bomb, powerful navies and large armies were the attributes of a leading power. With the advent of nuclear weapons neither became quite as important as they had been through World War II. Had there been no atom bomb, Britain with its powerful navy might well, for a few years at least, have remained in the forefront of the Western powers.

Although it came later, after David Greenglass and Klaus Fuchs hastened a Soviet A-bomb, Hiroshima was responsible for the arms race between the two leading world powers, Russia and the United States, the monstrous cost of which would dwarf any similar contests in world history. The race between the two powers combined with the costs of Korea and Vietnam, as well as military aid throughout the world, would bleed the United States and force it to abandon internal problems of a compelling nature. Much of the

[3] Hanson W. Baldwin, *Hiroshima Plus 20* (New York, Delacorte Press, 1965).

dissension that today plagues these United States stems from the A-bomb and Hiroshima.

Today both Russia and the United States possess sufficient nuclear weapons to destroy life on earth. The two great powers have become mutually restrained from reckless conduct. Even the most irresponsible of statesmen must pause with the thought that his actions could result in the end of civilization.

Can anyone doubt that the specter of a World War III, and the consequent use of nuclear weapons, deterred the hand of Khrushchev from the reckless course he had been following before and during the Cuban Missile Crisis? Can there be any question but that the United States would have long since crossed the North Vietnamese border, had it not been for the fear that such an action might result in Soviet or Chinese nuclear retaliation?

Dr. Luis Alvarez of the University of California, who played a key role in the development of the first two atom bombs, said in 1965: "The World has not had a major war in the past twenty years, and most responsible people feel the risk of a World War III has diminished steadily with time in these same years. I am confident that both of these admirable situations are already traceable to the existence of nuclear weapons."

Many of us today decry the possession by man of the means of his own destruction. Thermonuclear and nuclear weapons have, however, since the detonation at Hiroshima and Nagasaki, brought a sort of "Peace on Earth" between the great powers.

7.

DRAGON TEETH— THE COMMUNIST TAKEOVER OF CHINA

Should Western civilization, as we have known it, come to a screeching halt, the roots of its death will not be entirely found in the lack of vision of its leaders, the fantastic ingenuity of its scientists, or even in the writings of Karl Marx and Lenin, but in the complex and incomprehensible history of China. One quarter of the human race—more than seven hundred million people— steeped in hate, and with a rapidly growing industrial might, pose a threat to life as great as modern man has yet faced.

Communism is not the driving force of the Chinese. Rather it is a vehicle that a downtrodden and subjugated people seized to shake off the chains of centuries. Nor is communism just the product of the terror-filled twentieth century. Three thousand blood-drenched years have gone into the making of the Chinese People's Republic and we are reaping dragon teeth that have been sown from time immemorial.

The written history of China begins with the defeat by the warrier Wu, on the plain of Mu in northern Honan, of the last of the Shang kings, Choo Hsin, about 1100 B.C. Wu was later to establish both the Chou dynasty and a feudal system that included five orders of nobility among whom the land was divided. Chou rule of the middle kingdom was to see the development of an empire and the absorption of many states only partially Chinese. However, Chou influence was not nearly as great as the birth at Lu, between 551 and 479 B.C., of the philosopher Confucius.

A government official and teacher in the midst of tyranny and corruption, Confucius argued for a morality that would bring peace, justice, and order. He urged man to develop a system of "right relationship" or sympathy between each other, and to treat inferior individuals as you would wish superiors to treat you. Filial piety and respect, as well as an avoidance of extremes, were also a part of his philosophy. The theory of respectful relationship gradually solidified into an approval of the existing social order. Originally agnostic, his doctrines later took on a religious hue and by the first century A.D. Confucius had become deified.

Following the end of the Chou dynasty, the Prince of Ch'in, in 221 B.C., declared himself the first Emperor of China. A man of indescribable cruelty, he was, nevertheless, able to bring internal peace to China and establish a form of government that continued into the twentieth century, in which the country was divided into thirty-six provinces administered by officials responsible to the Emperor. It was Ch'in who met the threat of the encroaching Huns by building the Great Wall of China.

Ch'in died in 210 B.C., and after a bloody eight years of civil war was succeeded by Liu Pang, first emperor of the Han Dynasty that ruled the country for the next four hundred years. During their reign Korea and Turkistan were conquered and annexed, but the last years of the Han Dynasty and the three centuries that followed have been described as the Dark Ages of China. War lords fighting for their own survival successfully dismembered the Empire, with northern China being conquered by Tartar princes and divided into small kingdoms.

During this Dark Age, Buddhism with its emphasis on self-denial and compassion reached China from India in the first century A.D. In 581 A.D., the Sui Dynasty brought China under one emperor, but in 874 a civil war, lasting for a decade of terror, again resulted in a division of the country. Five separate dynasties, one of Turkish origin, ruled during the next fifty years.

Kublai Khan, a Mongol and the grandson of Genghis Khan, was the next emperor of all China. Building his capitol at Cambuluc, now Peking, his reign saw the flowering of Chinese cultures. His death in 1355 was followed by a rebellion led by a Buddhist monk, Chu Yuan-chang, who, as Emperor Hung Wu, established the

114

Ming Dynasty that reigned until 1644. With the prestige of having expelled the hated Mongols from China, the Ming empire extended from Burma to Korea, but oppressive taxation and corruption eventually brought about their downfall.

The Ch'ing, a Manchurian dynasty that was to govern until the twentieth century, had consolidated its power over all China by 1664. Under Emperor Ch'ien-lung the realm stretched from beyond the Amur river in the north through Indo-China to the south. Like most of its predecessors, the government was oppressive and harsh, and it became one of the most hated dynasties in the long history of China.

Modern Chinese history may be said to date from 1840, which saw the start of the infamous Opium War with Great Britain. For centuries China had restricted Western traders to Canton where they bought her silks, porcelains, tea, and rhubarb. To pay for these articles and create a favorable balance of trade, the British East India Company introduced opium from India. The trade flourished. In 1750 the total opium import was less than four hundred chests. By 1821 the amount had risen to five thousand and by 1839 had mushroomed to forty thousand chests. With this income from opium importation there came a corresponding increase in its use. By 1835, it was estimated that more than two million Chinese were addicted to smoking the poppy seed.

Over the years, the government in Peking had issued a number of decrees forbidding the importation or smoking of opium, but these edicts were never enforced. In 1821, when Emperor Tao Kuang ascended the throne, he issued another decree against its use but it was not until 1839 that any action was taken.

In that year, Lin Tse-hsu, the Imperial Commissioner at Canton, confiscated and destroyed the foreign merchants' supplies of opium. It never occurred to the Chinese, least of all the Emperor, that the traders could or would retaliate. After all, was not the Empire invulnerable? Certainly barbarians would not face the might of the imperial armies.

With little knowledge of the nineteenth-century world, the Emperor and his people underestimated both Western power and the determination of Victoria—the pious Queen of Great Britain and Ireland—to protect the commercial interests of her subjects.

In June, 1839, a British fleet arrived at the mouth of the Canton river. War and negotiations dragged on for two years with defeat and disaster the final outcome for China. Aboard a British ship of the line on August 29, 1842, an emissary of the Emperor Tao Kuang signed the first of the so-called unequal treaties that began a century of humiliation for China.

Hong Kong was ceded outright to the British crown with Amoy, Foochow, Ningpo, and Shanghai added to Canton as open ports. China agreed to pay an indemnity of twenty-one million silver dollars. Custom duties were to be determined by an equitable arrangement and, in deference to the conscience of the English Queen, the subject of opium that precipitated the war was not even mentioned in the Treaty of Nanking.

A supplemental treaty—that of Bogue—was signed the following year. The "equitable arrangement" of customs agreed upon provided for a five percent tariff on the value of imported goods. It also specified that British citizens should be subjected to their own laws under the jurisdiction of their consuls. The treaty further carried a "most favored nation clause," under which any right granted to other countries would be equally enjoyed by Great Britain.

Other nations quickly followed the British example. In 1854, first the United States and then France concluded treaties with China. With the exception of the war indemnity and acquisition of Hong Kong, their provisions were similar to the treaties of Nanking and Bogue. The French, however, insisted on a clause admitting missionaries into China.

To the downtrodden Chinese peasant accustomed to the submission required by Confucianism, Christianity was a revolutionary doctrine. Although unwilling to accept its teachings in their entirety, he welcomed many of its tenets and these were to be the motivating force of the bloodiest civil war in China's history.

Hung Hsiu-chuan, the leader of the Heavenly Kingdom or Taiping Rebellion, son of a small farmer, was born in a village thirty miles from Canton in 1814. Unable to pass the civil servant examination, his disappointment resulted in a long illness during which, in a delirium, he saw a venerable old man who commanded him to save humanity. Hung became a schoolteacher in his native

A U.S. Air Force Lockheed P-80B "Shooting Star" jet-propelled fighter plane flies over California during first months of the plane's production.

(U.S. Air Force Photo)

Smoke streams from the bellies of four Thunderjet fighter bombers as they show how aircraft can lay a screen for advancing ground troops, during a demonstration in 1951 by the 136th Fighter-Bomber Group, based at Langley Field, Virginia.

(U.S. Army Photo)

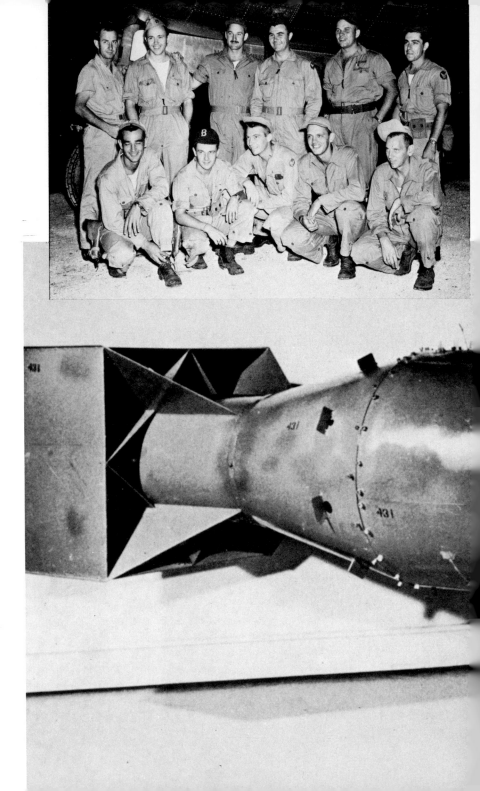

The crew of the *Enola Gay,* the U.S. B-29 bomber that dropped the atom bomb on Hiroshima. Left to right, standing: Lt. Col. John Porter, ground maintenance officer; Major (then Capt.) Theodore J. (Dutch) Van Kirk, navigator; Major Thomas W. Ferebee, bombardier; Col. Paul W. Tibbets, 509th Group CO and pilot; Capt. Robert A. Lewis, co-pilot; and Lt. Jacob Beser, radar countermeasure officer. Left to right, front row: Sgt. Joseph S. Stiborik, radar operator; S/Sgt. George R. Caron, tail gunner; Pfc. Richard H. Nelson, radio operator; Sgt. Robert H. Shumard, assistant engineer; and S/Sgt. Wyatte Duzenbury, flight engineer. *(U.S. Air Force Photo)*

(Below) Nuclear weapon of the "Little Boy" type, the kind detonated over Hiroshima, Japan, in World War II. The bomb is 28 inches in diameter and 120 inches long. The first nuclear weapon ever detonated, it weighed about 9,000 pounds and had a yield equivalent to approximately 20,000 tons of high explosive. *(U.S. Atomic Energy Commission Photo)*

A lone Japanese civilian sits on a broken section of curbstone beside trolley tracks amid the ruins of Hiroshima. *(U.S. Army Photo)*

A view taken from the Chamber of Commerce and Industrial Building after the atomic bombing of Hiroshima. Remains of the Agricultural Exposition (extreme left) overlook the Matoyasu River. The Ota River is in the background. *(U.S. Air Force Photo)*

Generalissimo and Madame Chiang Kai-shek and Lieutenant General Joseph W. Stilwell, Commanding General, China Expeditionary Forces, in Maymyo, Burma, following Japanese bombing attack on April 9, 1942.

(U.S. Army Photo)

Mao Tse-tung, Chinese Communist party chairman, climbs into jeep at Yennan Airfield after welcoming U.S. Ambassador Patrick J. Hurley and General Chang Chih Chung of the National Forces to Yennan on August 27, 1945. Colonel I. V. Yeaton, commanding American observers at Yennan, prepares to drive visitors to U.S. compound.

(U.S. Army Photo)

Major General A.C. Wedemeyer, Commanding General, U.S. Forces, China theater, talks to an old Chinese villager on July 22, 1945, while on inspection tour of American and Chinese installations in Southeastern China.

(U.S. Army Photo)

C-47s in the unloading line at Tempelhof during the Berlin Airlift (OPERATION-VITTLES). *(U.S. Air Force Photo)*

Partial view of a twenty-five-ton load of flour for Berlin flown by a C-74 Globemaster on August 17, 1948. *(U.S. Air Force Photo)*

The last OPERATION-VITTLES flight left Rhein/Main Air Force Base, Frank-furt, Germany, on September 30, 1949, at 18:45 hours as sister planes of Berlin Airlift flew overhead in formation, marking the end of a dramatic chapter in air history. *(U.S. Air Force Photo)*

village and, influenced by a Christian religious tract, "Good Words Exhorting the Age," was converted to Christianity. Recalling his dream, he concluded that the venerable old man was God, and he himself was the younger brother of Christ.

After spending two months studying Christianity under the tutelage of the Reverend Issacher J. Roberts, a Protestant missionary, Hung returned to his native village where he soon gathered a following of disciples who at first concentrated their efforts on smashing idols in the local temples. When the authorities took action, the converts followed Hung into the nearby hills where they were joined by other peasants who had been driven from their villages after local uprisings.

The times were ripe for Hung. There had been widespread drought and famine from 1846 to 1848. The exorbitant exactions of the landlords and tax collectors had reached an unprecedented high, and competition from foreign imports was beginning to hurt. Never far from starvation, Chinese peasants were now dying by the thousands, and for this Hung blamed the Manchu whose weakness allowed the entry of the hated Western barbarians into the Empire.

Hung's teachings began to take on more and more of an anti-Manchu complexion and by 1851 he was in open rebellion against the ruling dynasty. His followers rapidly grew in numbers and by 1853, in an advance up the Yangtze valley, the city of Hankow was captured and burned. In March of the same year, the rebels took Nanking and Hung made it his capital.

Preaching a doctrine of land redistribution, and a type of semi-Christianity, from which was deleted any concept of love thy neighbor or forgiveness, Hung's advancing troops captured province after province. The Emperor soon found that his warriors were no match for the fearless, fanatical Taiping soldiers and half of China was soon in revolt.

Because of the Christian slant of Hung's doctrine, the Western foreigners at first favored a takeover of China by the Heavenly Kingdom, but they soon realized that a reborn China might undermine their commercial interests. The Taiping Revolutionists, with their plans for land distribution and an end of privilege, also incurred the bitter opposition of the Chinese scholars, and civil servants, as well as members of the landlord class. The end result was that they joined in defending a corrupt dynasty for which they had little or no respect.

Bending their efforts toward the defense of the treaty ports, the Western foreigners were soon actually cooperating with the ruling Manchu. An army of mixed Chinese and foreign adventurers was organized, and command of it was given to Frederick Townsend Ward, an American from Salem, Massachusetts.

Born in 1831, after a sound military education at Norwich University in Vermont, Ward had seen service with William Walker in Nicaragua and later with the French in the Crimea. He dubbed his new Chinese command "The Ever Victorious Army" and, with the brevet rank of brigadier general, successfully led his force in a number of engagements with Taiping.

When he was mortally wounded in an attack on the city of Tzeki in September, 1862, the command of his army eventually devolved on Charles George ("Chinese") Gordon of later Khartoum fame. Under both Ward and Gordon, the Ever Victorious Army gained unenviable fame for their merciless slaughter and looting.

With the Taiping forces fast disintegrating, Hung killed himself on July 19, 1864, and while pockets of resistance still held out, the war virtually came to an end. More than ten million people died in the Taiping Civil War and many of China's towns and cities were devastated.

While siding with the Manchu during the years of its life-and-death struggle with the Heavenly Kingdom, the Western foreigners did not miss the opportunity presented by a prostrate China. Seizing on an incident at Canton on October 8, 1856, they pressed new demands on the Emperor. In the absence of its skipper, Belfast-born Thomas Kennedy, *The Arrow*, a lorcha or small ship of about one hundred tons that plied between Canton, Hong Kong, and the Portuguese colony of Macao, was boarded by Canton police who arrested its twelve crewmen.

Before debarking with their prisoners, the police struck the British colors. On October 23, 1856, a British naval fleet moved up the river from Hong Kong, capturing and dismantling four Chinese forts five miles from Canton. On the 27th, they opened fire on the city's wall and the Viceroy's residence. The Arrow or Second Opium War had begun.

In mid-March 1857, forty-five-year-old James Bruce, eighth Earl of Elgin, the former Governor of Jamaica and Governor General of Canada, was named as a special plenipotentiary to deal with the Chinese government. Bruce was instructed to treat directly with the Emperor; demand an indemnity for losses suffered; strict observance of all treaties including the right of British subjects to enter the city of Canton; and the opening of additional ports to British commerce.

With fifteen hundred British marines and support from the French, who were protesting the murder of the Abbé Chapdelaine —a Catholic missionary who had been arrested, disemboweled and then executed by a local official in the province of Kwangsi—Lord Elgin, in early May, 1857, captured the city of Canton. Thereafter, he dispatched a note to Peking demanding permission for foreign representatives to reside in the capital; full freedom for them to travel and trade throughout China; opening of more treaty ports and readjustment of the tariffs.

The Allied force, accompanied by Russian and American plenipotentiaries, next moved northward up the Chinese coast. On May 30, the fleet bombarded Taku and, after a spirited resistance, the British and French flags were raised over the city. Advancing up the river, the Allies reached Tientsin where representatives of the Emperor hastened to meet them. The Anglo-Chinese Treaty of Tientsin, signed on 26 June, met all British demands. A British minister would reside in Peking, ten additional treaty ports were opened, freedom of travel and the right to engage in missionary activities were granted foreigners. British subjects charged with crimes were to be dealt with by the British consuls and Great Britain was to be paid an indemnity of $4 million. The treaties signed by the other powers followed the same general tenor. In subsequent conferences at Shanghai, representatives of the Emperor agreed to legalize the opium trade.

Tientsin did not see the end of the Arrow War. Peking was far from the presence of the hated Western barbarians and the Emperor took advantage of the distance. Accordingly, while he delayed ratifying the treaties his representatives had negotiated, he used the time to strengthen the defenses of Taku. In mid-September, 1859, a British naval force carrying the new minister, Frederick Bruce, brother of Elgin, to Peking for the final ratification of the treaty was fired upon by the forts below Taku. Three British gunboats were sunk in the brief action with a heavy loss of life.

Under Lord Elgin, the Allies took no chances. With a force of two hundred warships and transports carrying ten thousand British and six thousand French troops, an amphibious landing was made in August at Pehtan. The Manchu forces were commanded by a blood-and-guts type of general, Seng-ko-lin-ch'in, who seemed to be in a continuous state of confusion. He was soon to be known among the British troops as Sam Collinson.

During the fighting near Sinho, a British buck private was to gain a kind of immortality. An Irish sergeant and a Private Moyse of the Buffs, guarding the regiment's rum ration from all but themselves, became drunk and lost their way on the march. Captured by a troop of the Manchu cavalry, they were taken before a mandarin and were ordered to kowtow. Moyse refused and was beheaded; the sergeant complied and later escaped. When the story became known and was reported in *The Times*, Private Moyse became the toast of London.

Three weeks after the landing at Pehtan the formidable forces at Taku were assaulted from their land sides and, following a spirited Chinese defense, were defeated. The Allies suffered about four hundred casualties. The march to Peking was marked by a number of engagements in which the soldiers of Sam Collinson were bested.

By the time the Allies had arrived on the outskirts of Peking, the Emperor had fled north. While waiting for the surrender of the city, Lord Elgin brought down the opprobrium of history on his head. Incensed at the Chinese treatment of his envoys and the execution of prisoners, Elgin ordered that the Emperor's palace, already stripped of its priceless possessions by the invading army, be burned to the ground. Built in the eighteenth century by Jesuit and Chinese artists, "Round Bright Garden" was considered one of the wonders of the world, and its wanton destruction by Elgin was remembered long after his other accomplishments were forgotten.

Prince Kung, the twenty-eight-year-old brother of the Emperor, who remained to defend the city, surrendered the Chinese capital

120

at noon on 13 October, 1860. He also had no other alternative than to accede to all the victors' demands. The 1858 Treaty of Tientsin was reaffirmed, but the indemnity was increased to $8 million for each ally. Tientsin was made a treaty port, missionaries were allowed to build churches in all provinces, and Kowloon, on the mainland across from Hong Kong, was ceded to Great Britain.

Meanwhile, the Russians were not content to sit on the sidelines and watch the despoliation of China by the other great powers. As early as 1850, they penetrated into Chinese territory in Manchuria as far south as the Amur river, where they established the town of Nikolayevsk on its banks.

In May, 1858, Count Muravyev, the former Governor General of Siberia and then Governor General of the new province of Amur, met with a Manchu envoy under the protection of the guns of five Russian warships near Aigun. After six days of fruitless negotiations, the Russian ships conducted a mock bombardment that reduced both plenipotentiaries and the inhabitants of the town to jelly. The next day Russian terms were agreed upon.

Land north of the Amur river was ceded to Russia; the area along the south bank between the Ussuri river and the sea became a condominium; and navigation on the Amur was restricted to Chinese and Russian vessels. In March, 1859, a Romanoff envoy, Perofski, reached Peking by way of Siberia and the 1858 Chinese-Russian Treaty of Tientsin was ratified. In the convention of Peking, two years later, Russia was granted the entire coast of Manchuria to the Korean border.

Russian encroachments on Chinese territory continued into the twentieth century. When the trans-Siberian railroad was completed in 1895, Russia was granted the right to administer connecting rail lines through Chinese Manchuria. In 1898, the Manchu leased the cities of Darien and Port Arthur to the Tsar and, in central Asia, Russian forces seized large areas of Chinese Turkestan. In 1915, the Celestial Emperor's province of Outer-Mongolia became a Russian protectorate. Today, Soviet troops still dispute with their supposedly ideological bedfellows the territory of the Chinese People's Republic.

The remaining decades of the nineteenth century were also to witness a continuing and relentless penetration of China by Great Britain and France. During the 1880s, Great Britain began her penetration of Chinese-held Tibet that ended in 1904 with the capture of its capital, Lhasa. In 1885, after a short war, France established a protectorate over the Chinese tributary state of Vietnam and started a chain of events that would ultimately, a century later, seriously involve and imperil the United States. In the following year, a treaty between China and Britain recognized the latter's occupation of Burma.

Nor were Western imperialistic ambitions limited to Britain, France, and Russia. In 1897, two German Catholic priests were murdered in Shantung and the Kaiser sent his fleet into Kiaochow, forcing the Chinese government to give him a ninety-nine-year lease on that port. The Germans also obtained railroad rights in Shantung province.

For centuries the Chinese had considered the Japanese as rather unimportant and contemptible barbarians, although their history, culture, and religion were somewhat similar. Japan, like China, had been isolated for centuries from the rest of the world. However, the Nipponese reaction to the West, after Commodore Perry's visit in 1853, differed from that of China. Quickly imitating superior techniques, the Japanese soon built a formidable army, navy, and industrial complex.

Japan also copied some of the less wholesome attributes of Western civilization and declared war on China in 1894. The troops and ships of the Chinese were no match for the modernized Western-oriented enemy. Following the end of these hostilities, Korea became a Japanese puppet, with Tokyo annexing Formosa, the Pescadores Islands, and the Liaotung Peninsula.

In 1915, while the West was occupied with World War I in Europe, Japan submitted "Twenty-One Demands" to the President of China, Yuan Shih-k'ai. This Nipponese ultimatum demanded that China cede all German rights in Shantung; that Japanese nationals have rights of residence, landholding, and mineral explorations throughout Soviet Manchuria; that the great Hanyehp'ing Iron Works in Hupei be turned over to a joint Sino-Japanese company; that China agree not to lease coastal areas to any third nation; that the policing of important places in China should be a joint responsibility of the two nations; that Japan should have the first option of developing railroads, mines, and harbors in the province of Fukien; that Japan be allowed to develop railroads in central China south of the Yangtze; and that the Japanese military be permitted to supply the Chinese Army with equipment and advisers. Japan was, in effect, insisting that China become a Japanese protectorate.

When Chinese President Yuan did not promptly accede to the proposals, an Imperial Japanese naval force entered and blockaded all Chinese coastal ports from Amoy to Taku while the Mikado's land forces were redeployed in South Manchuria. Yuan had no alternative but to comply with Japan's demands, although he was able to postpone acquiescing to the policing, military aid, and railroad rights in central China.

There were, however, many voices of protest throughout China insisting that her isolation of centuries was irrevocably gone and that if she were to survive she must imitate the West. They were confident that this could be accomplished without loss of Chinese values. As early as 1864, Li Hong-chang, a soldier, had addressed a memorial to the Emperor's brother, the Regent, Prince Kung:

> It is my submission that to turn China into a strong country we must acquire the use of modern weapons, and for this we must install machinery for making these weapons. By learning foreigners' methods for ourselves, we shall no longer depend on their service. In order to get these machines and the experts to use them, we shall create a special branch of the mandarinate, entry to which will be open to candidates qualified in these technical studies, who will thereafter have their careers assured.[1]

Prince Kung was impressed, but opposition to such a policy was formidable. The Manchu, as well as their principal supporters—the scholars, civil servants, and the landlord classes with privileges based on the teachings of Confucius—were adamantly against change. Factories and arsenals might see the end of absolutism in government and Chinese values.

The Emperor, Hsien Feng, who ascended the Dragon throne in 1850 and who fled north from the approaching Allied armies in 1860, never returned to Peking. When news of his brother Prince Kung's surrender of the city and the burning of the Summer Palace

[1] Henry McAleavy, *The Modern History of China* (New York, Frederick A. Praeger, 1967), p. 116.

reached the Emperor, Hsien vowed that he would never receive representatives of the nations who had humiliated him and he set out on a debauchery that led to his death at Jehol on 22 August, 1861. He was succeeded by his five-year-old son, Tung Chih, whose mother, Tzu Hsi, or Yehonala, was the Emperor's favorite concubine. After Hsien's death, she became joint regent along with the Empress Dowager.

Ignorant, venal, greedy, and cruel, Yehonala and her eunuch, Te-hai, played a stultifying role to any possible modernization of China. She claimed the Empire as her private estate and used its income for her own selfish purposes. She pocketed the taxes on goods entering Peking, and a large sum raised by a tax to build a new Chinese Navy was diverted by Yehonala to build a new Summer Palace with a marble pavilion, in the form of a ship, in the garden—the only vessel China ever saw from the levy.

When her son died in 1875 (some people said he was killed by his mother to prevent the end of her regency), Yehonala installed Kuang-hsu, her nephew, on the throne and continued as regent. In 1889, he became of age and Yehonala retired.

After the shock of Japan's victory in 1895, another movement sprang up for the modernization of China, this time led by Kang Yu-wei, a scholar from Canton. The reformers finally convinced the young Emperor in 1898 to issue a series of proclamations intended to reform Chinese society,

Once again the old order rose in wrath against any inroads on their privileges, and this time they took their grievances to the aging Yehonala. With the aid of the military, the young Emperor was imprisoned in the Imperial Palace at Peking and Yehonala again took over the reins of government, nullified the reform decrees and beheaded many of the reformers.

As it became more and more apparent that the Manchu would only continue to reign under sufferance of the Western powers, a number of secret societies opposed to both the dynasty and foreign encroachments came into existence. Among these was the I Ho Chuan or Righteous Harmony Band. Called "Boxers" because of their high regard for physical exercise and the art of self-defense, they entered into open rebellion at the turn of the century and seized a large part of the North China countryside. Killing more

8.

COLD WAR VICTORY— THE BERLIN AIRLIFT

The flag that was raised at the American Headquarters in Zehlendorf, Berlin, on July 20, 1945 had been flying on the Capitol dome in Washington when the Japanese attacked Pearl Harbor, and was flown in Rome after the Eternal City's capture in 1944 by the Fifth Army.

To those present that day for the brief ceremony, the sight of the Stars and Stripes over the once proud capital of the Reich represented not only victory in Europe and the end of a long hard road, but it was also an outward and visible sign of the nation's determination that this time there would be no precipitous withdrawal to "Fortress America." In cooperation with our allies who had helped to make the day possible, we would see that the Germans would never again be permitted to terrorize Europe.

On August 12, when French troops arrived in their sector, the four-power administration of Berlin agreed upon at Yalta was officially in operation. Furthermore, the Western Allies were determined that quadripartite control would work.

It wasn't easy. In hundreds of small, irritating ways Soviet officials seemed to exert themselves in an effort to harass their counterparts in the Western military governments. The Russians, having arrived first, had filled the municipal government positions with Communists and after the Western powers took over, they found these local officials still taking their orders from the Soviet Military

Administration. Until the Communist faithful were replaced, they would remain a constant source of irritation.

Nor were the officers of the Western powers in agreement with many of the local political maneuvers of the Soviet officials. Anticipating that the Berliners would soon be permitted to elect their own mayor and municipal assemblymen, the Russians attempted to merge their Communist party early in 1946 with the Social Democrats in such a manner that the former would assume a dominant role in the government.

Initially, it appeared the move would be successful. Fighting for their very survival and their families, most Berliners were little interested in partisan politics, and the British, French, and American Occupation authorities were, at first, apathetic. However, a small and determined group of the Social Democrat leadership stirred up opposition to the Russian plan and finally forced a vote of the entire party membership. The referendum was held on March 31, 1946, and with 75 percent of the members voting, the merger was defeated by a margin of better than 9 to 1. In spite of their defeat, the Russians went ahead and combined the two parties in East Germany and in their Berlin zone.

Meanwhile, the occupying powers had prepared a constitution for Berlin. It provided for city-wide elections, which the Russians were able to delay through the use of the veto in the Allied Kommandatura. However, in the Allied Control Council the Soviet representative, Marshal Sokolovski, finally gave his consent and the elections held on October 20, 1946, were the first free elections since Hitler had consolidated his control in 1933.

The Western powers, except for seeing that a fair and free plebiscite took place, refrained from electioneering. However, the Russians, conducting a Tammany type campaign, made every effort to secure a majority for their Communist party, now named the Socialist United party or SED. They nevertheless suffered a crushing defeat with SED able to obtain only 19.8 percent of the vote. Thereafter, the Russians never allowed city-wide elections in Berlin.

The city government that was formed following the October, 1946, election was a coalition of all four parties including the Communists, and the first Lord Mayor, Dr. Otto Ostrowski, tried to steer a neutral course between the occupying powers. The

142

Russians were dissatisfied and were finally successful in forcing him to sign an agreement pledging his cooperation with the Communist party. When this agreement became known, it was repudiated in the city assembly by a vote of 85-20 and the Lord Mayor was forced to resign.

Ostrowski's successor was Dr. Ernst Reuter, a Social Democrat who had formerly been a Communist but had left the Party— something the Russians could never forgive. By the use of their veto they were able to prevent him from taking office. As a consequence, the duties of the mayor were assumed by Deputy Mayors Louise Shroeder, a Social Democrat, and Ferdinand Freidensburg, a Christian Democrat.

As the year 1946 continued, it became increasingly evident that Russia had no intention of keeping the agreements that had been made at Yalta and Potsdam, but rather was using her occupation forces as a leverage for the extension of world communism. As Jean Edwards Smith wrote:

> Indeed, Soviet motives had become increasingly plain. People's governments already had been established in Poland, Rumania, and Bulgaria; and Hungary would soon fall completely into the Soviet orbit. In Greece, the Russians were openly promoting civil war against the established government; Turkey was being pressed for concessions in the Dardanelles which would jeopardize her independence.[1]

In the Russian zone of Berlin the situation was essentially the same as in the other Soviet-occupied areas. The Communist party took control of all parts of the government and, wherever possible, threw up road blocks to any German economic recovery. In the Allied Kommandatura and Allied Control Council, the Soviet veto had reduced those bodies to impotence. Four Power control of Berlin had become a complete and absolute failure.

Fortunately for the free world, the office of President of the United States was then occupied by one of our ablest and strongest Chief Executives, Harry Truman. In the waning months of his life, Franklin Delano Roosevelt had clung to a policy of accom-

[1] Jean Edwards Smith, *The Defense of Berlin* (Baltimore, The Johns Hopkins Press, 1963), p. 99.

143

modation with the Soviet Union—hoping it might lead to a truly peaceful co-existence and permanent cooperation after the war. When Truman succeeded to the Presidency, he tried to continue this policy, but by late 1946 he had become firmly convinced that cooperation with "the bear" would only result in a Communist-dominated world.

On September 6, 1946, with Truman's approval, Secretary of State James F. Byrnes, in a speech at Stuttgart, warned the Russians that as a result of the excessive use of their veto, the Allied Control Council was: "neither governing Germany nor allowing Germany to govern itself." It would be necessary, Byrnes added, as of January, 1947, to merge the British and American zones for economic purposes.

During February and March of 1947, the Truman Doctrine, extending economic and military aid and advice to Greece and Turkey that eventually saved those nations for the free world, was promulgated. As he stood before a joint session of Congress, President Truman said:

> The world is not static, and the status quo is not sacred. But we cannot allow changes in the status quo in violation of the charter of the United Nations by such methods as coercion, or by such subterfuges as political infiltration. In helping free and independent nations to maintain their freedom, the United States will be giving effect to the principles of the Charter of the United Nations . . . .

On June 5, 1947, speaking at the Harvard Commencement, Secretary of State George C. Marshall proposed a program of financial aid for European nations to promote their recovery. This offer was tendered to all the nations of Europe, East and West alike, whose economy had been disrupted by war. Neither Truman nor Marshall expected the American offer to be accepted by either Russia or its satellites and they proved to be right. Russia could ill-afford to admit that she needed or could use the financial assistance of capitalist America.

In the fall of 1947, a session of the Council of Foreign Ministers was held in London. Although a possible peace treaty for Austria and Germany was part of the agenda, it was finally concluded by the Western representatives that such a treaty could not be obtained except "under conditions that would enslave the German people."

When Lieutenant General Lucius DuBignon Clay, a Georgian and a 1918 U.S. Military Academy graduate, became Deputy Military Governor of the United States zone in Germany in 1945, he had little understanding of the ways of diplomacy.

An exceptionally able officer, Clay, like most of the American military at the time, was intolerant of politicians and political considerations in government. He had been handed a policy by his superiors and, as a professional soldier, would do his best to implement it and make four-power occupation a success.

By 1947, however, Clay reached the conclusion that not only were the Russians systematically wrecking the occupation, but that, if Germany was ever to recover economically, she would need American financial assistance.

Late that year, the general was in Washington for discussion of Marshall Plan aid for Germany. At the time he warned both the President and Marshall that Russia would not be satisfied until she had ousted the Western powers from Berlin.

January, 1948, saw the Russians imposing stringent curbs on civilian passenger traffic on inter-zonal trains in Germany. This was followed by Soviet inspectors boarding U.S. military trains and insisting on their right to inspect the papers of passengers. General Clay countered by putting armed guards on the trains to bar the inspectors. Frequently when the train commanders refused to allow the inspectors aboard, the train would be moved to a siding where it was delayed for several hours.

In the Eastern zone of both Germany and Berlin during this period, Western newspapers, magazines, and books were seized and burned. In the Allied Control Council, Marshal Sokolovski denounced the economic merger of the British and American zones that Secretary Byrnes had proposed at Stuttgart the year before.

On February 25, 1948, another nation, Czechoslovakia, succumbed to Russian domination. Two weeks later, its beloved leader Jan Masaryk was pushed to his death through a small bathroom window, although the Communists claimed it was an accident.

In spite of increasing vexations, there were still those in Washington who hoped for a rapprochement with the Soviet Union.

Their complacency was shattered on March 5, 1948, when the following message was received from General Clay:

> For many months, based on logical analysis I have felt and held that war was unlikely for at least ten years. Within the last few weeks, I have felt a subtle change in Soviet attitude which I cannot define but which now gives me a feeling that it may come with dramatic suddenness.
>
> I cannot support this change in my own thinking with any data or outward evidence in relationships other than to describe it as a feeling of a new tenseness in every Soviet individual with whom we have official relations. I am unable to submit my official report in the absence of supporting data but my feeling is real. You may advise the Chief of Staff of this for whatever it may be worth, if you feel it advisable.

A truly remarkable message from a professional soldier. Coming almost immediately after the Communist coup in Czechoslovakia, it did stir up the bureaucracy in Washington. As Smith notes: "This was one of the rare cases in recent American history when the responsible commander on the spot had not only sensed something that the intelligence experts had overlooked but also dared to communicate this feeling to his superiors."

Sokolovski continued his attacks in the Allied Control Council. Following a tirade on March 20, the marshal led the entire Soviet delegation from the conference room and they never returned.

Meanwhile, back in Washington, Clay's insistence on a firm stand was creating considerable consternation. In fairness to the timid bureaucrats, the crisis could not have developed at a more inopportune time. The advocates of "more bang for a buck" had had their way and the Defense Department was unable to transfer more than a division out of the United States without at least partial mobilization.

On March 30, the Department of the Army requested Clay's views on the withdrawal of military dependents from Berlin. The general strongly opposed such an action, saying, "Withdrawal of dependents from Berlin would create hysteria accompanied by a rush of Germans to Communism for insurance." The Department of the Army reluctantly went along with the American Military Government.

The following day, Clay was advised by Lieutenant Mikhail I. Dratvin, the Deputy Soviet Governor for Germany, that as of April 1, the identification papers of all passengers on military trains passing through the Russian zone would be inspected. Baggage and freight shipments would also be subject to a similar check.

In notifying Washington, Clay again favored a hard line and suggested that a train with armed guards be sent across the border as a test case. Secretary of the Army Kenneth C. Royall reluctantly agreed and on April 1 this was done, but the Soviets merely shuttled the train to a siding where it remained for several days until it withdrew under its own power.

On April 2, Clay was again asked by Secretary Royall if dependents should be withdrawn. Clay reaffirmed his previous stand "that we could support the Americans in Berlin with a very small airlift and that we should not evacuate our dependents. . . . Evacuation in the face of the Italian elections and the European situation is to me unthinkable."

The Russians closed the freight lanes from Hamburg and Nuremburg to Berlin on April 3, and six days later announced that all German freight trains on the one remaining line would require clearance from the Soviet authorities.

Secretary Royall again queried Clay as to his position and again the General's reply was adamant:

> When Berlin falls Western Germany will be next. If we mean to hold Europe against Communism we must not budge. . . . If we withdraw, our position in Europe is threatened. If America does not understand this now, does not know that the issue is cast, then it never will and Communism will run rampant. I believe the future of democracy requires us to stay . . . .

Early in April the "Little Airlift" that Clay had recommended was put into operation. Throughout May it continued to function, bringing in supplies for American personnel. Soviet pressures, however, continued to increase. On April 20, added restrictions were placed on barge traffic between Western Germany and Berlin, and in May the Soviets required additional redtape documentation for freight shipments into the former German capital.

When Russian troops attempted to remove locomotive engines and cars from the western sector on June 10, they were stopped by American MPs. The next day all rail traffic between the West and Berlin was halted, but permitted to resume two days later. On the pretext that repairs were necessary to the Elbe River bridge, the Berlin-Melmstedt Autobahn was closed. On June 16, the Berlin Soviet Commander walked out of the Kommandatura and four-power control of the city came to an end.

In 1945 the Allies had given the Russians a duplicate set of plates for the printing of Occupation currency. During the months of the 1948 crisis the Soviet authorities had been using these plates to undermine Allied currency by issuing quantities of notes that were redeemable at face value on the United States Treasury. The result had been an inflation spiral that bid fair to nullify any financial assistance to Germany. Accordingly, on June 18, Great Britain, France, and the United States announced a currency reform for their respective German zones, not including Berlin.

Soviet reaction was prompt. On June 23, they issued a new currency for their Eastern zone and for all Berlin. In reply that same afternoon, General Clay and Sir Brian Robertson, the British Military Governor, declared that the Western Powers' currency reform would be extended to all Berlin.

At six o'clock the following morning the Russians announced that all traffic to and from Berlin was terminated, and that the flow of electric current from the Berlin power plant, which was in the Soviet sector, could only be expected between the hours of 11 P.M. and 1 A.M. On June 24 the Berlin Blockade began.

While Clay and his deputy, Colonel Frank Howley, had consistently maintained that Berlin must be held, and that in the event of a blockade this would be possible by an airlift, there was certainly a lack of unanimity of opinion on the subject, not only among the Allied officers but also within the general's own staff. At a briefing on the morning of June 24 there were a number who felt the Allied position in Berlin was untenable, and that the United States and the West should withdraw before the situation deteriorated further.

Following the staff meeting, Clay conferred with Ernst Reuter whom the Russians had successfully prevented from assuming the office of Lord Mayor. Reuter assured the general that the people of Berlin would make the necessary sacrifices to protect their rights. Without consulting the Pentagon, Clay phoned General Curtis LeMay, the Air Force commander at Wiesbaden, and asked him to start the lift of supplies into Berlin the next day on as large a scale as the aircraft at his command would permit.

During this period government officials in Washington, with the exception of Harry Truman, spent most of their time wringing their hands, and a good proportion of General Clay's waking hours were devoted to teletype conferences with Royall in the Pentagon assuring the Secretary of the necessity for taking a firm stand. Nor was Secretary of Defense James Forrestal any more decisive. At a special meeting of the Service Secretaries and the Chiefs of Staff at the Pentagon on Sunday, June 27, all agreed that General Clay's opinion would again be solicited and they would meet with the President the following morning. As the Russians had hoped, the men of the Pentagon were paralyzed with fear that any firm stand on their part might lead to all-out war. Smith writes:

> Significantly the decision to act in Berlin had been made by the commander on the spot. His staff had been divided. Washington had offered no encouragement, and the Allies—Great Britain and France—were still pondering what to do. With very little more to guide him than his own conscience and the opinion of a Socialist politician, General Clay had resolved to begin the airlift. By so doing, he set in motion one of the great victories which the West was to achieve over Communism.[2]

No one could call President Truman indecisive. He ordered the airlift put into full-scale operation and, at the meeting with the Secretaries and Service Chiefs on June 28, directed that there be no discussion of whether we would stay in Berlin. "The United States," he said, "is going to stay. Period."

On June 30, British Foreign Secretary Ernest Bevin spoke in the House of Commons about the determination of His Majesty's Gov-

2 *Ibid.*

ernment and her allies to remain in Berlin. The only alternative, he said, was abject surrender. The Labor Government's stand was supported by the Conservative opposition led by Sir Winston Churchill.

Meanwhile, General Clay became convinced that the Russians were avoiding any confrontation involving force that could possibly provoke a war. Accordingly, he proposed to the Pentagon that the Soviets be informed that an armed convoy would move by road through their Eastern sector of Germany to Berlin on a specific date. The general advised the Department of the Army that he did not believe the Soviets would stop the column and the highway blockade would thereafter be ended. While Washington had by this time veered around to Clay's viewpoint, our top officials were unwilling to go quite this far, and the general's proposal was vetoed. He renewed his recommendation on the 19th and was again told, "No!"

On June 20, the Russians announced that food would be available for the people of Berlin in their zone. The only requirement of any Western zone resident was to come to the Eastern zone and register. Thereafter, he could purchase such foods as he might need and pay for it with the depreciated Eastern currency.

The Soviet move was immediately recognized as an effort to break down morale in the Western zone, but the Berliners stood firm. During the entire eleven months of the blockade only 85,000 people, or 3.2 per cent of the Western zones' population, requested food from the Russians.

At a conference on August 2 that the ambassadors of Great Britain, France, and the United States had requested with Stalin, the aging dictator told the emissaries that he might be willing to open the road and rail traffic to Berlin provided the Western powers would agree to accept the Eastern mark as the currency for all Berlin. Stalin at a later meeting, on August 23, further agreed that the West could share in the control of the currency. On the basis of Stalin's proposal, negotiations continued in Moscow during the month of August, but the agreement, as finally worked out, did not include the promise of four-power control of the currency.

The acceptance of the East zone currency for all of Berlin without quadripartite control would have represented a surrender.

There were, however, those in Paris, London, and Washington who were convinced that the airlift could not succeed, that the Western position in Berlin was militarily untenable. These groups were willing to accept any face-saving device to achieve a rapid settlement of the Berlin problem. Both Secretary of State George Marshall and Ambassador to Russia Bedell Smith held this opinion.

General Clay, however, insisted that Allied control of the currency become an integral part of the agreement. His firm stand scuttled the whole proposal since the Russians had no intention of allowing the Western powers to participate in control of the currency. The blockade continued.

Meanwhile, the airlift grew in size. The first American planes that began to arrive on June 25 were small transport aircraft with a capacity of only two and a half tons. It was estimated that four thousand tons of provisions would be required daily for the citizens of West Berlin, and five hundred tons for the Western forces. Since only about one hundred transports were initially available, the situation looked hopeless. Only General Clay, Colonel Howley, and President Harry Truman seemed to believe that the beleaguered city could be supplied by air.

It was not until October, upon orders of the President, that the slow C47s or Gooney Birds, with their limited capacity, were replaced by larger air transports. The combat-minded U.S. Air Force had not realized the potentials of their newest weapon, the troop-carrying C-54.

Templehof Airport, the principal terminus of the airlift, was probably as ill-suited for its role as is possible to imagine. Located in downtown Berlin, it was surrounded on three sides by high apartment buildings with the added hazard of a 400-foot brewery smokestack just off the runway. Nevertheless, at the peak of the airlift a plane was landing or taking off from Templehof every ninety seconds. A second Berlin airport, Gatow, a former training college of the Luftwaffe, was situated about fifteen miles from the center of the city. A third airfield, Tegel, was later built in the French Zone.

The 2,000-acre Rein-Main airfield was the principal airlift departure point in the American occupation zone of West Germany. Called Rein-Mud in the wet fall of 1948 by the GIs, it had been the home port of the ill-fated zeppelin *Hindenburg*. Situated opposite the southernmost of the three air corridors to Berlin allotted to the Western occupation powers, it was 267 miles from the city.

Wunstorf, the first of the airfields in the British Zone of West Germany to participate in the airlift, was located near Hanover and 150 miles from Berlin. It had been built for the light bombers of the Luftwaffe and its accommodations were almost luxurious. Its mess hall, set on a wide lawn, included a bar, and personnel quarters were scattered among the pines. Later, as the need arose, other airfields throughout the British Zone were to be included in the airlift.

The danger of heavy, two-way traffic in the three corridors to Berlin was recognized from the start of the airlift. Acordingly, it was agreed that the northern corridor should be used by the British flying into Berlin, the southern by the Americans, and the central for flying away from the city. By October, it was also concluded that the airlift could more efficiently operate under an overall command and the Combined Airlift Task Force was set up. Major General William Tunner, named commander of CATF, had directed the American-Chinese airlift during the Second World War, and had as his deputy Air Commodore J. W. Merer of the Royal Air Force Transport Command.

The airlift became truly a joint operation between the two nations. USAF planes were based on R. A. F. airfields, British and American ground crews working together—bare to the waist under their grime—could not be told apart, and the controllers of the two forces sat in the towers side by side. The cooperation was magnificent and the few irritants between the groups were mostly of a humorous nature. The American GIs did not particularly relish kippers for breakfast nor did the British lads have a desire for ham and eggs.

By January the airlift was operating with 225 American C-54s and about 150 British planes of all makes and description. One of the stories that circulated among the airmen told of a Texas pilot who was approaching Berlin when he saw a British plane of unfamiliar shape.

He immediately called up the British control tower and asked, "What's this coming in now, fella?" He was told it was the

Wayfarer. "Did you say the *Mayflower?*" replied the Texan. "You guys sure are throwing in everything."[3]

While the Americans, with more and larger aircraft, carried more tonnage than the British, the latter's real contribution to the airlift cannot be determined on that basis. Because their zone was nearer to Berlin, the British took over the major share of the ground work which was equally, if not more, important than the actual flying.

The American pilots in 1948 were still the happy-go-lucky, generous, crushed cap fly boys of the Second World War. Their lack of formality was a continuing source of amazement to their British counterparts. British air controllers often shook with amusement at the tart replies of the American flyers. One of their favorites was the story of a wisecracking pilot who, when told by the controllers, "If you read the tower, flap your wings," replied, "Roger tower and if you read the ship, flap your tower."[4]

Others told of a gabby, flip pilot who, when informed over the radio by an officer who pompously identified himself as Lieutenant Colonel Jones to end his chatter and "stop saying Roger, dodger," replied, "Roger, dodger you old codger, I'm a Lieutenant Colonel, too."

Unfortunately, the daily estimate of 4,500 tons needed for Berlin had not taken into consideration the fuel that would be vital through the winter months. Coal had already been airlifted for the generation of electricity, but mere subsistence would require almost doubling the tons daily airlifted into the city. The American and British pilots were doing their best but the prospects for a truly successful airlift still appeared very dubious.

Back in June, Generals Clay and Robertson had instituted a counter blockade. They had ordered all shipments between West Berlin and the Russian sector terminated. On July 8 reparation deliveries to the Soviets from the Western zones were discontinued. By December the movement of goods from West to East became a mere trickle.

Nor were the blockade, the counter-blockade, and the airlift

---

[3] Dudly Barker, *Berlin Air Lift* (London, His Majesty's Stationery Office, 1949), p. 6.
[4] Frank Donovan, *Bridge in the Sky* (New York, David McKay, 1968).

General Clay's only problems. Two months after the first plane had brought supplies through the corridor to the relief of Berlin, the Russians began an intensive campaign to take over the municipal government.

On August 26 a crowd of six thousand Soviet-directed protesters demonstrated outside the Municipal Building where the City Assembly was convening. A week later two similar protest meetings were held. On September 3, the Soviets announced that they could no longer be responsible for order in the area surrounding City Hall. On September 6, after Communist thugs invaded a session of the City Assembly and drove the members out of the building, the meeting reconvened in the Western zone. There it was agreed that all future meetings would be held outside the Russian sector.

Three days later more than 300,000 Berliners stood in a drenching rain before the blackened ruins of the Reichstag to protest the forcing of their City Assembly from the City Hall. Following this mass demonstration, a segment of the crowd marched into the Russian zone cheering as two boys tore down the Russian flag from the Brandenburg Gate. Russian troops retaliated by firing into the crowd and were only stopped when the British deputy provost marshal leaped in front of the Russian soldiers and ordered a cease-fire.

Having failed to intimidate the Assembly, the Russians next determined to at least control the municipal government of East Berlin. By the end of October more than two thousand non-Communist officials in the eight boroughs of the Soviet zone had been dismissed and replaced by the Party faithful.

The Western Allies finally took the growing Berlin problem to that greatest of all debating societies the world has ever known—the United Nations Security Council. On October 22, Sir Alexander Cadogan of Great Britain, Alexander Parodi for France, and United States Representative Dr. Philip Jessup presented the Western case. On the 21st, the Council proposed: (1) that all restrictions of ground traffic to Berlin be raised; (2) that talks between the four military governors regarding the currency question be resumed; (3) and that the Council of Foreign Ministers reconvene to discuss the subject of Germany. All three recommendations were vetoed by Andrei Vyshinsky, the Soviet delegate.

154

Despite the Russian veto, the neutral nations on the Security Council continued a futile effort toward reaching an agreement. A committee was formed to consider the problems involved in a Berlin settlement. Headed by Dr. Gunnar Myrdal of Sweden, the one Scandinavian country that can always be depended upon to be neutral—against the United States—the Committee called for Soviet currency to be the medium of exchange in all Berlin. To this proposal, President Truman replied with an emphatic, "No."

Through November the Russians continued their efforts to separate the government of their East zone from that of the West. They formally dismissed all heads of the various city departments. When this action was not recognized in the Western zones, they appointed new chiefs for the bureaus. On the last day of the month they called together what they termed an "extraordinary session of the City Assembly," consisting of fifteen hundred selected Communists. The group elected Fritz Ebert, Jr., son of the President of the late lamented Weimar Republic, as mayor, and named a new City Council. Two city governments now existed within Berlin.

On December 5, the Western Powers held elections in their sectors. With 86.3 per cent of the voters turning out, the Social Democratic party received 64.5 per cent of the ballots cast. Thereafter, the Allied Kommandatura was reestablished on a three-power basis.

During the waning months of 1948, success or failure of the airlift hung in the balance. Weather—thick, impenetrable fog—grounded the aircraft as many days as they flew during November and December. By January, the severely rationed coal had fallen to a critical point with only one week's supply on hand. In spite of all the superhuman effort that had gone into the airlift, it looked as if the Western allies would still be forced out of Berlin.

However, there was still a thirty-day supply of food on hand, and General Clay and recently promoted Brigadier General Howley ordered the importation of food cut in favor of coal. With the weather improving so that the planes could fly every day, resources gradually began to increase.

When the airlift had first started in June, the daily average of supplies delivered to the city had been barely 300 tons. By January, 1948, the average had risen to 4,500 tons; by March, 8,000 tons were delivered. On April 12, 1948, 12,941 tons in 1,398 sorties—a record—were carried in by air. During the blockade, between two and three million tons were delivered to the city—two-thirds carried by the U.S. Air Force while the British Royal Air Force brought in the remainder. The airlift had succeeded far beyond the expectations of even Generals Clay and Howley.

At the start of the blockade and subsequent airlift most Berliners, preoccupied with the currency reform, had missed the significance of the developing crisis. Some felt the Russian pressure was just another passing incident, others that it was a dispute between the occupying powers and no concern of theirs. With every new day, however, as event succeeded event and it became abundantly clear that the Reds were planning to gobble up the whole city, more and more of the city's citizens were jolted out of their complacency.

At first there was skepticism as to whether the Western powers could or would resist the Soviet move. When, however, they became convinced that the United States and Britain intended to stand firm and that an airlift was feasible, the vast majority of the people committed themselves to the Western cause and expressed their determination to hold out until the blockade was broken. And that was not easy.

The failure of their electrical supply, the absence of fresh milk for their children, the scarce dull food, and the insufficient coal for heat during the bitter cold months of winter were not insignificant sacrifices. Once having committed himself, the average Berliner came to feel a part of the airlift, a partner with his former enemies, and he went "all out" to support his stand.

In spite of increasing deprivations and unemployment, the morale of the people of the beleaguered city seemed actually to improve as the months went by. Pride, which had been absent since the defeat of Germany, seemed to have returned to the people of Berlin.

Working on the airlift at the fields were some thirty thousand Berliners. They were particularly proud of their part in the airlift and often, as a contribution, remained on duty hours after their daily tour had ended.

Pilots engaged in the airlift, in their few hours off, were feted as heroes in Berlin. They were particularly worshipped by the children who followed them about the city with adoring eyes and often presented them with gifts from their meager possessions. The pilots, in turn, showed their appreciation by organizing, under the leadership of First Lieutenant Gail S. Halvorsen of Garland, Utah, a little airlift for the children of Berlin. Candy and chocolate bars with handkerchief parachutes were dropped and eagerly retrieved by the city's youth.

By January the airlift had become a two-way street with the returning planes carrying products manufactured within the city and all stamped "Made in Blockaded Berlin." Light bulbs, electrical appliances, small locomotives, and a host of other goods were all carried to the outside world.

By the end of January, 1949, it was apparent to the Russians that the airlift was successful and that the Western Allies were not going to abandon their position in Berlin nor yield to a settlement short of the lifting of the blockade. Only by force of arms could they be made to pull back; and Russia was not prepared for such a gamble. The Western powers' counter-blockade was also beginning to hurt.

Through the medium of an interview with Kingsbury Smith of International News Service, Stalin announced that if the Western powers agreed to the postponement of the establishing of a separate West German state until a meeting of the Council of Foreign Ministers had been held to consider the German problem as a whole, and the Western counter-blockade was ended, the USSR would raise the Berlin blockade. For the first time, Stalin had omitted any currency demands from his terms of settlement. March and April were consumed while talks between Dr. Jessup and Jacob Malik took place at the United Nations.

On May 5, an official statement announcing the end of the blockade as of May 12, was simultaneously issued in Washington, London, Paris, and Moscow. It provided that the blockade and counter-blockade would end as of May 12 and that eleven days thereafter (May 23, 1949) a meeting of the Council of Foreign Ministers would be held in Paris, "to consider questions relating to Germany, and problems arising out of the situation in Berlin including also the question of currency in Berlin."

Without a transition period and unrecognized in the free world, the Cold War started long before World War II ended. The few who realized that Yalta and Potsdam were only engagements in a new conflict were ignored by most of us, for we wanted to believe the world would be hereafter as we wished it to be. Even the vision of Franklin Roosevelt, whose perception had twice saved the nation, became myopic when, with dreams of "Peace on Earth" beclouding his sight, he gazed at our monolithic ally.

Harry Truman, "The Captain with the mighty heart," as Dean Acheson calls him, had at first, as President, tried to follow the Roosevelt Russian policy. Fortunately, he was one of the few who early came to recognize the ineluctable Soviet menace that faced us. The perception, the stubborn courage of the little man from Independence, Missouri, in the Cold War saved the world from a Communist takeover.

The Berlin Airlift was only a battle of that war. It was, of course, not a conflict in the sense that one side shot at the other, although seventy-nine British, American, and German pilots and crewmen lost their lives in defeating the blockade. However, more was dependent on its outcome than in many bloodier engagements of the past. The Truman Doctrine had been promulgated before the Berlin crisis, but its outcome was still in the balance. The successful airlift represented the first important Western Allied victory of the Cold War.

The Berlin Blockade should have taught the Western Allies that their reaction to each Russian move in the Cold War would determine the next Soviet move. Concessions only led to the necessity of further appeasement. When we acted firmly, resolutely, and with courage, the matter was ended. When we wavered, were afraid and acted on that fear, we only made future problems for ourselves.

Unfortunately we have not always heeded this lesson. Our failure to move when the Berlin Wall was erected in 1961 led to the Cuban missile crisis; our acceptance of less than victory in Korea brought us to Vietnam. A unilateral withdrawal there will someday end in Israel, the Philippines, or Australia.

Although the British and American stand in defending Berlin from a Communist takeover was dictated by self-interest, there can be no question but that it gained us an ally in the Cold War. In effect, it came to represent our commitment to our former enemy, the German people. It convinced them of our friendship and our desire to help them in the rebuilding of their nation. The airlift, combined with the Marshall Plan, can be said to be principally responsible for Germany being today a powerful economic barrier to Soviet encroachment in Western Europe.

The successful Berlin Airlift did not win the Cold War but its failure could well have lost it. Had it failed, all Germany—and perhaps all Europe—would have been lost to freedom. Succeeding, it ultimately resulted in NATO and the containment of Russia to East Germany and the Balkans. Millions today live in comparative freedom because of the vision and courage of President Truman, Generals Clay and Howley, and the pilots and their crewmen who flew the planes in the Berlin Airlift.

9.

TWILIGHT OF
THE GODS—
DIEN BIEN PHU

At exactly 4:45 P.M. May 7, 1954, short, heavy-set Joseph Laniel, Prime Minister of France, mounted the tribune of the French National Assembly. News that Laniel would deliver an important address on the situation in French Indo-China had been circulating throughout Paris since noon and the chamber and visitors' gallery were crowded. A strained quiet that could almost be heard seemed to grip the room as the grim-faced minister began to speak in a low tone:

> The government has been informed that the central position of Dien Bien Phu has fallen after twenty hours of uninterrupted combat.

An audible sob filled the room and the deputies rose to their feet. The Prime Minister's voice trembled as he continued:

> . . . All of France shares the anguish of the families of the fighters of Dien Bien Phu. Their heroism has reached such heights that universal conscience should dictate to the enemy— in favor of the wounded and of those whose courage entitles them to the honors of war—such decision as will contribute more than anything to establish a climate favorable to peace.

Laniel's words had signaled the end of the Third Republic's colonial empire and France went into mourning. Bells tolled, on

161

television and radio only requiems were broadcast, and masses were said in the churches for the soldier dead. There were few who did not realize that here was the end of the Republic's greatness—that henceforth she would be little more than a second-rate power.

Vietnam, which stretches like an elongated hourglass for twelve hundred miles, almost the length of America's Pacific Coast, covers an area of 127,300 square miles with a width varying from thirty-three to as much as three hundred miles.

From 111 B.C. until A.D. 939, most of the country was administered as a Chinese province. In the later years a successful Vietnamese revolution threw off the yoke of China.

Penetrating to the south, the Vietnamese defeated the kingdom of Champa in 1471, and by the seventeenth century reached the Cambodian-controlled Mekong River delta. In the seventeenth and eighteenth centuries, Vietnam was divided into the North and South under two hostile governments whose capitals were Hanoi and Hue respectively. In the first half of the nineteenth century, the Emperor Gialong reunited the country and ruled from his capitol at Hue until the arrival of the French.

With the exception of French Catholic missionaries, Vietnam had little contact with the West prior to 1858. A representative of the Roman Emperor, Marcus Aurelius Antoninus, visited there in A.D. 166. Portuguese Captain Antonio de Faria, emissary of the Duke Albuquerque, landed at Faifo in 1535, and later, rival Dutch and Portuguese trading posts were established.

A permanent Catholic mission was started in 1615. Eleven years later Monsignor Alexander de Rhodes, said to have been a Jewish convert, arrived in Vietnam. When he died in 1660, Roman Catholicism had a firm base in Vietnam. However, foreign missionaries were often viewed with suspicion and occasionally persecuted.

Using the murder of several Catholic missionaries as a pretext, the French attacked and captured Danang on August 31, 1858, and six months afterward occupied Saigon. Cochin, the southernmost province of China, became a French colony, and in 1883 the French moved against the remainder of Vietnam. The following year Annam and Tonkin became French protectorates, but it was not until 1917 that they were completely pacified.

French rule in Vietnam, though authoritative and despotic, was benevolent. Frenchmen occupied civil offices as low as the village level, and by 1830 there were as many civil servants in Vietnam as British colonial officials in all India. Taxes were high but the French built roads, laid rail lines, improved health facilities, and instituted flood control. In the field of education, however, they did little. When the Japanese arrived in 1941, there were only fourteen secondary schools and one university—Hanoi, founded in 1917.

France did not exploit Indo-China, for year after year she poured more money into Vietnam than she received in returns. Why did she remain? Principally because of the prestige involved in ruling an empire. As Bernard Fall wrote: "It was largely a matter of 'keeping up with the Jones's'—even if this analysis does not fit in with the Marxist theories on the purpose and aims of imperialism."

Perhaps France's greatest weakness in governing Vietnam stemmed from her instability at home. French governments were not long-lived and with each succeeding administration, a new governor was dispatched to Vietnam. Between 1902 and 1945, twenty-three governors arrived there from Paris. Consequently there was no continuity of policy and French rule largely depended on the enthusiasm and ability of the current Viceroy.

During the First World War, 100,000 Vietnamese recruits were sent to France for military service. Upon their return, many of them had become ardent nationalists and actively worked for an end to French rule. In the 1920s they formed the Vietnam Quoc Dan Dang, or the Vietnamese National party, modeled on Chiang Kai-shek's Kuomintang. In February, 1930, a revolt led by soldier members of the National party was suppressed by the French at Yen Bay in North Central Tonkin and the Quoc Dan Dang was effectively destroyed. Thereafter, anti-French efforts were confined to the Communist party, whose leader was Ho Chi Minh.

Unlike most public figures, Ho always preferred to remain mysterious and the known facts of his early life are sparse. He was born on May 19, in either the year 1890, '91 or '92, in the village of Him-Lien, province of Nghe-Anin, in central Vietnam. His father was a well-to-do mandarin who was dismissed from government service because of his anti-French activities. To support his family after his dismissal, he began the practice of oriental medicine. Ho attended the Lycée at the provincial capital of Vinh.

There is some evidence that he was later a student at Lycée Quoc-Hoc in Hue, probably Vietnam's best secondary school, but in 1910 he was expelled for anti-French activities.

For a short period he was a teacher and later attended cooking school. In 1912 he secured passage on a French passenger liner as a messboy, finally settling in London where he was employed as an assistant chef at the Carlton Hotel. Ho next came to the United States and for a time lived in Harlem.

In France during the First World War he became a photographer's assistant, and was soon politically active in the Vietnamese colony in Paris. During the Versailles Conference in 1919, Ho addressed a memorandum to the great powers, advocating the application of Woodrow Wilson's principles to Vietnam. Joining the French Socialist party, he became a member of the faction in 1920 that split to form the Communist party.

In 1923, he was a delegate to the Peasants International in Moscow, and in 1924, to the Fifth Congress of the Comintern. In 1935, he was sent to Canton, China, where he became an interpreter and secretary for Mikhail Borodin, the Russian advisor to Sun Yat-sen. During this time, Ho formed a group of Vietnamese political refugees into an organization he called the Vietnamese Revolutionary Youth, the forerunner if the Indo-Chinese Communist party.

When Chiang Kai-shek succeeded Sun Yat-sen after his death, and many Communists were executed, Borodin broke with Chiang and returned to Russia. Ho then went to Hankow and then on to Moscow where he remained until 1928. Becoming a political agent of the Comintern, he was in Hong Kong in June, 1931, where he was arrested by the British and imprisoned for eighteen months. After his release, he went to Shanghai and later returned to Moscow. During 1937 and 1938 Ho carried on his work throughout northwest China, but after the Japanese occupation of Vietnam in 1940, Ho returned to his native country where he resumed leadership of the Communist party.

The Japanese had entered Vietnam under the September 22, 1940, agreement with the Vichy government whereby administration was left in French hands while the Nipponese controlled the country's military and economic resources. Ho's Communist party became the sole opposition to both the Japanese and French officials.

In May, 1941, Ho met with the leaders of his party near the border of Tonkin in South China where he organized a popular front group he named the Vietnam Doc Lap Dong Minh Hoi or Volunteer Independence League. The new party, later called the Vietminh, became Vietnam's principal instrument in her thirteen-year struggle for independence.

During the winter of 1944–45 the Vietminh gained control of three northern Vietnamese provinces. As the only large force opposing the Japanese in this area, Ho's army was supported by the United States Office of Strategic Services, the OSS. In return for supplies, Ho's men helped rescue downed pilots from the Japanese. One American OSS officer was later to speak of Ho as "an awfully sweet guy," whose outstanding quality was his gentleness.[1]

In March, 1945, with their world collapsing around them, the Japanese seized and interned most of the French troops and officials. Simultaneously, in an effort to enlist Vietnamese support, the Japanese announced the formation of an independent government at Hanoi headed by Bao Dai, the former French-controlled Emperor of Annam.

Two days after the Japanese surrender, the Vietminh seized Hanoi, ousted Bao and proclaimed the establishment of the "Provisional Government of the Democratic Republic of Vietnam." In the South, Vietminh elements under the command of Tran Van Giau took Saigon, harshly suppressing any dissidents.

The Vietminh had confidently expected Allied support and recognition, but following Potsdam they received a rude awakening. France was determined to reassert her authority over Vietnam and the Allies—including Russia—were more interested in good relations with France than with the Nationalist forces in Southeast Asia. They agreed in July, 1945, that, following the defeat of Japan, British forces would occupy Vietnam south of the 16th parallel with Chiang Kai-shek's troops garrisoning the northern part of the country. Both armies were, however, restricted to accepting the surrender of Japanese troops and the "recovery of Allied prisoners of war and internees."

Major General D. D. Gracey, the British commander, didn't quite see it that way. He rearmed the five thousand French troops

[1] Bernard B. Fall, *The Two Viet-Nams* (New York, Frederick A. Praeger, 1963), p. 82.

who had been interned in the Saigon area, and allowed them to seize the city and several outlying areas. By December, 1945, when the British withdrew, French forces in the South numbered fifty thousand men.

Chiang Kai-shek's representatives handled the situation somewhat differently in the North. While Chinese troops were allowed to loot at will, and while some Communist officials were replaced, the Vietminh Republic was recognized as the *de facto* government of Vietnam. On February 28, 1946, under an agreement with the French, Chiang withdrew his forces from Vietnam.

With the country ravaged by both the Japanese and the Chinese, the war-weary economy became badly weakened. Furthermore, the Allied bombardments of the river control system had resulted in the flooding of vast areas of land. As a result, Ho felt it necessary to make some rapprochement with the French. Accordingly, on March 6, 1946, an agreement was concluded whereby France could move fifteen thousand troops into northern Vietnam to relieve the Chinese, provided that three thousand of these troops were withdrawn thereafter yearly. Ho's Democratic Republic was recognized under this agreement as "a free state, having its own parliament, army, and treasury, forming part of the Indo-Chinese Federation and the French union."

In early June, 1946, France clearly indicated that she had no intention of permitting a free Vietnam when her viceroy in Indo-China, Admiral G. Thierry D'Argenlieu, set up a puppet republic in Cochin. Thereafter the rapidly deteriorating relations between the French and Ho culminated, in November, with a French naval bombardment of the port of Haiphong resulting in the death of six thousand Vietnamese. Ho retaliated with attacks against the French in Hanoi.

In the war that followed, France was able to hold the cities and many of the towns, but the Vietminh dominated most of the villages and the rural areas. By 1947, the French realized that military measures alone were not enough. If she were to reconquer the country, it would be necessary to throw some sop of appeasement to the Vietnamese nationalists.

Resurrecting the former Japanese puppet, Bao Dai, France established a new Vietnamese government as a rival of the Vietminh. Not quite the quiescent and conciliatory vassal of previous years,

Bao only agreed to cooperate if the new state included Cochin, Tonkin, and Annam, and was independent within the French union. France, of course, had no intention of permitting the formation of a Free Vietnam and, accordingly, retained control of foreign relations, finances, the armed forces, and maintained the right to keep her troops within the borders of the newly defined state. The United States recognized Bao Dai's government on February 7, 1950, as did thirty other nations.

Also realizing that a war cannot exclusively be won by the military alone, Ho made a vigorous effort to rally the peasants to his banner. Outlining his aims as not only the defeat of the imperialists, but also the overthrow of the feudal landlord classes, the reduction of interest rates and rents, and the redistribution of land in the area he controlled, Ho broadened the base of his support among the peasants.

September, 1950, saw Ho's forces move from the defensive to the offensive. By the end of the year, fort after fort along the Tongking-China border had fallen to his army in the Red River delta while thousands of French troops were killed or captured.

The fall of Dong Khe on the Lang Son-Cao Bang border road split the French main border garrison, preventing not only reinforcements, but also withdrawal. A French column fighting its way to the provincial capital of Cao Bang was ambushed and completely destroyed. Long Son, another provincial capital, was reduced by October 1 and ten days later Dinh Lap was similarly brought under Ho's control. In a period of less than six weeks, a hundred miles of highway had been secured by the Vietminh for supplies and a gateway opened into Red China.

When General Jean de Lattre de Tassigny arrived in Indo-China in mid-December of 1950 as high commissioner and commander of the French forces, the morale of French troops was at its lowest ebb. One of World War II's truly great figures, the aristocratic de Lattre, an idealist and an inspiring leader, believed that he had come to Indo-China to lead a crusade—a crusade against communism—to save Vietnam "from Peking and Moscow."[2]

In the short year that de Lattre was in Vietnam he accomplished miracles. Following their successful operation in the Red River

[2] Robert Shaplen, *The Lost Revolution* (New York, Harper & Row, 1965), p. 80.

Delta, the Vietminh decided to launch an all-out offensive to retake Hanoi. On January 16 and 17, French troops decisively defeated the Vietminh forces at Vinhyen, killing more than six thousand of the enemy. In succeeding engagements the French, as well as their Vietnamese allies, repulsed attack after Communist attack and, by June, the Vietminh were forced to retreat to the mountains and again switch to defensive tactics. Unfortunately, toward the end of 1951, de Lattre became ill and in December asked to be relieved of his duties. He died of cancer in Paris on January 11, 1952.

General Raoul Salan, an unimaginative officer, succeeded de Lattre and once more the French position began to deteriorate. The Vietminh Army commander, General Vo Nguyen Giap, refused to meet the French in a head-on battle and, instead, advanced into the Thai highlands toward Laos, and continued his infiltration of the Red River Delta and other sections of central Vietnam. By May, 1953, the French were again confined to a narrow coastal enclave and Salan was replaced by General Henri Navarre.

The fifty-five-year-old Navarre, son of the Dean of Letters at Toulouse, was a graduate of Saint-Cyr. He had seen combat in World War I and in the Riff campaign, but his service subsequently had been entirely as a staff officer. This had not, however, interfered with his advancement, and at forty-seven he became a brigadier general. Of small stature, he had a charming personality and had successfully ingratiated himself with his civilian superiors in Paris.

The new commander at first proved to be a considerable improvement over his predecessor. Making a number of mobile stabs at the enemy's positions in the Red River Delta, he soon had thrown Giap off balance. The Red commander, however, retaliated by setting in motion a fresh and large-scale invasion of Laos.

While Navarre's instructions included the defense of Laos they were hedged—he was not to endanger the safety of the Expeditionary Corps. He knew that he could not defend Laos by a campaign of movement or by a defensive line. He thereupon determined that his only option was the establishment of a strategically located strong point which he hoped would prevent at least a massive invasion of that country. He also had high hopes that he could draw Giap into a set battle.

Like most of his predecessors, Navarre underestimated the Red general. Born of a well-to-do family in Anxa in the province of Quang Binh in central Annam in 1910, Giap took his bachelor and a law degree at Hanoi. Rejecting a proffered scholarship for further study in Paris, he became a teacher of history in a private school and married the daughter of Dan Tai Mai, a dean at Hanoi University.

A professed revolutionist, Giap served a term of imprisonment for his political activities, and upon his release was sent by the Communists to a Chinese military academy. In his absence his wife was arrested, sentenced to hard labor, and died in prison. Giap was not only a great strategist and a master tactician but was thoroughly schooled in guerrilla warfare.

Navarre selected for his strong point the area around the small village of Dien Bien Phu. Located in a valley measuring approximately ten by five miles, it was a poor choice. Not only was the valley ringed by hills from which the enemy could fire down on the position, but it was more than two hundred miles from the nearest French air bases and, accordingly, at the extreme range of fighter aircraft.

The French general also clearly misunderstood the quantity and use of enemy artillery. Giap had obtained from the Chinese far more guns than French Intelligence realized and their deployment was so unconventional as to create a grave crisis for the French command which operated by the methods recommended by war manuals.

Using their pieces in direct fire rather than indirect fire as practiced by the conventional French and Americans, the Vietminh completely surprised their enemy. Instead of placing batteries behind the hills which would have put the French forts out of range, they moved the guns at night to the forward slopes. In that position the carefully camouflaged single pieces fired pointblank at the French with devastating effect. The Vietminh were thus able to neutralize the French artillery and, consequently, creep closer to the enemy, as well as place their anti-aircraft weapons sufficiently close to the strong point to hamper French air supply.

With the French artillery neutralized, Giap was able to push forward an intricate system of trenches and dugouts, which slowly spread toward the enemy position. From these trenches he launched the first of his massive infantry attacks against the French in March. Two outposts, Beatrice and Gabrielle, fell and the French finally realized how tenuous was the position they occupied.

American policy during the war in Vietnam can best be described as one of vacillation. We wanted an independent Vietnam and such freedom to be granted without strings on a definite date in the future, but we lacked the courage to take a firm stand with the French. Had we insisted on Vietnamese independence in the early stages of the conflict, perhaps thousands of lives and billions of dollars might have been saved.

On May 15, 1950, we agreed to furnish aid, but the assistance was mostly economic and "too little and too late." On March 20, 1954, General Paul Ely, the French Chief of Staff, informed President Eisenhower that only by massive intervention on our part could France hope to prevent a defeat at Dien Bien Phu.

The possibility of a Communist victory in Vietnam provoked a sharp debate in American official circles. Admiral Arthur B. Radford as well as Vice President Richard Nixon and Secretary of State John Foster Dulles were in favor of prompt military intervention, but it was apparent that such a step would not have the full approval of Congress and that our ally, Great Britain, would not go along. The President accordingly said, "No."

In May Giap launched the final attack and, on May 6, the last French troops surrendered. French casualties totaled about twelve thousand men killed and taken prisoner. Vietminh casualties were about twice that figure.

The fall of Dien Bien Phu signaled the end of the French Empire —the death of French colonialism. Although the rebels in North Africa were never to administer a defeat of French arms as had the troops of Giap, the loss of the African colonies became inevitable as the last "poilu" surrendered at Dien Bien Phu. May 8, 1954, was also to set into motion events that will eventually lead to an end of all empires.

The fragmentation of Africa can be traced to the impact of that battle on peoples given too little preparation for the responsibilities of self-government. Not many of us believe in "the white man's burden," or that peoples should be subjugated to the will of others, but it is unfortunate that so many in the world were precipitously hoisted into their freedom with so little preparation or education.

The tragedies of the Congo and Biafra all had their conception at Dien Bien Phu.

The French defeat in Vietnam, as well as the American defeat in Korea, completely changed both for himself and for the world the image of the Oriental soldier. Until the guns were silenced at Dien Bien Phu, he was pictured as a small inept man who could fire a gun and run, but little else. Today, with his vast numbers and his newly acquired confidence, he is looked upon with respect and awe by the powers of the world.

The cool relations that have existed between the United States and France since the middle fifties also stem from Dien Bien Phu. France is convinced the United States let her down and she may well have a point. The jaundiced eye that Charles de Gaulle cast at the United States was not the product of the Second World War or Franklin Delano Roosevelt, but rather had its inception in Southeast Asia. At least France can have the satisfaction that we have made as many mistakes in that distant country as did she.

Probably more important than all the other consequences of the battle is that it marked the passage of responsibility for Southeast Asia to the United States. Today in our effort to stem the tide of Communist totalitarian expansion we have probably extended ourselves far beyond our military strength. Forty thousand lives and billions of dollars later, it is now necessary that we coldly ask ourselves if it is possible for a democracy to fight a prolonged limited war no matter how moral or necessary may be its ultimate objective. America refused to learn from the French and may well have a Dien Bien Phu in its future.

10.

AMERICA'S BLACKS —THE 1954 SUPREME COURT DECISION

The heat in the gymnasium of Rutgers University in August, 1947, was so oppressive it felt almost rancid. Oliver Randolph, a tall man with crinkly gray hair, rose to address the New Jersey Constitutional Convention on an amendment he and a co-sponsor had introduced to the Bill of Rights. A delegate from Essex County, he moved forward to the speaker's lectern.

The son of a slave, a graduate of Wiley College in Marshall, Texas, and Howard University Law School, Randolph, a Newark lawyer active in the NAACP, was a leader of the state's anti-discrimination forces. He had devoted all his adult life to those he called "my people," but it had only been during the last few years that he could see any results of his efforts. In 1922, as a member of the legislature he had managed to secure the passage of the New Jersey Anti-Lynching Law, but then even the bigots were against murder.

In the last few years, however, he had detected a change in the attitude of his white friends. They seemed to be more willing to acknowledge that his race had received unfair treatment for centuries and were more receptive to proposals to correct inequalities of decades. Randolph hoped that this change of outlook was the result of their own innate fairness and not a conciliatory gesture to the black veterans who had not been hesitant to speak their minds—sometimes, in Randolph's opinion, too violently.

Our modern activists would call Oliver Randolph an "Uncle

173

Tom," for he was willing to accept the aid of the white man for his cause. Actually, he would have welcomed the support of the devil himself, if it would help to end the discriminating practices against his people.

On that hot, sultry afternoon the Negro barrister told the eighty-two assembled delegates about practices in New Jersey that most would have condemned, had they known of their existence in the deep South. He spoke of the still large number of segregated schools throughout the state, one of which was in the supposedly enlightened borough of Haddonfield, the home town of the governor. He emphasized the discrimination practiced in the New Jersey National Guard—how black enlistees were placed in segregated units, usually with their headquarters in the oldest and most dilapidated armories. Uniforms, equipment, and weapons were only turned over to the Negro units when they were practically worn out and unfit for use.

There was some feeble opposition to Randolph's proposal, but it stemmed mostly from delegates from the southern end of the state, below where an extension of the Mason-Dixon line would cut through New Jersey. Of interest today is the fact that the leader of those opposed to Randolph's antidiscrimination amendment was Mrs. Marie H. Katzenbach of Princeton, whose son, Nicholas deB. Katzenbach, led the civil rights forces in the Kennedy administration a decade and a half later.

When the convention adjourned that evening, the first amendment to the New Jersey Bill of Rights in over a century had been adopted. It read:

> No person shall be denied the enjoyment of any civil or military right, nor be segregated in the militia or in the public schools because of religious principles, race, color, ancestry, or native origin.

Segregated schools were gone in New Jersey by the time the new constitution took effect on January 1, 1948, but there still remained some sticky hurdles before the state could have an integrated National Guard. While most of the field grade and general officers of the Guard were bitterly opposed to any change, this didn't pose a problem. They could be given specific orders by which they would be compelled to abide. The real stumbling block was in Washington where the National Guard Bureau insisted that desegregated units were contrary to Department of Defense regulations. Since most of the supporting funds came from federal sources, an enforcement of the constitutional mandate might well end New Jersey's State Militia.

Governor Alfred E. Driscoll was not, however, to be intimidated. Shortly after the first of the year he sent for the Guard's commanding general, Clifford Powell, who had been a leader of the opposition to the constitutional enactment. Driscoll told the general that, unless the segregated units were de-activated and the remaining units opened to all persons regardless of race, he would order the State Police to seize all the armories and hold them until the law was fully obeyed. By way of General Powell, news of the governor's stand soon reached the Pentagon. The following weekend, Driscoll received a telegram from Secretary of Defense James Forrestal authorizing the desegregation of the New Jersey National Guard. Not only did Governor Thomas Dewey of New York follow New Jersey's example but also a number of chief executives of other states. Shortly thereafter, President Harry Truman issued an executive order desegregating all the active military services.

Nor was the climate in other parts of the nation north of the Mason-Dixon line different from that which prevailed in New Jersey. In 1947, many whites were deeply troubled by the fact that in one third of our states, blacks were excluded from decent schools, hospitals, restaurants, hotels, and public parks. Over a large part of the country Negroes were forced to sit in the rear of buses, travel in separate railroad cars, and were excluded from voting. In both North and South they were largely restricted to menial employment, and could only serve in segregated units in the National Guard and the military forces of the United States. Even in Washington, the capital of the nation of which they were citizens, Negroes were not permitted to lunch at drugstore counters nor attend motion picture performances at the main downtown theaters.

While racial discrimination in the United States troubled the conscience of many white Americans and aroused the ardor of most Negroes—particularly the recently discharged veterans of World War II—it wasn't enough. Even actions like those of the

New Jersey Constitutional Convention could only make a small dent in the problem. To really solve anything as deeply ingrained as Negro discrimination as practiced in America in 1947, with centuries of usage behind it, would take a social revolution.

Revolutions, bloodless or otherwise, are seldom just the products of a momentary flash. Change does not start at a given point, but rather "builds on history." There were many factors at work in America after 1945 that made a racial explosion inevitable. The returning servicemen who had experienced equality in foreign nations, the growing visual awareness of underprivileged blacks —via the motion picture and TV screens showing how the "other half" of America lived—a continuing industrial prosperity bringing some Negroes security, as well as educational opportunities offered by the GI Bill, all were contributing factors to racial unrest. Only a spark was needed to set off an explosion. It came in the decision rendered by the Supreme Court in the case of *Oliver Brown et al* vs. *The Board of Education of Topeka, Kansas.*

The Thirteenth Amendment adopted immediately after the end of the Civil War in 1865 enfranchised the Negro, but the South responded by the enactment of the Black Codes designed to prevent Negroes from owning land, or doing work other than farming without a license.

Congress, dominated by the Radical Republicans, reacted in 1866 by passing the first Civil Rights Act. It provided that Negroes should have the same rights as whites, to make and enforce contracts, sue, give evidence, inherit, purchase, lease, sell, hold and convey real and personal property, and "shall be subject to like punishments, pains and penalties and none other, any law, statute, ordinance, regulation, or custom to the contrary notwithstanding."

On the ground of its dubious constitutionality, President Andrew Johnson vetoed the Act, but Congress passed it over his objection. That there might be no question of constitutionality, Congress thereafter proposed the Fourteenth Amendment which was ratified in 1868. It provided:

> All persons born or naturalized in the United States and subject to the jurisdiction thereof, are citizens of the United States and of the state wherein they reside. No state shall make or enforce any law which shall abridge the privileges or im-

munities of citizens of the United States, nor shall any state deprive any person of life, liberty, or property, without due process of law, or deny to any person within its jurisdiction the equal protection of the laws....

In the Slaughter House cases, where a butcher's monopoly granted by the State of Louisiana was attacked as a violation of the Fourteenth Amendment, the Supreme Court by a 5 to 4 majority held in 1873 that the Amendment did not extend to economic restriction not related to race. In 1880, the Court, with only two dissents, held that a West Virginia law excluding Negroes from jury duty was unconstitutional. Justice William Strong speaking for the majority in *Strauder* vs. *West Virginia* said:

> The law in the states shall be the same for the black as for the white; that all persons, whether colored or white, shall stand equal before the laws of the states, and, in regard to the colored race, for whose protection the Amendment [XIV] was primarily designed, that no discrimination shall be made against them by the law because of their color....

Strauder vs. *West Virginia* marked the end of the post Civil War period. Most of the North, and certainly the Republican party, had lost interest in the Negro cause. The sanctimonious Rutherford B. Hayes had in 1876 stolen the Presidency from his Democratic opponent, Samuel B. Tilden, by his unholy deal with the southerners. It was agreed that the Republicans could have the Presidency and the South could do as they pleased with the Negro. An era of decency had come to a dirty end.

More interested in defending the business community from state regulations than the Negro from his oppressors, the Court in the following decades redefined the Slaughter House cases and included corporations under the protective wings of the Fourteenth Amendment. Like the rest of the nation, the Justices had become more interested in economic rather than human rights.

It was in such a climate that, with one dissenting vote, the Court decided the case of *Plessy* vs. *Ferguson* in 1896. Homer Adolph Plessy, who was one-eighth Negro, entered a car reserved for whites and was arrested under Louisiana's "Jim Crow" Act. Plessy's

177

challenge of the Act was carried to the Supreme Court which held the Act to be valid.

The separate but equal doctrine that states might keep the two races apart, providing accommodations were equal, as enunciated by the Court, had no basis in law. It was as without legal foundation as the Warren Court's one-man one-vote decision in *Reynolds* vs. *Sims* in 1964.

As Dr. Robert J. Harris, Professor of Political Science at Vanderbilt University, writes: "The opinion of the Court in the *Plessy* case is a compound of bad logic, bad history, bad sociology, and bad constitutional law."[1]

It was, however, in keeping with the spirit of the times. The average white American in that callous age was in full accord with Justice Henry B. Brown's majority opinion. The Court, in effect, overruled the Fourteenth Amendment.

That all white Americans were not in accord with the majority of the Court or with the majority of their fellow citizens was evidenced by the strong dissenting opinion of Justice John Marshall Harlan, of which Harris writes:

> . . . was characterized by sound logic, accurate history as far as it went, correct constitutional law, and, above all, those high moral assumptions and aspirations. "The destinies of the two races," Harlan wrote, "and the interest of both require that the common government of all shall not permit the seeds of race hate to be planted under the sanction of law. What can more certainly arouse race hate, what more certainly create and perpetuate a feeling of distrust between these races, than state enactments which in fact proceed on the grounds that colored citizens are so inferior and degraded that they cannot be allowed to sit in public coaches occupied by white citizens? That, as all will admit, is the real meaning of such legislation as was enacted in Louisiana . . . . The thin disguise of 'equal' accommodation for passengers in railroad coaches will not mislead anyone, or atone for the wrong this day done."[2]

Plessy vs. *Ferguson* was to remain the law for fifty-eight years, and during that time was extended to the public schools, but it was

[1] Robert J. Harris, *The Quest for Equality* (Baton Rouge, La., Louisiana State University Press, 1960), p. 101.
[2] *Ibid.*, p. 102.

178

never to have a fair trial. The South and parts of the North made no pretense at equality as between the accommodations furnished the two races:

In 1915 South Carolina spent $23.76 on the average white child in public school, $2.91 on the average Negro child. As late as 1931, six southeastern states (Alabama, Arkansas, Florida, Georgia, North and South Carolina) spent less than a third as much per Negro public school pupil as per white child. Ten years later spending for the Negro had risen only to forty-four percent of the white figure. At the time of the 1954 decision the South as a whole was spending $165.00 a year for the average white pupil, $115.00 for the Negro.[3]

Nor were the other accommodations provided for the Negro any better than those given their children. Negro hospitals were clearly inferior to those provided for whites, railroad coaches and waiting room facilities were filthy and dilapidated. Blacks were excluded from public parks and could not even be buried in public cemeteries. Justice Harlan had been prophetic when he predicted a growth of race hatred stemming from the *Plessy* case. Every effort in the South was directed to keeping the Negro "in his place." Blacks in wholesale numbers were disenfranchised and by 1900 the number of lynchings rose to an average of one hundred a year.

Southern excesses gradually aroused public opinion and the Supreme Court who, as Mr. Dooley said, "follows election returns the same as anyone," began in 1917 to erode the base of the *Plessy* decision. In that year a Louisville, Kentucky, ordinance forbidding both Negroes and whites from moving into a block occupied by the other race was declared unconstitutional. A decade later the Court held state laws forbidding blacks to vote in primary elections invalid.

In 1938, the Court decided that Missouri had not met the separate but equal test by offering to pay the tuition of a Negro at an out-of-state law school, rather than permitting him to attend the law school of the University of Missouri.

In 1950, the Court further undermined *Plessy* by holding that a

[3] Anthony Lewis, *Portrait of a Decade* (New York, Random House, 1964), p. 20.

new law school established for Negroes in Texas was not equal to the prestigious University of Texas and, accordingly, blacks could not be excluded from the latter. The case made the reversal of the doctrine in *Plessy* vs. *Ferguson* inevitable. How could any one school be characterized as equal to another?

The National Association for the Advancement of Colored People now grasped an opportunity. It had previously directed its attacks against the inequalities of particular schools and teacher salaries. The Texas law school decision impelled it to move against the entire institution of school segregation.

The first of the famous school cases was brought to the Supreme Court in 1951. Clarendon County, South Carolina, with 6,630 Negro and 2,375 white students was spending $375,000 yearly for the white schools as compared to $282,000 for the black. There were no drinking fountains, inside latrines, auditoriums, or gymnasiums in the Negro schools as there were in the white. Two out of the three black schools were without desks. The District Court upheld the South Carolina law segregating the two races by a two-to-one vote,[4] but ordered prompt action to equalize the two school systems. When the case came before the Supreme Court in 1952, it was remanded to the lower court which was asked for an opinion of a report filed by the Clarendon County School Board on a program for the equalization of the white and black schools.

By the fall of 1952, the case was again before the Supreme Court together with similar ones from Delaware, the District of Columbia, Kansas, and Virginia. The Kansas case—*Oliver Brown et al* vs. *The Board of Education of Topeka, Kansas*—listed first, gave the litigation its name. It was first heard early in 1953, but was put over for reargument in the October term. Meanwhile, two events of significant importance occurred. Dwight D. Eisenhower became President of the United States, and Chief Justice Fred Vinson, a segregationist, died. His successor on the bench was the liberal California Governor Earl Warren.

On May 17, 1954, Chief Justice Warren delivered the Court's opinion in the *Brown* case:

[4] The dissenter, Judge J. Waties Waring, of Charleston, S. C., was not only ostracized by his Southern neighbors for his courage, but eventually driven from the state.

180

. French Foreign Legion tank (U.S. gifted), with attached Vietnamese personnel, stops for a map reading during an operation against Vietminh forces in French Indo-China in 1954. *(Fred Sparks—PIX Photo)*

(Below) Two young girls, armed with machetes and smoke grenades, as they appeared before going on night duty to guard against Communist guerrilla attacks in the town of Thuy-Nhai in the Red River rice delta in 1954 during the French Indo-China conflict. *(Fred Sparks—PIX Photo)*

(Right) Paratroopers escort Negro students to classes at Central High School in Little Rock, Arkansas, in September, 1957.

(United Press International Photo)

(Bottom right) U.S. marshals search a group of prisoners in Oxford, Mississippi, in October, 1962, after they were taken into custody following riots in the wake of the enrollment of James Meredith, a Negro, in the University of Mississippi. *(Wide World Photo)*

(Below) Desegregation at work in an elementary school playground at Janney School, Washington, D.C., in October, 1967.

(Washington Evening Star Photo)

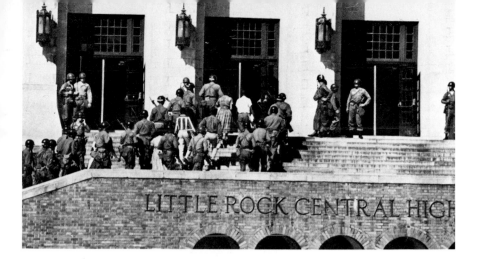

The Russians' Sputnik I. *(Photo by Novosti Press Agency)*

Robert Goddard, famous rocket scientist, with the world's first liquid-propelled rocket at Auburn, Massachusetts, on March 16, 1926. The projectile traveled 184 feet in 2½ seconds.

(U.S. Air Force Photo)

A Jupiter-C rocket on the launch pad at Cape Canaveral prior to launching an eighteen-pound satellite into Earth orbit. The satellite was launched January 31, 1958. Explorer I discovered the first two circular radiation belts surrounding the Earth. *(Photo by NASA)*

MEDIUM RANGE BALLISTIC MISSILE BASE IN CUBA

A medium-range ballistic missile base photographed in Cuba by American U-2 spy planes during the Cuban missile crisis.

(U.S. Air Force Photo)

Close-up of rear deck of Soviet ship *Divinogorsk,* showing two missile transporters with their canvas-covered missiles.

(U.S. Navy Photo)

We cannot turn the clock back to 1868 when the Amendment [XIV] was adopted, or even to 1896 when *Plessy v. Ferguson* was written. We must consider public education in the light of its full development and its present place in American life. Today education is perhaps the most important function of state and local governments . . . . In these days, it is doubtful that any child may reasonably be expected to succeed in life if he is denied the opportunity of an education. Such an opportunity, where the state has undertaken to provide it, is a right which must be made available to all on equal terms.

We come to the question presented: does segregation of children in public schools solely on the basis of race, even though the physical facilities and other "tangible" factors may be equal, deprive the children of the minority group of equal educational opportunities? We believe that it does . . . . We conclude that in the field of public education the doctrine of "separate but equal" has no place. Separate educational facilities are inherently unequal.

The doctrine of "separate but equal" had been set aside, and the Supreme Court ushered the nation into a new era. It also kindled a spark that ignited a revolution, the ultimate outcome of which cannot be predicted even today.

The South at first greeted the Court's decision with stunned silence. Even that staunch segregationist of the Byrd organization, Virginia's Governor Thomas B. Stanley, spoke out with moderation on the day following the *Brown* decision: "We will consider the matter and work toward a plan which will be acceptable to our citizens and in keeping with the edict of the Court."

A month later Stanley appeared less temperate. "I shall," he announced, "use every legal means at my command to continue segregated schools in Virginia."

Stanley's reversal was typical of leaders throughout the entire South. One by one they took a stand for "the southern way of life" and vowed that the perfidious federal government would ultimately find it impossible to force integration on their fair state. President Eisenhower did not help matters when he made the chance remark that laws could never change men's hearts.

In the border states with few Negroes, and where segregation was under local option, there were rapid steps toward desegregation. Kansas, Arizona, the District of Columbia, and the City of Baltimore all moved toward ending separate schools. Between 1954 and 1956 more than two hundred school districts in the South abandoned segregated classes.

Hoxie in Lawrence County,[5] Arkansas, was one of the first southern towns to desegregate its public schools. With few Negroes in the county, the Board of Education announced, on June 25, 1955, that it would integrate its classes—as economically practical, legally required and "right in the sight of God."

At first integration proceeded smoothly, but within a few days local rednecks had stirred up enough opposition to the school board's action that local protest meetings were held. A white student boycott of the school was begun and parents set up picket lines around the school. The school board had the courage to stick to its guns and within weeks the desegregated school was operating smoothly.

The Supreme Court, when it decided the *Brown* case, ordered arguments held at the next session on problems implementing the decision. On May 15, 1955, it finally disposed of the case by directing that the litigation be remanded to the trial courts to solve local problems. The Court did not, however, require the presentation of desegregation plans within a specified time but rather that they proceed with "all deliberate speed." Perhaps, if the Supreme Court had fixed a specific day for the final end of segregation, and the President of the United States had enforced the Court's decree, the ultimate outcome might have been far different.

In September, 1956, Clinton, Tennessee, under a Federal District Court order, began the desegregation of its schools in what the town fathers had determined would be "a smooth and peaceful transition." Three weeks after the decision, "John Kasper, a twenty-six-year-old northerner from New Jersey, whose confirmed hates included integration, and 'pink punks, freaks, golf players, poodle dogs, hot-eyed Socialists, Fabians, scum' came to town and began making phone calls."[6]

[5] Lawrence is one of the poorest counties in the United States. Accordingly, school sessions are held during the summer months in order that the students can assist with the spring planting and the fall harvest.
[6] George Barrett, *The New York Times Magazine* (September 16, 1956).

Kasper, after forming a White Citizens Council, was able within a few days to completely disorganize the town. The school integrated peacefully enough until pressure was applied—high school students, forced to pass through picket lines accompanied by taunts and insults, boycotted classes, and a week after Kasper's arrival in Clinton a mob of three thousand shouting men, women, and children ran wild, abusing Negroes and cursing anyone who didn't join their ranks as "nigger lovers."

Fortunately there were a few responsible whites in Clinton. A group led by the mayor's son, Buford Lewallen, an attorney and former speaker of Tennessee's House of Representatives, along with another member of the bar, Lee Grant, Jr., a decorated war veteran, formed a posse and were able to hold the mob in check until the arrival of State Police and the National Guard. Clinton integrated its schools but later, on the night of October 5, 1958, its high school was bombed and destroyed.

Southern resistance to the Supreme Court decision began to crystallize. Fewer voices of moderation were heard and the years following 1956 were filled with hate and violence. Additional white citizens councils were formed and signs reading "Impeach Earl Warren" were displayed on practically all Southern highways. Virginia's Senator Harry Flood Byrd, who was probably the only leader south of the Mason-Dixon line whose words would have been heeded had he spoken for the compliance of the law, declared for total resistance. Voluntary integration in hundreds of school districts came to a complete halt by the autumn of 1957. The South had set a course that later almost brought the nation to disaster.

In early September, 1957, the city of Little Rock, Arkansas, was prepared to put into effect a court-approved plan for the gradual integration of its schools by the admission of a few black children into the Central High School. On September 2, the day before the school was scheduled to open, the supposedly liberal Governor Orval Faubus made a televised address. While there had been no rumors of disorder, he declared that it would "not be possible to restore or maintain order (in Little Rock) if forcible integration is carried out tomorrow," and that accordingly he was ordering the National Guard to be posted around the high school.

No Negro children attended the school the first day, but Federal Court Judge Ronald N. Davies ordered the designated plan into effect "forthwith." The following day National Guardsmen barred the entrance of the school to the nine scared, trembling black children who tried to attend classes. Again President Eisenhower sang his old refrain, "You cannot change men's hearts merely by law," although he did meet with Faubus in Newport, Rhode Island, where he was vacationing.

On September 20, Judge Davies granted an injunction enjoining Faubus from using his National Guardsmen to prevent integration at Central High School. The militia vacated the area, and the nine Negro students attended classes on Monday, September 23. However, by mid-morning a mob of more than a thousand collected outside the school shouting, "Get the niggers out, lynch them." Because of the threat of violence the children were spirited from the school at noon.

That evening President Eisenhower publicly denounced the mob's actions as a "disgraceful occurrence." Four days later he ordered federal troops sent to Little Rock and called up ten thousand Arkansas National Guardsmen. Under the command of Major General Edwin Walker[7] these troops were the first sent into the South since Reconstruction Days. Protected by twenty-three paratroopers of the 82nd Airborne Division, the nine black children returned to Central High School on September 25. While the battalion of paratroopers was later withdrawn, it was necessary to keep a reduced force of the federalized Guard stationed in the area during the remainder of the school year.

A climate had now developed in the South wherein men of good will were afraid to speak out for moderation, and those who did had to clothe their utterances in the shibboleths of the segregationists.

Following Little Rock, the scene shifted to Montgomery, Alabama. Here the banner of Negro non-violence was raised and Dr. Martin Luther King, Jr. was projected into national leadership. The Negro, scoring a decisive victory in the bus boycott in Birmingham, Alabama, gained confidence in himself and in his own power, for the triumph had been his alone.

[7] General Edwin Walker's combat leadership of the First Special Service Force in France during World War II, won him his first star. In 1962, he was charged with taking part in the anti-integration riots at the University of Mississippi.

184

Neither the passage of the Civil Rights Act of 1957; the federal vote registrants in 1960 and 1964; the Greensboro lunch counter sit-ins; James Meredith and the 1962 riot at Ole Miss; nor the emotional and futile stand of George Wallace on the steps of the Administration building at Tuscaloosa, Alabama, in June, 1963, convinced the South of the dangerous course it was pursuing.

And it was not just the rednecks or the demagogues who were flouting the law and refusing to accept the inevitable. Over a decade and a half after the *Brown* decision, the citizens of the supposedly enlightened city of Wilmington, North Carolina, were still dragging their feet on integration and protesting the "illegal acts" of the federal government.

Meanwhile, a reign of terror erupted throughout the entire South. The murder of Medgar Wiley Evers; Virgil Wade, a thirteen-year-old Negro boy; sixteen-year-old Johnny Robinson; the Philadelphia, Mississippi killings; the bombing of a Negro church in which four little girls died, and a host of other acts of violence in Georgia, Alabama, Louisiana, and Mississippi were all the products of defiance of the nation's law, encouraged and abetted by irresponsible southern leadership.

Under Dr. King the Negroes, in the main, met their white enemies' violence with a steadfast policy of non-violent resistance. It was, however, inevitable that some members of the Negro community would break the bonds of restraint. The first important departure from Dr. King's doctrine occurred on Maryland's eastern shore in July, 1963.

Cambridge, a town of 15,000, is traditionally southern and segregational. Led by Mrs. Glorie H. Richardson, the town's Negroes demonstrated for the integration of schools, restaurants, and the Volunteer Fire Company. Two hundred and fifty blacks staged a freedom walk at the Dorchester County Court House, where they were jeered as well as pelted with eggs and rocks. Using shotguns, the Negroes fired on their white adversaries, wounding six. The National Guard sent to Cambridge by Governor J. Millard Tawes finally put down the rioting but not until they, too, had been fired upon by the angry blacks. A social revolution had finally degenerated into a bloody revolt that was to eventually split America apart.

Following Cambridge, those who were later to be called the

black militants not only favored meeting force with force, violence with violence, but assumed more significant roles of leadership within the Negro ranks. Stigmatizing the older, more conservative, and moderate leaders of their race as "Uncle Toms," they moved toward the left, and many—particularly the Black Panthers—loudly called for the overthrow of the government and an end to Whitey's dominance. The riots that erupted all over the country following the assassination of Dr. King in 1967 were in this pattern, and with his death died the hopes of the many sincere and concerned individuals of both races for a peaceful reconciliation.

To every action there is a counteraction, and the violence of the Negro militants led to a blacklash in the North. Many who had previously considered equal treatment of black and white as essentially fair, began urging a need to slow down the process of integration. The astronomical vote for "Little George" Wallace in the 1968 election indicated the wide base of this reaction.

It was, perhaps, unfortunate that the Department of Health, Education, and Welfare and some of the Federal District Courts in the late 1960s went beyond the scope of the Supreme Court's decision in the *Brown* cases. They insisted that in order to create a balance between the two races, children should be carried by bus to other school districts.

While this had little effect on rural areas in the South where most blacks and whites live interspersed with few residential concentrations, it placed a heavy burden on large cities such as Los Angeles, San Francisco, or Mobile, where to achieve this balance it might be necessary to transport children from twenty to forty miles. In some situations, as in Los Angeles, it jeopardized the entire school system.

The issue became a focus for criticism of the whole integration program. On March 24, 1970, President Richard Nixon announced that while school segregation must be ended "at once," the problem of dealing with school segregation resulting from busing patterns must be left mainly to local communities.

The President firmly stated, "Past policies have placed on the schools and the children too great a share of the burden of eliminating racial disparities throughout our society." The unanticipated mild reaction of many of the black leaders to the President's announcement may well indicate they, too, are just as happy to see the "busing" issue resolved.

It is easy to speculate that had the Supreme Court in 1954 ordered all segregation terminated by a specific date, and had the President been less concerned with men's hearts and more with a desire to rigidly enforce the law, we would not today be facing an abyss. Unfortunately, however, the problems of racial discrimination were far too complex to be so easily resolved.

That there has been a failure or absence of both black and white leadership in the North and South is obvious. They were sad days for America when assassins' bullets struck down John F. Kennedy and Dr. Martin Luther King, Jr., for they alone seemed to have a true insight into the magnitude of the problems we face.

The consequences flowing from centuries of injustice and the *Brown* case will be with us for years to come and we know they have brought America to the brink of disaster. Even were the lion to lie down with the lamb, the segregationists to moderate their differences with the militants (which we know to be impossible), the scars from the blows we have endured will remain for generations and the gulf dividing us will continue for decades.

In the fall of 1968 a Mrs. Charles A. Smith of Topeka, Kansas, appeared with her young son at the Monroe school to enroll him in the kindergarten. Mrs. Smith was the daughter of Oliver Brown who, in her behalf, had brought the suit that has become known as *Brown et al* vs. *The Board of Education of Topeka, Kansas*. Linda Brown (Mrs. Smith) had graduated from Monroe before the Supreme Court decision, but her son was now to become the first of his family to attend a desegregated elementary school.

Too often we are inclined to see only the bigoted resistance that followed the *Brown* decision. We fail to realize that along with the sound and fury, progress has been quietly made, that this is a better nation because of improvements that have stemmed from *Brown et al.* Today there are thousands of Negro children receiving an education that is, indeed, equal to that given their white peers.

Probably even more important than these increased educational opportunities is the pride in self that has flown from these black children being accepted as equals—not as children apart. The very thought that we permitted a large segment of our children to be stigmatized as inferior is not only horrible but degrading to all of us who "passed on the other side of the road."

Nor are the black children the only ones who have gained from the decision in Linda Brown's case. There is much that the black race has to offer the white. If, however, our children gain nothing but the knowledge that skin pigmentation is of little importance, the nation will have profited.

There are, of course, other dividends that can be traced to that judicial milestone. From it has stemmed (even if indirectly) improved job opportunities for the Negro, an end of housing restrictions, and an increased number of black industrial and political positions of responsibility.

Oliver Brown et al vs. *The Board of Education* has, indeed, changed our world, and the changes will go on and on as the Negro finds himself more and more in the mainstream of American life.

11.

MOON DUST—SPUTNIK

October 4, 1957, was a black Friday for many thoughtful Americans. When they contemplated the future, they could not suppress a chill of fear. Russia, our archenemy, had accomplished the impossible. A nation, many of us felt, of semi-barbarians without technical skill had accomplished an engineering feat that had put American technology to shame. The Soviet Union had not only been the first to put an artificial satellite in orbit, but it had been a large 190-pounder, while those the United States contemplated sending skyward weighed only 31 pounds.

There was born that day the fiction of the "Missile Gap" that was to help deny Richard Nixon the White House in 1961, and start the United States on a vast space program, the cost of which even today staggers the imagination.

The reaction on the part of the nation was violent. Newspapers in large black headlines charged, "Another Pearl Harbor," and usually economy-minded Senators stormed that "something must be done, no matter the cost."

Only Dwight D. Eisenhower in the White House, to his credit, kept his cool. At his press conference five days later, he told the assembled journalists that the successful launching of Sputnik had not affected the security of the United States "one iota." George Humphrey, Secretary of the Treasury, saw it all as a Communist plot to start us on a spending spree that would ultimately bankrupt the nation.

Russia, however, did have a long list of past scientific accomplishments. Starting from scratch after World War II, she had duplicated our atom bomb by 1949, and by 1953, detonated a thermonuclear device. But these we naïvely concluded were not her own achievements, but rather the products of her devious ways. We decided both were made possible by the spies, Fuchs and Greenglass, or by the efforts of the scientists she had kidnapped from Germany. To our amazement, the USSR's far-flung espionage net could not be credited with the result, for she had by far exceeded our own plans.

The United States was not just piqued over losing the first round in a game, but plagued by a well-grounded fear that the Reds had developed a rocket thrust that would soon give them an intercontinental ballistic missile that, combined with a nuclear warhead, could put the United States at their mercy.

President Eisenhower at first endeavored to beat a delaying action in resisting the clamor that had arisen, but even he had to finally capitulate. On November 27, 1957, he pushed the panic button and ordered the Army's Jupiter and the Air Force's Thor into production.

Rockets invented in China had their first military usage in A.D. 1232. They were employed by the Tartars against the Poles in the battle of Liegnitz in A.D. 1249. During the Napoleonic Wars in 1807, 25,000 incendiary British rockets destroyed the city of Copenhagen. In the War of 1812, the "rockets red glare" at Fort McHenry became a part of our national heritage. Although they were extremely inaccurate, the use of Congreve rockets by the British in the Battle of Bladensburg on August 24, 1814, was principally responsible for the fear that gripped the American militia, causing them to throw down their rifles and desert the battlefield en masse. A company was formed to manufacture rockets in Russia in 1826, and thousands of St. Petersburg rockets were employed in the Russo-Turkish War of 1826–29.

Although the Russians are inclined to boast that they were the first in various fields, they can in all honesty claim they were pioneers in considering the possibility of using rockets for interplanetary space exploration.

Konstantin Eduardovich Tsiolkovski is generally acknowledged to be the father of space flight. Born in the village of Izhevsk, province of Ryazanskii, on September 5, 1857, Tsiolkovski, the son of a poor forester, was stricken with a virulent type of scarlet fever that left him totally deaf when he was a boy of ten. His affliction had its compensations, however. Unable to compete in sports with other boys, he turned to reading and studying. In the process he was able to acquire a remarkable self-taught education. In 1871, he passed the required teacher examinations and for forty years taught mathematics and physics in the town of Borovsk, Kaluzhsgii province.

Tsiolkovski first was interested in dirigibles and in 1891 constructed the first Russian wind tunnel. In 1895, he turned to the science of astronautics and published an article in a popular magazine on the possibility of flight beyond the earth. In 1898, he designed a space ship propelled by liquid fuels that bears a remarkable similarity to those used in our Apollo program. Another article, "Exploitation of Cosmic Expanse via Reactive Equipment," was given considerable attention by the scientific world. By 1911, Tsiolkovski was writing of nuclear engine propulsion for space vehicles and the development of electronics and ionic engines as a source of rocket propulsion in deep space. When he died in September, 1935, the Soviet Government inscribed his own words on his tomb:

> Mankind will not stay on the earth forever, but, in the pursuit of the world and space, will at first timidly penetrate beyond the limits of the atmosphere and then will conquer all the space around the sun.

In the United States, at the very time that Tsiolkovski was continuing his theoretical studies of the basis of rocketry and flight into space, Dr. Robert Hutchings Goddard was actually testing rockets.

Born in Worcester, Massachusetts, in 1882, Goddard as a boy—after reading Jules Verne's *From the Earth to the Moon*—became interested in space flights. As a graduate student, he reached the conclusion that rocket propulsion was the key to astronautics. Using a ballistic pendulum in his experiments, he proved that a rocket could and did work in a vacuum.

While professor of physics at Clark University, Worcester, he wrote a technical paper on the potentials of rockets and was awarded a grant of $5,000 by the Smithsonian Institution. In November, 1918, two days before the Armistice of World War I, Dr. Goddard demonstrated before representatives of the War Department a solid fuel rocket using nitroglycerin and gun cotton.

At Auburn, Massachusetts, on March 16, 1926, he sent aloft the world's first liquid propelled rocket. His projectile traveled 184 feet in two and a half seconds. Because of the fire hazard, the State of Massachusetts prohibited any future rocket launchings in 1929. With the financial support of the Guggenheim family, the Carnegie Foundation, and Clark University, Dr. Goddard resumed his experiments in Roswell, New Mexico, where his eleven-foot rocket, traveling at a speed of five hundred miles an hour, reached an altitude of nine thousand feet.

During his lifetime, Dr. Goddard's efforts received little government encouragement or support. Often dubbed "moon-mad," he was considered an eccentric whose experiments had little practical value.

When he offered his services to the United States at the beginning of World War II, he was assigned an inconspicuous slot at the Naval Ordnance Research Station in Annapolis, Maryland. His patents were, however, used by the Nazi government in its V-2 rocket program and later by the United States in its space probe efforts. Fifteen years after Dr. Goddard's death in 1945, the United States awarded his estate the sum of a million dollars for past infringements and future license of his patent rights, and the Space Flight Center at Greenbelt, Maryland, was named in his honor.

In 1923 considerable interest was aroused in Europe by the publication of *The Rocket into Interplanetary Spaces*. The author, Rumanian-born Dr. Hermann Oberth, wrote: "Spacecraft can be built to rise beyond the limits of the atmosphere," and "will be able to carry men." The Organization of the German Society for Space Travel in 1927 was a direct result of Oberth's book and within a year it had a membership of five hundred, including many non-Germans.

The Berlin Rocket Testing Station was established in 1930 by Rudolf Nebel. Among Nebel's assistants was a young man, Wernher von Braun, who had previously helped Dr. Oberth with his experiments. Born in Wirsitz, Posen, on March 23, 1912, von

Braun was the son of Baron Magnus Freiherr von Braun who moved his family to Berlin after he became a member of the Cabinet of the Weimar Republic.

Young von Braun's later triumphs in the science of rocketry could not have been prophesied when, as a student in the Berlin French Gymnasium,[1] he failed in both physics and mathematics. That was, however, before he discovered Oberth's *The Rocket into Interplanetary Spaces*. On that day von Braun's subsequent career in rocketry was born.

In 1932 the Reich centralized its rocket research program under Colonel Walter R. Dornsberger with von Braun as his assistant. Their work together was to eventually result in the development of the first 46-foot long, 28,250-pound V-2 which, fired from a distance of 188 miles, hit London on the night of September 7, 1944. Altogether a total of some 4,300 V-2s were fired against England and 2,100 against Antwerp—the last on the night of March 27, 1945.

Russia, no stranger to rocketry, made extensive use of rockets during the Second World War. When Field Marshal General Friedrich von Paulus' Sixth Army was trapped in "Fortress Stalingrad," the Red troops are said to have thrown "fantastic quantities" of rocket shells into the German enclave.[2]

Soviet rockets were launched from racks on lend-lease Studebakers and many of the rocket parts were made in Tennessee factories. Probably the deadliest of all the Soviet weapons was the "Stalin Organ" launcher which was simple to operate and maintain. Mounted on a truck, it was completely mobile, and thirty organs could launch more than 14,000 rockets within a minute.

Peenemünde, the birthplace of the V-2, was captured by the Russians at the end of World War II, and most of its scientists taken to Moscow. Von Braun, however, fled to the American lines and subsequently came to the United States where he directed the program at the Redstone Arsenal that produced the Jupiter ICBM. In April, 1970, he joined the staff of NASA.

Following the Second World War, Red rocketry experimentation achieved notable success. The 103 motor was capable of a

[1] A school established by Frederick the Great for the education of the children of Huguenots driven from France by the harsh measures of the Catholic Louis XIV.
[2] Martin Caidin, *Red Star in Space* (New York, Crowell-Collier Press, 1963).

thrust of 240,000 pounds as compared with North American Aviation Corporation's improved A-4 motor with a thrust of only 75,000 pounds. It is also believed that Russian engineers later developed a motor with a thrust of 550,000 pounds.

A skeptical United States public greeted the Russian announcement on August 27, 1957, that their scientists had successfully fired an intercontinental ballistic missile that could reach any city in the world. The more knowledgeable, familiar with Red rocket research, were concerned when it was further claimed that the missile had an accuracy of not less than two-thousandths of the range or within twelve miles of any target. Generally, however, American citizens dismissed it as just another wild boast of Communist officials.

Sputnik, fired from an area in the vicinity of the Caspian Sea, was soon circling the earth every hour and thirty-six minutes. Its altitude varied in orbit between 585 and 140 miles above the earth and radios sent off constant signals on two wave lengths.

Any lingering doubts of Russian technological capabilities were dispelled when Sputnik II was launched on November 3, 1957. The new satellite's chamber contained pressurized spheres and its total weight was estimated at between 8,000 and 14,000 pounds. Obviously the USSR had achieved a breakthrough in thrust. Sputnik II also carried a dog passenger named Laika, whom American newspapers soon nicknamed Mutnik or Dognik.

Following Sputnik I, the White House issued orders for a crash program that would place a satellite in orbit within ninety days. Von Braun and his team did not quite make the deadline but on January 31, 1958, Explorer I was launched. It was a piddling thing compared to the Russian effort, for its total weight was only 31 pounds. Cylindrical in shape, it took one hour and fifty-four minutes to orbit the earth and like Sputnik I sent out signals from two radios. Unimpressive as it was in size compared to its predecessor, it was, nevertheless, responsible for the discovery of the earth's inner radiation belt.

The third Sputnik launched on May 15, 1958, weighed 3,350 pounds. Sputnik IV followed on May 15, 1960, with a payload of 10,000 pounds. The five-and-a-half-ton Sputnik V, carrying two dogs, mice, rats, and insects, went into orbit in August, 1960. It was recovered five days later with its passengers reported unharmed. Thus another Russian first had been achieved. The Soviets launched another animal-cluttered Sputnik on December 1, 1960. Unfortunately for its dog passengers, Pehelka (Little Bee) and Mushka (Little Fly), and the other animals, Sputnik VI proved a failure for it returned "along an uncalculated trajectory and burned out."

There was a missile gap in the fifties but it wasn't quite as the Alsop brothers described it. With the exception of a few enthusiasts, the United States had never been rocket-minded. Certainly our military establishment had shown little interest in the rocket as a weapon. In 1926, when Dr. Goddard had approached the War Department with the results of his experiments, he had been told that the next war would be fought with trench mortars.

A rocket research project did get underway at the California Institute of Technology in 1939 under the direction of Dr. Theodore von Karman and General H. H. (Hap) Arnold, but it was never given any great priority. During the war the United States Navy developed a rocket battery for use on its ships, and the Army's bazooka—an anti-tank rocket similar to Goddard's 1918 device—gave good service, but there seemed to be little military interest in long-range rockets.

It was not until the closing months of hostilities in Europe that a high-altitude rocket carrying twenty-five pounds of equipment to an altitude of nineteen miles was produced. Facetiously named the WAC Corporal, it was successfully tested at White Sands Proving Grounds in the fall of 1945, and while it actually went to a height of forty-three and a half miles in vertical flight, it was not in the same league with the German V-2. The United States military establishment was just not rocket-minded.

As late as March, 1947, the distinguished American scientist, Dr. Vannevar Bush, in testifying before Congress, spoke words that he was later to regret when he said that an intercontinental ballistic missile, ". . . is impossible for many years to come and I think we can leave this out of our thinking."

In 1957, the United States, in addition to its manned bombers, had four long-range nuclear delivery systems—the Polaris submarine, the Atlas, Titan, and Minuteman ICBMs—in various stages of planning. Furthermore, the strategic problems of the Soviet Union and the United States were entirely different. Russia was ringed by allies of the United States from whose bases American pilots could reach any Soviet city of importance. To the manned-aircraft-minded generals who had seen the effectiveness of the B-29s' mass attacks on Japan, the manned bomber was a logical carrier for the nuclear bombs against the enemy. The Soviet Union, on the other hand, without this strategic weapon, and with the United States thousands of miles away from the nearest Communist base, saw the development of the intercontinental ballistic missile as their only alternative.

Even though the Soviet Union's decision to produce an ICBM was more in step with modern technology than the United States' reliance on the manned bomber, the Reds made some serious errors before completing their program.

In the late 1940s atomic bombs weighed around ten thousand pounds and the lifting power required to transport this weight over intercontinental distances made the missile not only costly, but expensive to deploy and maintain. The first Russian ICBM was obsolete almost before it went into production and only a score were ever built. At about the time the Red planners ordered a "go ahead" in 1953, nuclear scientists had mastered the technique of producing thermonuclear bombs from lighter elements. Consequently, when Eisenhower gave the directive for the manufacture of the ICBM in 1954, the United States was almost on a par with the Soviet Union in the rocket field. If there was a "missile gap," it was not in military hardware but in vehicles for propelling satellites skyward.

Nevertheless, in this country there was a belief that a military missile gap existed, that the Republicans had bungled things, and the security of the nation was threatened. The young and vigorous Democratic hopeful, Senator John F. Kennedy, hit hard on this charge during the 1960 presidential campaign and promised to "get the nation moving." The "missile gap" probably had more to do with the defeat of Richard Nixon than any other issue of the campaign, for it was difficult to meet the charge without revealing top secret intelligence.

Once he was elected, Kennedy had no other alternative but to move to end the alleged gap. On May 25, 1961, in a special message to Congress he said:

This nation should commit itself to achieving the goal before this decade is out, of landing a man on the moon and returning him safely to earth . . . . We propose to develop alternate liquid and solid fuel boosters much larger than any now being developed, until certain which is superior. We propose additional funds for other engine developments and for manned exploration—explorations which are particularly important for one purpose which this nation will never overlook; the survival of the man who first makes this daring flight. But in a very real sense, it will not be one man going to the moon—if we make this judgment affirmatively, it will be an entire nation, for all of us must work to put him there.

America was committed. With its industrial might, its technological knowledge, and its vast wealth, it could not fail in the objective it had set for itself. Sputnik I as it passed around the earth forced the United States into a course of action from which it could not withdraw.

Sputnik had represented a great technological triumph for the Soviets, but the ultimate result was far different from that which Khrushchev had contemplated. Had the United States been the first to put an artificial satellite into orbit, it would have been no more than the world expected of the computerized and technological colossus of the West. To such an accomplishment, there would have been little reaction either here or abroad.

But the impossible had been accomplished by our supposedly backward ideological enemies, and the reaction was both prompt and violent. Russia, by her triumph, had irrevocably forced the United States and its military establishment into rocketry and in a race to the moon. That economic necessity and the needs of her military later forced the USSR to abort the contest does not change the picture. Once committed, there was little doubt about the United States winning the race to the moon. The factor that is important to the Russians is that the intercontinental ballistic missiles now guarding America were conceived as Sputnik I began her violent but graceful ascent into outer space.

Unfortunately, the intense competition between the Soviets and the United States—amplified by mutual distrust and suspicion, and a constant round of action and reaction—has led to the deployment of tremendously sophisticated weaponry that includes MIRV

(Multiple Independently Targeted Re-entry Vehicles), which is capable of being fitted with as many as twelve separate warheads, and such ABM systems as America's soon-to-be-installed Safeguard installations, and the Russian Galosh system.

Following the launching of the first Sputnik, many of the non-communist nations, especially in Africa and Asia, withdrew into neutrality. Russia's technological triumphs made them pause. Even some of our envious allies found it hard to suppress their glee over the humbling of the overconfident United States. These reactions, however, were short-lived as we gradually caught up in the race and regained scientific prestige.

The principal long-range effect of Sputnik I—other than its role in accelerating the arms and space race between Russia and the United States—was the impact on our educational establishment. As artificial Russian satellites streaked through the sky, America indulged itself in an orgy of self-negation. As always, when there is a setback in this country, there must be a scapegoat, and it was not long before our system of higher education filled the role.

Throughout the nation, and particularly in the halls of Congress, it was charged that our colleges and universities—failing to produce sorely needed trained engineers and scientists—had overemphasized the classical and social sciences. The results of the debate were threefold. Congress moved into the field of higher education, educators began stressing the scientific disciplines, and the states, with federal funds available, entered into a program of mass college education.

Within three months after Sputnik, in the summer of 1957, Congressional hearings on higher education were underway in both the Senate and the House, and for once the educators played second fiddle to the scientists. Among the witnesses—including Detlev Bronk, President of the National Academy of Sciences, Lee Dubridge, I. I. Rabi, Wernher von Braun, and Edward Teller—there was considerable unanimity on the problem. They were in agreement on the need for more trained engineers and scientists, and additional qualified secondary-school teachers. But there was little agreement on solutions.

A number of the experts who appeared before the Senate committee opted for a federal scholarship program, but their estimate of the numbers required varied between 1,000 and 400,000. Others

198

suggested that the main problem had its base in our secondary schools rather than in the universities and that federal aid should go to the high schools rather than the colleges.

Out of a welter of proposals there finally emerged the National Defense Education Act, signed by President Eisenhower on September 2, 1958. Acknowledged by its proponents to be a "stop gap" —an emergency piece of legislation—the act provided for 1,000 to 1,500 graduate fellowships in each of the three succeeding years; grants to states for laboratories and equipment; aid to secondary schools for guidance counseling, testing, language instruction, and vocational training of scientific technicians. In addition, the Act established a national student loan program.

The effect of Sputnik was also felt in the universities and colleges. After a period of soul-searching, with an eye on proposed federal funds, a curriculum revision followed. The social sciences were de-emphasized, with a broadening of the scientific. Many of the heretofore liberal arts colleges, by placing more and more emphasis on the mathematical and the scientific, became mere trade schools with no effort expended toward producing a well-rounded and mature graduate.

Sputnik's impact also profoundly influenced the programs for higher education in the states. Almost overnight a host of small colleges sprang up with little or no educational requirements for student admission or retention. The uneducable were educated and a college degree had soon dropped to the status formerly held by a high school diploma. The frustrations of young adults mentally unable to cope with the requirements of higher education eventually led to demands for more and more snap courses—an end to grades, a place to congregate rather than to study. The disorders that are today besetting our many seats of learning may well have been partially due to the emergence of Sputnik.

Having accepted the challenge of the race to the moon, we could not withdraw without serious damage to our international image. President Kennedy tried to back down from our commitment and still save face by proposing to the United Nations in 1963 that Russia and the United States make a joint effort to reach the moon. How this could have been accomplished without the United States assuming a disproportionate share of the project is hard to understand, but nevertheless the Reds didn't buy the proposal.

The United States had thus been maneuvered into a program that it could ill-afford, and which was of dubious scientific value. What $40 billion could have done toward the eradication of the domestic problems that are tearing us apart today is obvious. The end of the urban ghettos, of marginal starvation, inadequate educational facilities, and a real attack on our environmental problems might all have been accomplished by the judicious use of the funds that brought us moon dust.

12.

EYEBALL TO EYEBALL —THE CUBAN MISSILE CRISIS

During the evening of Monday, October 15, 1962, Edwin M. Martin, Assistant Secretary of State for Inter-American Affairs, was addressing Sigma Delta Chi, the National Journalism Society, at the National Press Club in Washington, D.C. He confirmed the newspaper stories that five thousand Russian technicians were building anti-aircraft missile sites in Cuba and that the Soviets had given Castro MIG fighter planes and rocket-launching torpedo boats. But these, he said, posed no threat to the United States.

"This military buildup is basically defensive in character," he added, "and would not add more than a few hours to the time required to invade Cuba successfully, should that become necessary. . . . Taken together, the present military capabilities in Cuba would not materially increase the Cuban ability to undertake offensive action outside the island."

Martin was in the middle of his speech when a telephone call came for him from Roger Hilsman, director of the State Department's Office of Intelligence and Research. An aide took the message with instructions that the speaker was not to be interrupted, but the call must be returned as soon and unobtrusively as possible.

On the pretense that he must let his wife know when he would be home, Martin called Hilsman. He was advised that the two U2 aircraft that had flown over Cuba the previous day had returned with films that indicated the Russians were constructing medium

201

range ballistic missile sites on the island—information that made the speech he had just delivered pure nonsense.

Only the previous day McGeorge Bundy, former Dean of Harvard and Presidential Assistant for National Security Affairs, in a televised interview with Edward P. Morgan and John Scali of ABC, had said: "I know there is no present evidence, and I think there is no present likelihood that the Cubans and the Cuban government would, in combination, attempt to install a major offensive capability."

Martin's speech had only reiterated the Administration's view and had merely repeated the words of the President himself.

There were those in government, who, unlike Martin, had not been repeating the Administration's line. In the dying hours of the 87th Congress, Senator Kenneth Keating of New York made a direct charge that there were six intermediate range ballistic missile sites under construction in Cuba. Beginning on the last day of August, Keating delivered a series of speeches before the Senate warning of a Russian buildup in Cuba. He insisted that his information came from an unimpeachable source, but the Senator refused to divulge that source even to the CIA. For his pains, Senator Keating had not only been ignored but ridiculed by the Administration.

John A. McCone, head of the Central Intelligence Agency and successor to Allen Dulles after the Bay of Pigs disaster, assured the President that there was little possibility of any such Soviet action. In August, a U2 photo-reconnaissance flight over the island revealed two SAM, or surface-to-air missile batteries, in position. Even so, McCone concluded that the emplacement of MRBM in Cuba by the Soviets would be contrary to Kremlin foreign policy goals. McCone and his CIA aides could not believe the Russians would show such audacity so close to the continental United States. As in the case of the 1961 Berlin Wall crisis, there were plenty of indications of Communist intent but the American Intelligence community underestimated Khrushchev's boldness.

There were also those in the Pentagon who felt that the introduction of SAMs into Cuba could be the first step toward the building of missile sites. Were this allowed to happen, it might well tip the balance of power in Russia's favor.

Keating's speeches failed to sway the Administration but their effect had been felt in the Kremlin. On several occasions Nikita Khrushchev had made a point of reiterating that there were no Russian bases in Cuba, which at the time was true. On 2 September, several days after the Senator's speech, the Russians stated in a communiqué that the Cuban government had asked for armaments and military advisors for training Cuban soldiers.

Two days later, the Soviet Ambassador to the United States, Anatoly Dobrynin, called on the President's brother, Attorney General Robert Kennedy. He told Bobby that Khrushchev wanted the President to know, "—there would be no ground-to-ground missiles or offensive weapons placed in Cuba." He further indicated that the Cuban military buildup, "was not of any significance and that Khrushchev would do nothing to interrupt the relationship of [the] two countries during [the] period prior to the election."[1]

Either because the Republicans had made the Russian buildup in Cuba an issue in the campaign or because he was dubious of Khrushchev's assertions, the President issued a statement before the day was over, to the effect that the United States would not tolerate the introduction of Russian offensive surface-to-surface weapons into Cuba. On 7 September, he asked Congress for and received the right to call up 150,000 reserve troops. On the 11th, the Kremlin disavowed any hostile attempt and stated there was no need for it to place nuclear missiles outside the Soviet Union.

At his news conference on 13 September, the President stated that the arms being shipped from Russia to Cuba did not constitute "a serious threat to any other part of the hemisphere." At this same conference he made it crystal clear that if Cuba became "an offensive military base of significant capacity for the Soviet Union, then this country would do whatever must be done to protect its own security and that of its allies."

Meanwhile, the CIA had been the recipient of a host of reports from Cuban exiles that missile sites on the island were in the process of being constructed. Most of these stories, however, were viewed with skepticism by the Intelligence agency. With no technical

[1] Robert F. Kennedy, *Thirteen Days* (New York, W. W. Norton, 1969).

knowledge, the reports of the refugees were often valueless and sometimes tinged with self-service. If the United States could be drawn into a war with Cuba, these refugees might be able to return to their homeland.

In the aftermath of the Bay of Pigs debacle, American Intelligence operatives had all but been annihilated by Castro, and the few remaining CIA agents had gone underground. Not until 21 September was the first report from a trained and reliable agent in Cuba received. On 12 September, the agent had personally seen the tailpiece of a missile larger than that of a SAM on a truck on a highway.[2] At almost the same time CIA had received word that Castro's pilot, while drinking at a bar, had boasted that Cuba now had atomic weapons.

McCone, a widower, had recently remarried and spent his honeymoon at Cap Ferrat on the Riviera. Returning to Washington early in October, he found that except for peripheral flights or those flown from outside the three-mile limit, western Cuba had not been overflown since September 5. The Administration had considered overflights too risky. McCone immediately recommended that the entire island be photographed. Not until a week passed did the Administration, on October 9, approve his recommendation.

In the Pentagon, Colonel Ralph Wright, Jr., a fifty-year-old, Virginia-born West Point graduate, had been recently assigned to the newly created Defense Intelligence Agency. Wright became intrigued by the deployment of the SAM disclosed by the September flight photographs. He noticed that near the town of San Cristobal the SAM locations followed a pattern similar to those which Gary Powers had photographed near missile sites in the Soviet Union. Wright suggested the San Cristobal area be given

[2] This agent was probably the former noncommissioned French officer who had served with the American Army in Germany whom Colonel Philippe Thyraud de Vosjoli, former Chief of French Intelligence in the United States, tells of in his article, "So Much Has Been Swept Under the Rug," that appeared in the April 26, 1968, issue of *Life* magazine. De Vosjoli passed on the report to the CIA. Arthur Krock, in his *Memoirs, Sixty Years on the Firing Line* (New York, Funk and Wagnalls, 1969, p. 378), suggests that with this information it is hard to understand why McCone would leave on his honeymoon but this occurred on August 30. It is, however, inconceivable that after receiving this report, the Administration continued to insist that the military buildup in Cuba was purely defensive.

U-2 photographic priority and this was subsequently incorporated into the over-flight plan.

Weather delayed the photo missions until October 14, when two U-2 planes, piloted by Air Force Majors Rudolf Anderson, Jr., of Spartansburg, South Carolina, and Richard S. Heyser of Battle Creek, Michigan, took off from Homestead AFB, Florida. Both officers, in their thirties, were veteran pilots. They were well versed in the intricacies of piloting the high altitude U-2. Their flight was uneventful and San Cristobal was given a good going-over. After their return to base, their film magazines were soon on a jet bound for Washington.

The following evening, 15 October, the date of Martin's Press Club speech, Roswell Gilpatric, Deputy Secretary of Defense, was dressing for dinner when he received a call from Lieutenant General Joseph Carroll, head of the Defense Intelligence Agency. Carroll told Gilpatric that the films taken that day were most disturbing and he was sending two photo interpreters with the exposed pictures to Gilpatric's apartment. They arrived before the Secretary had finished dressing.

Colonel Wright had proven prophetic. The San Cristobal negatives clearly revealed the construction of a medium range ballistic missile site. Erectors, launchers, and transporters were all there and a tent city had sprung up. Gilpatric realized that a major crisis was in the making but kept his cool. He called Carroll back, and directed him to have the photos restudied overnight and be prepared to brief Secretary of Defense Robert S. McNamara the next morning at seven thirty.

Soon after Gilpatric's briefing, McGeorge Bundy was called by Deputy CIA Director Ray Cline and given the same news. He was at home, the host of a dinner party in honor of Charles ("Chip") E. Bohlen, the new Ambassador to France. Bundy also directed that the films be re-checked.

Since the President had been out on the hustings the previous day, and looked tired, Bundy decided he would not disturb him until the following morning. Later when Kennedy asked why he had not been told of the situation the night before, Bundy replied, "I decided that a quiet evening, and a night of sleep were the best preparation you could have, in light of what you would face in the days ahead."

205

One by one the Administration leaders were told that evening of the photo interpreters' findings. General Maxwell Taylor, Chairman of the Joint Chiefs of Staff, was giving a dinner in his white-columned quarters at Fort McNair when he received his call. Among his guests were General Marshall S. Carter, Deputy Director of the CIA; U. Alexis Johnson, Deputy Under-Secretary of State; and General Carroll. They were told in Taylor's quarters of the impending crisis. The preoccupation of the men and their frequent trips to the telephone did much to spoil what was otherwise intended to be a very pleasant evening.

President Kennedy was sitting on the side of his bed in his pajamas when McGeorge Bundy entered his room early the next morning. Without any preliminaries, Bundy came right to the point. "Mr. President, there is now hard photographic evidence, which you will see later, that the Russians have offensive missiles in Cuba."

The President's reply has not been recorded, but his thoughts must have been bitter for again he had been "led down the primrose path." As with the Bay of Pigs, his Intelligence experts and his advisers had failed him. His reaction was immediate.

He directed Bundy to call a meeting that morning for eleven fifteen, and to include Vice President Lyndon Johnson; Secretary of State Dean Rusk; Robert McNamara; Robert Kennedy; General Maxwell Taylor; General Marshall Carter; Roswell Gilpatric; George Ball; Edwin Martin; the President's appointment secretary, Kenneth O'Donnell; Secretary of the Treasury, Douglas Dillon; Ted Sorensen; Bohlen; and Bundy. McCone's stepson, Paul J. Pigott, had been killed in a sports car accident in California and the CIA director had flown out to accompany the body to Seattle.

The group that met that morning was later to be known as the Executive Committee of the National Security Council. It was a flexible body with some of the membership changing from time to time. "Chip" Bohlen later left for his new post in Paris and his place was filled by Llewellyn Thompson, recently returned from Moscow. Paul Nitze, former head of the State Department Policy Planning Staff, and acting Assistant Secretary of Defense, joined the committee. Upon the President's invitation, Dean Acheson became a member of the group and Adlai Stevenson attended the meetings whenever his duties as Ambassador to the United Nations would permit. For the next twelve days this committee met continuously.

The discussions that first day seemed to go round and round, and accomplished little. Some of those present thought that Khrushchev's move was related to Berlin. When the missiles were in place, Nikita would offer a trade—their removal if the Western powers would get out of Berlin. Others felt that perhaps the Kremlin planned to withdraw their missiles if the American Jupiters based in Italy and Turkey were dismantled. McNamara insisted that the presence of the missiles in Cuba did not affect the balance of power —that "A missile is a missile. It makes no great difference whether you are killed by a missile fired from the Soviet Union or from Cuba."

In spite of the number of sharp differences of opinion, the committee agreed that the United States and Russia faced a serious confrontation and that the world was at the brink of a nuclear war. Douglas Dillon recalls, "The first reaction of the President and the others was that we simply could not accept the fact of the Soviet missiles in Cuba trained on the United States. Everyone around the table recognized that we were in a major crisis. We didn't know that day, if the country would come through it with Washington intact."

There was, however, that first day sharp disagreement as to how the President and the nation should respond. Those who went along with McNamara believed there had been little change in the balance of power and favored a cautious diplomatic approach. On the other side were those who felt that Khrushchev's daring had tipped the world power balance in Russia's favor and the only recourse was direct military action. Siding with McNamara were Ball, Gilpatric, and Bohlen. Opposing the lenient approach were Taylor, Nitze, and Dillon.

Before the session temporarily adjourned, President Kennedy directed that until he had determined on the course he would follow, not one word was to leak out of the meetings regarding the presence of Russian missiles in Cuba. He also ordered that twenty weekly U-2 flights were to be made over Cuba. As a cover, the President told the group that, as far as possible, he would try to follow his normal schedule.

In distant Moscow, Khrushchev, continuing his deception, called in Foy Kohler, the American Ambassador, and among other things assured him that Russian objectives in Cuba were entirely defensive.

On Wednesday, 17 October, the President was in Connecticut campaigning for Governor Abraham Ribicoff, Democratic candidate for the United States Senate. This long-standing commitment had to be kept, to allay any suspicions of the Washington press corps that anything was brewing. Meanwhile, the Executive Committee continued its meetings and covertly switched its locale to a conference room at the State Department.

The interpretation of additional U-2 films subsequently taken revealed twenty-eight launching pads under construction in the San Cristobal and Guanajay areas. For the first time missiles could actually be seen. They were of two types, the mobile 1,000-mile medium range (MRBM) and the 2,200-intermediate range (IRBM).

Various courses of action open to the President were thoroughly discussed that day with a number of alternatives receiving little support and being quickly discarded. Obviously, taking the matter to the Security Council of the United Nations would accomplish nothing. The endless debate, with the probability that at least some of the missile sites would be operational within a week or ten days, ruled out this course of action. There was also the certainty of a Russian veto of any action of the Council. The time element involved precluded any serious discussion of a possible ground invasion of Cuba. It would take days before such an assault could be put into motion—days that could not be spared.

To send an emissary to Khrushchev or Castro, to confront the Russian ambassador with the telltale photographs, were also considered, but each of these courses of action would telegraph our blows to the enemy allowing the Russians to mobilize the nonaligned nations. It was also believed that as long as military action remained a possibility it was foolish to give the Soviets advance warning.

The two alternatives that were given the most consideration both involved force. First: a blockade of Cuba to prevent the shipment of military matériel to that country. While this would involve a direct confrontation with Khrushchev rather than with Castro, it had several distinct advantages. It was less violent than a military attack on the island and no civilian casualties would occur. It would be easier to control, and could be graduated in intensity. On the other hand, it was argued that it was like "locking the barn door after the horse had been stolen," and would antagonize our maritime allies, and under international law was an act of war.

The final plan proposed—and this one had strong support—was for a pinpoint surprise bombing attack on the missile installations. Such a program would have the advantage of speed, but unfortunately would involve killing both Russian soldiers and Cuban civilians. An air raid would place Khrushchev under strong pressure to take counter measures and this could result in a nuclear world war.

There was another disadvantage. Bombing is considerably less than precise, and there could be no guarantee that all missile sites would be destroyed. Those that remained might well be aimed and fired at targets in the United States. At the very least, an air attack on Cuba would be grist for the Communist propaganda mill and the United States would be labeled an imperialistic bully.

Dean Acheson was the principal proponent of an air strike. He argued that such action was justifiable under the Monroe Doctrine, and necessary in light of the unmistakable danger created by the placement of the missile sites. At first, George Ball and, later, Robert Kennedy opposed an air strike. Both men insisted that such a step was contrary to every tradition of the United States, and regardless of the military outcome of an assault, it would place a blot on the United States that could never be eradicated. R.F.K. added somewhat dramatically and perhaps presumptuously, "My brother is not going to be the Tojo of the 1960s."

At the eleven o'clock morning session of the Executive Committee the next day, the President was told by the CIA that within eighteen hours the first of the medium range missiles in Cuba would be in position for firing and that, thereafter, more of these instruments of destruction would daily become operational.

As the morning wore on, there were discussions as to whether the alternatives that the President finally determined upon should be limited to a simple removal of the missile sites or should include an attempt to get rid of Castro. This would necessitate an armed invasion of the island. A pointless dispute also took place as to the legality of whatever action was finally taken.

Dean Acheson dryly commented, "A man with a dagger at his throat is seldom bothered with the niceties of the ultimate response."

The President did not attend the afternoon session. Andrei Gromyko, who had previously asked for an appointment, was scheduled for 5 P.M. During the two and a quarter hour session with the Soviet Foreign Minister, Kennedy was assured that Khrushchev would do nothing about Berlin until after the American elections; but that immediately thereafter, unless an agreement could be reached with the Western powers, Russia would feel "compelled" to sign a peace treaty with East Germany.

The President replied that while he always stood ready to talk with Russia about Berlin, the United States felt the city's very survival was dependent upon the presence of Western troops. The talk then turned to Cuba, Gromyko stating that he was under instructions to point out that military assistance given the island was solely for the purpose of strengthening its capacity to defend itself. The President was careful to give the Russian every opportunity to straighten the Cuban record, but Gromyko continued to insist that the help given Castro was purely of a defensive nature.

In the evening Secretary Dean Rusk gave a dinner for Gromyko while the Executive Committee was meeting in the same building. The members seemed to be pulling away from an air strike, although Bundy had come to favor this more forceful action. Douglas Dillon, who had supported such an attack, now changed his position and made the compelling argument that if the air strike was first, it foreclosed any other option. If a naval blockade was attempted and failed, it was still possible to level the sites from the air. Dillon's argument convinced Bundy as well as Robert Lovett, whom the President had added to the group.

Shortly after 9 P.M. the Committee left the State Department and reconvened at the White House where they continued their discussion with the President. At midnight, Thursday, Kennedy directed Ted Sorensen to begin working on a speech in which he would disclose the presence of the Russian missile sites in Cuba and tell the nation of the steps he was taking for their removal.

Still fearful that any change in his schedule might result in a premature leak to the press, the President went out on the campaign trail on Friday, October 19. Reporters and columnists were becoming suspicious that something important was brewing.

That morning the unsuspecting Pierre Salinger, the President's Press Secretary, denied that there was a movement of troops toward Florida. In the afternoon, following the appearance of an article by Robert S. Allen and Paul Scott, that missiles were in Cuba, the Department of Defense denied the truth of the column and insisted that "it had no information indicating the presence of offensive weapons in Cuba," and that no "emergency measures had been taken."

Both statements were, of course, bare-faced lies. In fairness it should be noted that Salinger and probably the Pentagon Public Information officers who released the statements, had not as yet been informed of the crisis. Six Army Divisions had already started their movements toward the southeast, and the Atlantic and Caribbean Commands had been alerted.

Meanwhile, that day the air strike proponents continued to lose ground. General Maxwell D. Taylor, a humane man, had concluded that such an attack could not be made unless a twenty-four-hour warning was given. By evening that Friday, most were in agreement that a naval blockade of Cuba should be the first step. Thereafter, if the Russians and Cubans continued with their work on the sites, an air strike would become necessary.

In Chicago, Saturday morning, the President received a call from his brother Robert asking him to come home immediately. Salinger was summoned and thereafter issued a statement that the President had "a slight upper respiratory infection and a one degree temperature." Since the weather in Chicago was raw and rainy his doctor had advised him to return to Washington.

By 1:45 P.M. Kennedy was in the White House and an hour later met with the Executive Committee. Two choices were presented: a naval blockade that, if necessary, would be followed by an air strike; or, an air strike that would require a follow-up amphibious invasion of the island.

Dean Rusk, who had remained relatively silent during the discussions but leaned toward an air strike, was now of the opinion that a naval blockade was the wiser course of action. He agreed with McNamara that it had the advantage of keeping the other options open. Stevenson also favored this course. Unfortunately, Adlai gained the reputation of an appeaser that he subsequently found difficult to live down because of his proposal that the President should consider giving up the Guantanamo Naval Base and the Jupiter MRBM bases in Turkey. Addressing himself directly to the United Nations Ambassador, the President assured him that such actions would not be taken under the threat of compulsion.

The matter was settled when Kennedy announced that he preferred the naval blockade as the first step. He decided it would preserve, for both himself and Khrushchev, alternate options and the Russians would not be forced into a precipitous reaction.

Prior to the meeting that morning, the Joint Chiefs of Staff, anticipating possible counteractions throughout the world, alerted all United States military commands. Later in the day, an additional thousand Marines were sent to Guantanamo Bay. That night (Saturday), naval ships began leaving Norfolk for their blockade stations in the Caribbean.

On Friday evening it appeared that the Executive Committee favored a blockade. Acheson had concluded his usefulness was at an end and returned to his home in Maryland. There, on Saturday, he was called by Rusk and asked to fly to Paris the next day to explain the American position to President de Gaulle. Walter Dowling, the American Ambassador to West Germany, was in Georgia visiting his mother when he was alerted to return to Bonn and brief Chancellor Adenauer. Livingston Merchant, the former Ambassador to Canada, was located in Princeton, New Jersey, and asked to leave for Ottawa and explain developments to Prime Minister Diefenbaker.

That the President still harbored some doubts of the course he was following was indicated on Sunday morning when he called a group of Air Force officers along with General Taylor, McNamara, and his brother Robert, for a conference. The President was reassured when General Sweeney, Commander of the Tactical Air Force, told him that an air strike could only be expected to eliminate 90 percent of the Cuban missiles, and that such a strike would of necessity include attacks on all Cuban airfields, some of which were in populated areas.

The Executive Committee spent most of Sunday editing the

speech that Sorensen had written for the President. At noon Kennedy left the group to meet with his good friend, Sir David Ormsby Gore, the British Ambassador, and tell him of the decision he had made. At 2:30 P.M. the National Security Council convened to formally ratify the actions of its Executive Committee.

Monday, October 22, was the day to which the week's talks and planning had led. It was now time for action. Acheson, on his way to Paris, met with David Bruce, the American Ambassador to the Court of St. James, at Greenham Common, briefed him on the crisis and left copies of both the missile site photos and the speech the President was to deliver that night. These Bruce took to the British Prime Minister, Harold Macmillan, at once. The PM had known of developments since Friday. While he was an extremely worried man, he promised the full cooperation of the British government.

Acheson, after briefing the American Mission of the North Atlantic Treaty Organization, met with de Gaulle, with whom Washington had expected difficulty. Quite the contrary was the case. After summarizing President Kennedy's planned speech, the reply from the French President brought relief to the American, "It is exactly what I would have done," and later to Acheson, "You may tell your President that France will support him. I think that under the circumstances President Kennedy had no other choice. This is his national prerogative and France understands."

While he did not admit it, de Gaulle, as a result of the reports from Colonel de Vosjoli, probably was informed of the existence of the missile sites before President Kennedy.

A similar response was received from Chancellor Adenauer in Bonn. Only Diefenbaker in Ottawa questioned the motives of the American President, but Merchant finally obtained an agreement that no Russian or Cuban aircraft would be allowed to land at Gander Airport.

Back at the White House the day was a busy one for President Kennedy. He met with the Executive Committee, the National Security Council, and his Cabinet. The finishing touches were made on the speech he was to deliver that night, and arrangements were made for it to be broadcast to Cuba and the rest of Latin America.

At five o'clock he met with congressional leaders and, much to Kennedy's annoyance, faced considerable opposition from his fellow Democrats. Senator Richard Russell of Georgia insisted that the blockade would accomplish little or nothing, and was only a halfway measure. The Chairman of the Foreign Relations Committee, J. William Fulbright, who had opposed the Bay of Pigs venture and was later to shepherd the Tonkin Bay Resolution through the Senate, supported Russell in his demand for more forceful action—for an invasion. Kennedy is said to have "left the room in a smouldering rage."[3]

At 6:00 P.M. Secretary Rusk met with the Soviet Ambassador and gave him a copy of the speech Kennedy was to deliver. Dobrynin left the State Department visibly shaken. At six fifteen, in State's International Conference room, George Ball briefed forty-six of the ambassadors of our allies, and forty-five minutes thereafter the President went on the air.

In simple but clear words, Kennedy told of the findings as revealed by U-2 photos. He recited the misleading assurances that had emanated from the Kremlin, and he outlined the steps he was about to take.

"All ships of any kind bound for Cuba from whatever nation or port will, if found to contain cargoes of offensive weapons, be turned back."

There was to be continued close surveillance; a missile attack on any nation in the Western hemisphere would be considered an attack on the United States; Navy dependents had been evacuated from Guantanamo; the United States was calling for an emergency meeting of the Security Council of the United Nations; and asking the Organization of American States to meet immediately. Few of the millions who listened to the President's speech on the evening of October 22, 1962, went to bed without grim forebodings.

The ambassadors of the Organization of American States met immediately after the President had gone off the air and heard Secretary Rusk explain the developments of the crisis. The initiative had now passed to the Soviet Union.

Tuesday, October 23, dawned with the Russian government accusing the United States of "unheard of violations of international law," and of acts that might bring about nuclear war. At

[3] Elie Abel, *The Missile Crisis* (Philadelphia, J. B. Lippincott, 1966), p. 120.

9:00 A.M. the Organization of American States convened. Rusk hoped to get fourteen votes of the twenty-one member nations. The vote was 19 in favor of the United States with none casting a negative vote. Later it was learned that Moscow was much impressed by the support given to the United States by its Latin American neighbors. In the United Nations Security Council, Ambassador Stevenson, with his talent for the dramatic, did a masterful job in confronting and confounding the representatives of the USSR.

The formal Blockade Proclamation was issued by President Kennedy that evening. He had delayed until the vote in the OAS.

As the crisis had developed, the President had put more and more pressure on the CIA for information out of Moscow.[4] He was relieved to learn that the Kremlin had made no plans for mobilization, nor had there been any change in the disposition of its forces.

The first actual day on which a confrontation between the United States and the Soviet Union might take place was Wednesday, October 24. Twenty-five Russian owned or chartered ships had been spotted by Naval Air Reconnaissance steaming toward Cuba. Waiting for them five hundred miles from the eastern end of the island were nineteen ships of the United States Navy under the command of Vice Admiral Alfred ("Corky") G. Ward, who had recently assumed command of the Second Fleet. The ships had also located and were observing a number of Soviet submarines that appeared in the area.

The first tentative intimation that there might be a peaceful outcome occurred that afternoon when the Navy reported a dozen of the Russian ships had stopped or changed course. Dean Rusk, who was meeting with the President along with several other of Kennedy's advisers, is said to have turned to McGeorge Bundy when the news was relayed and said, "We're eyeball to eyeball and I think the other fellow just blinked."

No indications, however, came from Moscow that the Soviet Union had softened. The Kremlin returned the proffered copy of

---

[4] The CIA in turn put pressure on our chief source of information in Moscow, Colonel Oleg Penkovsky. There are those who believe that Penkovsky's involvement resulted in his exposure, trial, and execution. The Russian State Security people have stated, however, that Penkovsky was arrested on October 22, 1962, which is six days before the missile crisis ended.

the President's Quarantine Proclamation to the American Ambassador declaring it unacceptable. Khrushchev sent for an American businessman, William Knox, President of Westinghouse International, who happened to be in Moscow, and subjected him to three hours of invectives and threats. He did admit that the USSR had missiles in Cuba, but insisted that if his ships were stopped, Russian submarines would retaliate by sinking American vessels. Knox reported his conversation to the White House the next day.

Throughout the world popular sentiment, for once, seemed to favor the American side of an issue, but fear of nuclear warfare tempered that support. France and West Germany, two of the most vulnerable nations to Soviet retaliation, as well as Latin America, were solidly behind the United States. In Britain, sentiment was divided; the government supported the American cause but the "Ban the Bomb" forces had been mobilized and under the leadership of Lord Bertrand Russell were vigorously defending the Russian position. Hugh Gaitskell, leader of the Labor party, spoke of "so-called missiles."

The Japanese were well aware of the effects of nuclear warfare and both pro- and anti-Communists seemed terrified the crisis might escalate into open conflict. As anticipated, sentiment in India was anti-American. Among the other non-aligned and neutral nations there appeared to be much sympathy for the United States.

At home support of President Kennedy's stand was all but unanimous, particularly after certain of the Republican leaders had been briefed and had seen the photos. The talk that Kennedy was engaging in a clever political trick had all but died out. But, as always, there were appeasers. The distinguished but aging columnist, Walter Lippmann, was one of a few who urged the withdrawal of the obsolete Turkish bases in return for the dismantling of the Cuban sites.

To counter any belief that the crisis might be a clever move to influence the American election, as many of the pro-Russians were charging, the President released aerial photos of the missile sites for publication. The United States Information Agency issued a total of fifty thousand of these photos throughout the world.

In the United Nations, U Thant, hopeful of being actual rather than acting Secretary General, played the Russian game. Sending identical letters to the White House and to the Kremlin, he asked that for two or three weeks Russia cease sending arms to Cuba and the United States suspend the blockade. This, of course, ignored the matter of continuation of work on the missile sites. Kennedy quickly vetoed any such suggestion unless the Soviets were willing to immediately dismantle or remove the bases.

The first interception of a ship bound for Cuba took place between 8:00 and 8:30 A.M. on Thursday, October 25. The Russian tanker, *Bucharest,* carrying oil, and the East German passenger ship *Voelkerfreund* were allowed by the blockading destroyers to proceed toward Cuba.

The first boarding and search of a Cuban-bound vessel occurred early Friday morning. The ship stopped had been carefully selected to give the least affront to Moscow, and yet show that we were resolute in going forward with the blockade. The *Marcula,* an American-built Liberty ship of Lebanese registry with Panamanian owners, sailed from the port of Riga under Russian charter. At 7:00 A.M. she was hailed by two U.S. destroyers, the *John R. Pierce,* and the *Joseph P. Kennedy, Jr.* A boarding party found that the *Marcula* carried no arms and she was allowed to proceed toward Cuba.

Aerial photographs still indicated that work was continuing on the missile sites. There was a general feeling in Washington that the blockade would not be effective—that further action, an air strike, would become necessary. Could it be that all the equipment for the sites was already in Cuba?

In the Executive Committee, the President continued his resolve to stay with the quarantine measure while at the same time exerting psychological pressure on Moscow. The State Department, the White House, and various congressional leaders all emphasized that, if the blockade failed to result in the dismantling of the sites, additional actions would become necessary. U Thant was privately and publicly told that the United States would not wait indefinitely.

Probably the most bizarre incident of the missile crisis happened on 26 October. John Scali, of ABC, was in the press room of the State Department when he received a call from Alexander S. Fomin, a counselor at the USSR Embassy. Fomin, believed to be the head of Soviet Intelligence in the United States, asked Scali to meet him at the Occidental Restaurant near the Willard Hotel.

"It's very important," Scali was told.

At the meeting place Fomin informed Scali the situation was ominous, "that something must be done." He asked the American if the Administration would agree to settle the dispute if the Soviet Union dismantled the sites and shipped the missiles back to Russia under United Nations supervision; Castro agreeing not to accept offensive weapons in the future; and the United States pledging itself not to invade Cuba.

Scali returned to State, where he joined Roger Hilsman. Then they both met with Secretary Rusk. The message Scali took back to Fomin was to the effect that the United States was interested in such a proposal but that time was of the essence.

A communication from Khrushchev was received at State that evening at six o'clock. It was directed to the President, and was long and rambling. Unquestionably it had been written by him personally and sounded as if he were thoroughly frightened. While the wording of the message was imprecise, there was no reference to the Jupiter missiles in Turkey. Together with the Fomin approach to John Scali there appeared a ray of hope—a possibility that the dispute might be compromised.

The Executive Committee reconvened the next morning (Saturday), and proceeded to draft a reply to the Soviet leader's message. They had not progressed far when a second message from the Kremlin dashed their former optimistic hopes. Russia was now asking that the missile sites in Turkey be withdrawn as the price of dismantling those in Cuba. This time, the letter was obviously not the effort of Khrushchev alone. Superficially there seemed to be logic in the Russian demands and the Jupiters were obsolete, but to agree to their removal under threat would only be construed as weakness and a betrayal of our Western allies.

The pessimism that now prevailed among the members of the Executive Committee was not lessened when word was received that U-2 pilot Major Rudolf Anderson had been shot down over Cuba by a Russian-fired SAM. The crisis had now assumed a new dimension. Complication compounded complication when it was learned later that another U-2, on an air-sampling mission from Alaska, had strayed over Russian territory and Soviet aircraft had taken off to intercept the intruder.

U.S. Air Force planes were trying to locate the U-2 and safely bring it back to base but the mistake could have serious consequences. The President, who had issued explicit instructions against provocative flights, when told of the mishap, could only bitterly repeat the old Navy-Marine saw, "There is always some son-of-a-bitch that doesn't get the word."[5]

Rusk, Thompson, Ball, and Bundy tried their hand at writing a reply to the first Khrushchev letter, but their effort proved unsatisfactory. The President finally turned the task over to his brother and Ted Sorensen. Their draft was dispatched to the Kremlin that evening about 8:00 P.M. Without saying so, the message assumed that the Fomin offer had been a part of the Soviet leader's proposal and stated that it was acceptable to the United States. The President, in effect, had accepted terms not offered.

When Ambassador Dobrynin was given a copy of the letter that evening by Robert Kennedy he was quite dubious about the Russian response. The Kremlin, he said, "was deeply committed." The members of President Kennedy's Executive Committee were pessimistic when they left for their homes. The dawn of Sunday, October 28, did not improve the spirits of those in Washington. Planning was well underway for the air strike to take place no later than Tuesday. Everything, including perhaps the survival of the human race, depended upon the Russian reply to the Kennedy-Sorensen letter.

Moscow radio began broadcasting the answer at 9:00 A.M. Monday (Washington time). In view of the assurance that there would be no attack on Cuba, "we [have] instructed our officers—to discontinue construction [of the sites]—dismantle them, and return them to the Soviet Union." Neither American government officials nor newsmen, in an effort to save face for Khrushchev, would publicly assert that this represented a complete capitulation on the part of the USSR. Without waiting for the official text, President Kennedy accepted the Russian proposal.

There were still a number of loose ends and details to be resolved. Late that bright Sunday afternoon, Communists and fellow travelers who "didn't get the word" were picketing the United Nations with placards reading, "End the Blockade."

Castro later kicked up his heels by refusing to allow a United

[5] Said to have first been repeated in the days of the sailing ships when, after a boarded ship had surrendered, an officer looked up and saw a marine, with one hand holding the rigging, slashing at his opponent with a cutlass.

Nations inspection team into Cuba and attempted to retain the Ilyushin 28 bombers the Russians had given him. Under a compromise the missiles were allowed to be visually inspected on Russian ships after they had left Cuba, and the fiery Cubans finally consented to the removal of the bombers on November 26. The Cuban Missile Crisis thus entered the pages of history.

In retrospect and with the advantage of hindsight, there are two principal questions to be answered. Why had not the government of the United States anticipated the placement of missiles in Cuba? Why had Khrushchev so underestimated the United States as to believe that it would weakly acquiesce to the existence of the sites after they had once been constructed?

Granting that Intelligence was faulty, there can be no question that the Administration should have considered it quite likely that Russia would place missiles in Cuba. Senator Keating believed it. Unfortunately, the Administration had reached a static state of mind. It was convinced that Nikita Khrushchev was an intelligent and logical leader who would not make an illogical move. Having once reached the conclusion that Russia would not give Cuba other than defensive weapons, our leaders refused to budge from their preconceived opinions—and this in spite of the report that was received from Colonel de Vosjoli as early as September 21, 1962.

Since World War II the leaders of this nation, with the exception of Harry Truman, have mesmerized themselves into believing that peaceful co-existence with the USSR is not only possible but eventually inevitable. One need not be an hysterical rightist to realize that such a concept is naïve. Soviet-provoked crises have studded the years since those of F.D.R.—each one followed by a period of comparative calm that camouflaged Russia's future intentions.

Communist ideology demands that capitalism be constantly kept on the defensive—to a point. When this point is reached, when it appears that a continuation of the adventure will no longer serve a useful purpose, a strategic Soviet withdrawal from the brink is made. However, this retreat only happens when our nation leads from strength and stands firm. Unless we want an all-out war, we must become reconciled to the nature of the world in which we live, and continuous harassment of this nation by the USSR is part of that world. The Kennedy Administration should have heeded the warnings of de Vosjoli, and realized that the Russian missile sites in Cuba were not only possible, but probable.

Khrushchev, on the other hand, had grossly underestimated the American President. He had evidently concluded that Kennedy was just a younger edition of Eisenhower. Had not this young man unleashed an ill-conceived landing at the Bay of Pigs, and then not had the guts to provide the air support so desperately needed? Had not Kennedy allowed him to build the Berlin Wall with nothing but a feeble protest? As Elie Abel has said: "There is no evidence to support the belief that Khrushchev ever questioned America's power. He questioned only the President's readiness to use it."

Fortunately for us, Khrushchev was wrong. John F. Kennedy "stood up." He refused to be intimidated and steadfastly stuck to his goal—the removal of the missile sites from Cuba. Had he wavered—had he conceded—the world in which we live today would be far different. Appeasement of Russia will always breed more harassment.

The most significant result of the Cuban Missile Crisis was the decision made in Moscow after the Russians finished studying the Cuban debacle. It is now apparent that a conscious decision was made by the Kremlin that never again would Russia be caught in a situation of strategic inferiority. In 1962, the Soviets had only a few intercontinental ballistic missiles. The "Missile Gap" alleged by John F. Kennedy in 1960 did not exist and its use as a campaign issue was absurd.

Totalitarian powers are not namby-pamby, and Khrushchev soon paid for his miscalculation. In October, 1964, he was dismissed from office and, while allowed to live, soon faded into obscurity.

The United States, for its part, witnessed a temporary renaissance. Its light previously dimmed by the Bay of Pigs fiasco and its bland acceptance of the Berlin Wall, now saw its image take on some of its former luster. America had again shown the world that it was ready and able to act when its national interest was at stake.

Our European and South American allies, many of whom had begun to question our determination, were served notice that when the chips were down, we could and would stand up and be counted. This new confidence in the United States was later to be eroded in the jungles of Vietnam, but that is another story.

Since October, 1962, the Soviets have embarked on a very deliberate course as to strategic nuclear rockets. In less than ten years the Russians have passed the United States in the number of ICBM launchers. In addition, the Soviet SS-9 has a bigger payload than any U.S. missile. In a confrontation today—say over the Middle East—the USSR would be at least in a position of strategic equality. If present trends continue, they may have strategic superiority by 1975.

The status of the Soviet strategic deterrent is a direct result of, and may be traced to, the embarrassment and shame Khrushchev felt in 1962. He had to blink! Nikita had too few rounds in his magazine.

BIBLIOGRAPHY

Abel, Elie, *The Missile Crisis*. Philadelphia, J. B. Lippincott, 1966.

Acheson, Dean, *Present at the Creation*. New York, W. W. Norton, 1969.

Adleman, Robert, and Walton, George, *The Devil's Brigade*. Philadelphia, Chilton, 1966.

Air Ministry, Great Britain, *Berlin Air Lift*. London, His Majesty's Stationery Office, 1949.

Alperovitz, Gar, *Atomic Diplomacy*. New York, Simon and Schuster, 1965.

Anders, General Wladyslaw, *Hitler's Defeat in Russia*. Chicago, Henry Regnery, 1953.

Bailyn, Lotte, *Mass Media and Children*. Washington, D.C., American Psychological Association, 1959.

Baker, Leonard, *Roosevelt and Pearl Harbor*. New York, Macmillan, 1970.

Baker, Liva, *Felix Frankfurter*. New York, Coward-McCann, 1969.

Baldwin, Hanson W., *Battles Lost and Won*. New York, Harper & Row, 1966.

———, *Hiroshima Plus 20*. New York, Delacorte Press, 1965.

Barclay, J. B., *Viewing Tastes of Adolescents*. Glasgow, Scottish Educational Film Association, 1961.

Barnouw, Erik, *A Tower in Babel*. New York, Oxford University Press, 1966.

Berg, Roland H., *Polio and the Salk Vaccine*. New York, The Public Affairs Committee, 1955.

Blakeslee, Alton L., *Polio and the Salk Vaccine*. New York, Grosset & Dunlap, 1956.

Brownlow, Donald Grey, *The Accused*. New York, Vantage Press, 1968.

Burkhead, Jesse, *Public School Finance*. Syracuse, New York, Syracuse University Press, 1964.

Bush, Vannevar, *Modern Arms and Free Men*. New York, Simon and Schuster, 1949.

Caidin, Martin, *Red Star in Space*. New York, Crowell-Collier Press, 1963.

Canning, John, ed., *100 Great Events That Changed The World*. New York, Hawthorn Books, 1965.

Carter, Richard, *Breakthrough*. New York, Trident Press, 1966.

Casamassa, Jack V., and Bent, Ralph D., *Jet Aircraft Power Systems*. New York, McGraw-Hill, 1957.

Charles, Max., *Berlin Blockade*. London, Allan Wingate Ltd., 1959.

Chen, Theodore H. E., ed., *The Chinese Communist Regime*. New York, Frederick A. Praeger, 1967.

Chiang Kai-shek, *Resistance and Reconstruction*. New York, Harper & Brothers, 1943.

Chinnock, Frank W., *Nagasaki*. New York, World Publishing Co., 1969.

Chuikov, Vasili I., *The Battle for Stalingrad*. New York, Holt, Rinehart and Winston, 1964.

Clark, Blake, *Remember Pearl Harbor*. New York, Harper & Brothers, 1943.

Clubb, O. Edmund, *Twentieth Century China*. New York, Columbia University Press, 1964.

Clutterbuck, Richard L., *The Long Long War*. New York, Frederick A. Praeger, 1966.

Communist Party, *The Siege of Stalingrad*. London, Communist Party of Great Britain, N.D.

Cooke, David C., *The Planes the Axis Flew in World War II*. New York, Dodd, Mead & Company, 1970.

Crawley M.I.E.E., Lt. Col. Chetwode, *From Telegraphy to Television*. London, Frederick Warne & Co., Ltd., 1931.

Daniel, James, and Hubbell, John G., *Strike in the West*. New York, Holt, Rinehart and Winston, 1963.

Davison, W. Phillips, *The Berlin Blockade*. Princeton, New Jersey, Princeton University Press, 1958.

Diamond, Edwin, *The Rise and Fall of the Space Age*. New York, Doubleday, 1964.

Dibold, Hans, *Doctor at Stalingrad*. London, Hutchinson, 1958.

Dizard, Wilson P., *Television, A World View*. Syracuse, New York, Syracuse University Press, 1966.

Donovan, Frank, *Bridge in the Sky*. New York, David McKay, 1968.

Duschinsky, Walter J., *Educational Television*. Houston, Texas, Privately Published, 1958.

Elton, Lord (Godfrey Elton), *Gordon of Khartoum*. New York, Alfred A. Knopf, 1955.

Emme, Eugene M., *A History of Space Flight*. New York, Holt, Rinehart and Winston, 1965.

Everson, George, *The Story of Television*. New York, W. W. Norton, 1949.

Fairbank, John King, *The United States and China*. Cambridge, Massachusetts, Harvard University Press, 1959.

Fall, Bernard B., *The Two Viet-Nams*. New York, Frederick A. Praeger, 1963.

————, *Hell Is a Very Small Place*. Philadelphia, J. B. Lippincott, 1966.

Farago, Ladislas, *The Broken Seal*. London, Arthur Barker Ltd., 1967.

Fisher, P. J., *The Polio Story*. London, William Heinemann Ltd., 1957.

Fitzgerald, C. P., *China*. New York, Frederick A. Praeger, 1935.

————, *Flood Tide in China.* London, Cresset Press, 1958.

————, *The Birth of Communist China.* New York, Frederick A. Praeger, 1964.

————, *The Empress Wu.* London, Cresset Press, 1968.

Flynn, John T., *While You Slept.* New York, Devin-Adair, 1953.

Fogelman, Edwin, *Hiroshima: The Decision to Use the A-Bomb.* New York, Charles Scribner's Sons, 1964.

Friendly, Fred W., *Due to Circumstances Beyond Our Control.* New York, Random House, 1967.

Fuller, Major General J. F. C., *Decisive Battles of the Western World;* Vol. III. London, Eyre & Spottiswoode, 1956.

Gable, Luther S. H., *The Miracle of Television.* Chicago, Wilcox & Follett Co., 1949.

Gartmann, Heinz, *Space Travel.* New York, Viking Press, 1962.

General Motors, *Story of General Motors.* Detroit, Michigan, General Motors, 1957.

Goerlitz, Walter, *Paulus and Stalingrad.* New York, Citadel Press, 1963.

Goldman, Sidney, and Crystal, Herman, *Constitutional Convention of 1947.* Trenton, New Jersey, State of New Jersey, 1951.

Goldston, Robert, *The Rise of Red China.* Indianapolis, Bobbs-Merrill, 1967.

Gray, Jack, and Cavendish, Patrick, *Chinese Communism in Crisis.* New York, Frederick A. Praeger, 1968.

Green, Edith, *Education and the Public Good.* Cambridge, Massachusetts, Harvard University Press, 1964.

Grime, Alan P., *Equality in America.* New York, Oxford University Press, 1964.

Groombridge, Brian, *Adult Education and Television.* London, National Institute of Adult Education, 1966.

Hachiya M.D., Michihiko, *Hiroshima Diary.* Chapel Hill, North Carolina, University of North Carolina Press, 1955.

Harris, Robert J., *The Quest for Equality*. Baton Rouge, Louisiana, Louisiana State University Press, 1960.

Hill, Norman, "Was There an Ultimatum Before Pearl Harbor?" *The American Journal of International Law*, Vol. 42 (1948).

Hilliard, Robert L., *Understanding Television*. New York, Hastings House, 1964.

Hoehling, A. A., *The Week Before Pearl Harbor*. New York, W. W. Norton, 1963.

Hofstadter, Richard, and Smith, Wilson, *American Higher Education*. Chicago, University of Chicago Press, 1961.

Holt, Len, *The Summer That Didn't End*. New York, William Morrow, 1965.

Hubbell, Richard W., *4000 Years of Television*. New York, G. P. Putnam's Sons, 1942.

Hurd, Douglas, *The Arrow War*. New York, Macmillan, 1967.

Ianniello, Lynne, ed., *Milestones Along the March*. New York, Frederick A. Praeger, 1965.

Jukes, Geoffrey, *Stalingrad, The Turning Point*. New York, Ballantine Books, 1968.

Kahin, George McTurnan, and Lewis, John W., *The United States in Vietnam*. New York, Dial Press, 1967.

Kempner, Stanley, ed., *History of Television*. Atlanta, Georgia, Television Encyclopedia Press, 1966.

Kennedy, Robert F., *Thirteen Days*. New York, W. W. Norton, 1969.

Kettering, Charles Franklin, and Orth, Allen, *American Battle for Abundance*. Detroit, Michigan, General Motors Corporation, 1947.

Kimmel, Admiral Husband E., *Admiral Kimmel's Story*. Chicago, Henry Regnery, 1955.

Klapper, Joseph, *The Effects of Mass Communication*. New York, Columbia University Bureau of Applied Research, 1959.

Kluge, Alexander, *The Battle*. New York, McGraw-Hill, 1967.

Knebel, Fletcher, and Bailey II, Charles W., *No High Ground*. New York, Harper & Brothers, 1960.

Krieger, Evgeni, *Battle on the Volga*. Moscow, Foreign Language Publishing House, 1943.

Krock, Arthur, *Memoirs, Sixty Years on the Firing Line*. New York, Funk and Wagnalls, 1968.

Lamb, Alastair, *Asian Frontiers*. New York, Frederick A. Praeger, 1968.

Lancaster, O. E., ed., *Jet Propulsion Engines*. Princeton, New Jersey, Princeton University Press, 1959.

Lewis, Anthony, *Portrait of a Decade*. New York, Random House, 1964.

Lifton, Robert J., *Survivors of Hiroshima*. New York, Random House, 1967.

Loh, Pichon, *The Kuomintang Debacle of 1949*. Boston, D. C. Heath, 1965.

Lord, Walter, *Day of Infamy*. New York, Holt, Rinehart and Winston, 1957.

MacNeil, Robert, *The People Machine*. New York, Harper & Row, 1968.

Magistrate of Greater Berlin, *Berlin Airlift*. Berlin, Verlags GMBH, N.D.

Marx, Joseph L., *Seven Hours to Zero*. New York, G. P. Putnam's Sons, 1965.

McAleavy, Henry, *The Modern History of China*. New York, Frederick A. Praeger, 1967.

McGinnis, Joe, *The Selling of the President 1968*. New York, Trident Press, 1969.

Mehling, Harold, *The Great Time-Killer*. New York, World Publishing Co., 1962.

Miller, John Anderson, *Men and Volts at War*. New York, McGraw-Hill, 1947.

Minow, Newton, *Equal Time*. New York, Atheneum, 1962.

Mooney, Booth, *Mr. Speaker*. Chicago, Follett Publishing Co., 1964.

228

Morgenstern, George, *Pearl Harbor, The Story of the Secret War.* New York, Devin-Adair, 1947.

North, Robert C., *Moscow and Chinese Communists.* Stanford, California, Stanford University Press, 1953.

Optowsky, Stan, *The Big Picture.* New York, E. P. Dutton, 1961.

Osada, Dr. Arata, *Children of the A-Bomb.* New York, G. P. Putnam's Sons, 1959.

Pantzer, Eric F., *The Debacle at Pearl Harbor.* Indianapolis, Indiana, Privately Printed, 1965.

Penkovsky, Colonel Oleg, *The Penkovsky Papers.* New York, Doubleday, 1965.

Pilat, Oliver, *The Atom Spies.* New York, G. P. Putnam's Sons, 1952.

Plievier, Theodor, *Stalingrad.* New York, Appleton-Century-Crofts, 1948.

Porteus, Stanley D., *And Blow Not the Trumpet.* Palo Alto, California, Pacific Books, 1947.

Reinfeld, Fred, *Miracle Drugs and the New Age of Medicine.* New York, Sterling Publishing Co., 1962.

"Report of the Joint Committee on the Investigation of the Pearl Harbor Attack, with additional views of Mr. Keefe, together with the Minority views of Mr. Ferguson and Mr. Brewster." Washington, D.C., Government Printing Office, 1957.

Reuben, William A., *The Atom Spy Hoax.* New York, Action Books, 1955.

Rivlin, Alice M., *The Role of the Federal Government in Financing Higher Education.* Washington, D.C., Brookings Institution, 1961.

Rodrigo, Robert, *Berlin Airlift.* London, Cassell & Company Ltd., 1960.

Rooney, Andrew A., *The Fortunes of War.* Boston, Little, Brown, 1962.

Rowland, John, *The Television Man.* New York, Roy Publishers, 1966.

Roy, Jules, *The Battle of Dien Bien Phu.* New York, Harper & Row, 1965.

Sakamaki, Kazuo, *I Attacked Pearl Harbor*. New York, Association Press, 1949.

Sammis, Edward R., *Last Stand at Stalingrad*. New York, Macmillan, 1966.

Sarnoff, Brig. Gen. David, *Pioneering in Television*. New York, Radio Corporation of America, 1948.

Schlesinger, Jr., Arthur M., *A Thousand Days*. Boston, Houghton Mifflin, 1965.

Schneider, Franz, trans., *Last Letters from Stalingrad*. New York, William Morrow, 1962.

Schramm, W., Lyle, J., and Parker, E. B., *Television in the Lives of Our Children*. Stanford, California, Stanford University Press, 1961.

Schramm, W., Lyle, J., and Pool, I. des., *The People Look at Educational Television*. Stanford, California, Stanford University Press, 1963.

Schroter, Heinz, *Stalingrad*. New York, E. P. Dutton, 1958.

Seth, Ronald, *Stalingrad: Point of No Return*. London, Victor Gollancz Ltd., 1959.

Shaplen, Robert, *The Lost Revolution*. New York, Harper & Row, 1965.

Simonov, K., *Stalingrad Fights On*. Moscow, Foreign Languages Publishing House, 1942.

Smith, Jean Edwards, *The Defense of Berlin*. Baltimore, The Johns Hopkins Press, 1963.

Snow, Edgar, *People on Our Side*. New York, Random House, 1944.

Snyder, Louis L., *The War, A Concise History, 1939-1945*. New York, Julian Messner, 1960.

Snyder, Louis L., ed., *Masterpieces of War Reporting*. New York, Julian Messner, 1962.

Soviet Army Correspondents, *Stalingrad*. London, Hutchinson & Co., Ltd., N.D.

Stanley, Raymond, director, *Exploring Problem Areas in Educational TV*. Madison, Wisconsin, The University of Wisconsin Television Laboratory, 1956.

Steinberg, Rafael, *Postscript from Hiroshima*. New York, Random House, 1966.

Sterling, D. and P., *Polio Pioneers*. New York, Doubleday, 1955.

Styler, Herman, *Plague Fighters*. Philadelphia, Chilton, 1960.

Sunderlin, Sylvia, ed., *Children and TV*. Washington, D.C., Association for Childhood Education International, 1967.

Swift, John, *Adventure in Vision*. London, John Lehmann, 1950.

Tanham, George K., *Communist Revolutionary Warfare*. New York, Frederick A. Praeger, 1962.

Tiltman, Ronald F., *Baird of Television*. London, Seeley Service and Co., Ltd., 1933.

Trefousse, Hans Louis, ed., *What Happened at Pearl Harbor*. New York, Twayne Publishers, 1958.

Tresolini, Rocco J., *Justice and the Supreme Court*. Philadelphia, J. B. Lippincott, 1963.

Utley, Freda, *The China Story*. Chicago, Henry Regnery, 1951.

Wallen, Vice Admiral Homer N. (USN Retired), *Pearl Harbor: Why, How, Fleet Salvage and Final Appraisal*. Washington, D.C., Naval History Division, 1968.

Warner, Denis, *Hurricane from China*. New York, Macmillan, 1961.

————, *The Last Confucian*. New York, Macmillan, 1963.

Weinert, Erich, *Stalingrad Diary*. London, I.N.G. Publication, 1944.

Werth, Alexander, *The Year of Stalingrad*. London, Hamish Hamilton, 1946.

White, Theodore H., *China, The Roots of Madness*. New York, W. W. Norton, 1968.

Williams, Greer, *Virus Hunters*. New York, Alfred A. Knopf, 1959.

Wilson, John Rowan, *Margin of Safety*. New York, Doubleday, 1963.

Windsor, Philip, *City on Leave: A History of Berlin 1945-1962*. New York, Frederick A. Praeger, 1963.

Wohlstetter, Roberta, *Pearl Harbor: Warning and Decision*. Stanford, California, Stanford University Press, 1962.

Woodbury, David O., *Battlefronts of Industry*. New York, John F. Wiley & Sons, 1948.

Wyckoff, Gene, *The Image Candidate*. New York, Macmillan, 1968.

Zaehringer, Alfred J., *Soviet Space Technology*. New York, Harper & Row, 1961.

Zhukov, Georgi K., *Marshal Zhukov's Greatest Battle*. New York, Harper & Row, 1969.

INDEX

237